Media Matter

TV Use in Childhood and Adolescence

COMMUNICATION AND INFORMATION SCIENCE

Edited by
BRENDA DERVIN
The Ohio State University

Recent Titles

Media Matter

TV Use in Childhood and Adolescence

KARL ERIK ROSENGREN
University of Lund

and

SVEN WINDAHL
University College of Växjö

with

Ulla Johnsson-Smaragdi, Inga Sonesson
University of Lund

and

*Bentil Flodin, Elias Hedinsson, Ingrid Höjerback,
Gunilla Jarlbro, Annelis Jönsson, Keith Roe*
University of Lund

 **ABLEX PUBLISHING CORPORATION**
NORWOOD, NEW JERSEY

Library of Congress Cataloging-in-Publication Data

Rosengren, Karl Erik.
   Media matter: TV use in childhood and adolescence/by Karl Erik Rosengren and Sven Windahl with Ulla Johnsson-Smaragdi . . . (et al.). p. cm.—(Communication and information science)
   Bibliography: p.
   Includes index.
   ISBN (invalid) 0-89391-449-1.—ISBN 0-89391-570-X (pbk.)
   1. Television and children—Sweden—Malmö—Case studies. 2. Television and children—Sweden—Växjö—Case studies. 3. Mass media surveys—Sweden—Malmö. 4. Mass media surveys—Sweden—Vaxjö.
I. Windahl, Swen, 1942- . II. Title. III. Series.
HQ784.T4R72 1989   88-38458
791.45'013—dc19   CIP

Ablex Publishing Corporation
355 Chestnut Street
Norwood, New Jersey 07648

Table of Contents

List of Tables

List of Tables, Appendix

List of Figures

Preface

This book is the outcome of a decade's studies by a Swedish research group concentrating its efforts on the media use of children and adolescents, its causes and consequences. The book is built on two premises, an evaluative premise and a cognitive one. We believe that what happens to children and adolescents is important. We also believe that the mass media, especially television, are important in the lives of children and adolescents. Kids matter very much to us and to society, and media matter very much in the lives of our kids. Those two premises form the raison d'être of our book.

The two premises have been with communication scholars and communication studies for a long time: at least since the Payne Fund movie studies were launched in the late 1920's, and very probably long before that (Charters, 1933; Dale, 1935; Peterson & Thurstone, 1933). For every new medium entering upon the scene, concern has been voiced that the minds and lives of children and adolescents run the risk of being corrupted by the new medium. The pioneering studies during the late 1950s of "Television in the Lives of our Children" were all triggered by this concern (Schramm et al., 1961). So were the important studies which followed in the late 1960's and early 1970s (Baker & Ball, 1969; Comstock & Rubinstein, 1971), which were followed up and summarized in a number of books and reports, overviews, and textbooks, most of them characterized by much the same concern (for instance, Comstock, 1980; Comstock et al., 1978; Murray, 1980; Pearl, Bouthilet, & Lazar, 1982).

All the studies cited so far were carried out in the United States. Parallel with this strong current of American research on children and mass media, however, a series of similar studies was undertaken in various countries in Europe and Asia. Sometimes these studies were inspired by their American counterparts, sometimes they preceded or even anticipated them. As often as not they were able to add new perspectives and deepen the theoretical arguments (Brown, 1976; Feilitzen, Filipson, & Schyller, 1979; Filipson 1980; Furu, 1971; Himmelweit et al., 1958; Sturm & Brown, 1979; Werner, 1972). Sometimes, by starting from different societal conditions, they were able to show that some results previously taken at face value by Americans and Europeans alike were probably the consequence of idiosyncratic American conditions rather than necessary concomitants of human behavior. In spite of such differences, however, the researchers from the old world shared with their American colleagues the concern for the young generation, and the belief that media matter in their lives.

We have already mentioned that we, too, share those concerns and beliefs. At the same time, however, our research differs from much of the research that has been briefly mentioned above. One reason for this is the simple fact that the research traditions we have just described originally stem from studies undertaken when television was a relatively new phenomenon, still an anomaly of sorts in a world which had never before seen the combination of living pictures and sound being mass-distributed into the homes of literally everybody. This perspective is most clearly seen in the first two classics of the genre, Himmelweit et al. (1958) and Schramm et al. (1961), but it has been with the tradition ever since. Indeed, one of the last great studies in this tradition, Williams (1986) is nothing more and nothing less than a careful and ingenious study of the introduction of television into three Canadian communities.

Our study is no study of television being introduced. On the contrary. It is a study of a quite normal, almost trivial phenomenon: television in the daily lives of children and adolescents living in a society which has been for decades a "television society." Our concern is with the causes and consequences of this everyday phenomenon. In order to sort out causes and effects among the confounding influence from a host of other variables, we have combined a panel approach with advanced statistical analysis. Our findings show that, in all its triviality, television may still have profound effects on the lives of children and adolescents—although these effects may sometimes be rather different from the ones observed in research carried out during an introductory phase, and in the research tradition growing out of such research.

Our study centers on the individual use made of television, a medium the shape of which is in an incipient process of thorough-going change. In the last wave of the panel studies reported in this book, the so-called new media appear on the scene. Video recordings, cable, and satellites are about to enter their (assumed) takeoff stages. Thus our studies may well be said to be located precisely on the threshold between two eras of mass communication: the era when national and local broadcast television reigned uncontested, and the era in which (presumably) these media will have to accommodate the new and partly unknown phenomena brought about by video recordings, cable, and satellite: time shifting, narrowcasting, teletext, videotex, zipping, zapping, and what not. In future studies of the initial stages of this assumed new era, our studies may well offer useful benchmarks against which the new developments may be assessed. Earlier studies, because of their greater temporal distance from recent developments, may be less suited to this role. This is one way in which our research undertaking differs from previous ones. There are other ways, however.

Although in retrospect one may construe some continuity in the history of mass communications research, what has predominantly characterized it is above all its adhoc nature. From time to time, governmental commissions have been appointed and cast their nets among research and researchers. From time to time the usual experiments or surveys have been undertaken by the doctoral candidates, supervised by their busy professors. This is characteristic of mass communications research in general, and also for research on the use made of mass media by children and adolescents. Consequently, the bulk of this research always runs the risk of becoming theoretically and methodologically naïve.

In contrast to this predominant trend, however, a relatively small number of long-range research projects may be found. Often such projects have been established in connection with panel studies, which by their very nature call for some continuity. Among the panel studies themselves there has been continuous methodological and theoretical development, reaching from the first crude cross-tabulations to cross-lagged correlations to path-analysis, to LISREL analysis based on explicit theoretical considerations, and so forth. During the last few years, as a result of a sustained interest in specific theoretical and methodological problems, a number of theoretically well-underpinned, methodologically quite sophisticated panel studies have been published, (for instance, Gerbner et al., 1980; Himmelweit & Swift, 1976; Huesman et al., 1984; Milawsky et al., 1982; Morgan, 1980; Tims & Masland, 1985; Williams, 1986). We like to see our research as a link in that chain.

Part of the reasons behind the incipient development of long-term research on the use of mass media by children and adolescents is the growing insight that in order to understand the phenomena under study, they must be followed as they develop over time. As a consequence of this insight, there has been a general trend toward the study of long-term effects on the minds and acts of the users of mass media. Having ourselves been part of this development, we wholeheartedly endorse it, hoping that our book will help keep the development going.

Concomitant with this development toward a long-term perspective has run a related development toward broadening the research perspective from the originally ameliorative, predominantly morally oriented interest in specific effects (violence, reading scores, etc.) toward broader and also more diffuse effects on the minds and acts of children and adolescents (ideas about the self, the surrounding society and the world at large; relations to parents, peers, and other agents of socialization). We feel we have been part and parcel of this development, too, and we hope that our book will help keep the development going also in this respect.

The developments just sketched are closely related. They also have a common prerequisite and a common consequence. An increased interest in sociologically oriented theory is both a precondition and an outcome of the gradual turn away from short-term, specific effects. This growth in theoretical interest, as well as the ensuing increase in theoretical sophistication, has taken several paths. While communications studies are gradually establishing themselves as a distinct academic discipline, the classical disciplines have still a vested and continuing interest in the field, especially, perhaps, psychology and sociology.

We are sociologists of communication, and some of us have also been working at departments of communication. Consequently, our main theoretical perspectives are both sociological and communicative. We believe that individual use of mass media is strongly influenced by the surrounding social structure, and by the individual's position in that structure. We also believe in the power of society and its culture to shape, not only the content offered by the media, but also the individual's perception, understanding, and use of that content. In our studies of media use we apply not only the structural perspectives of social class and culture, but also the processual perspective of socialization.

Theories of sociology and social psychology come naturally to us, then. Working for a decade or so with the use made of mass media by children and adolescents, we have, of necessity, also become deeply interested in the biological, psychological, and social phenomenon of development. Here we have no original expertise of our own, but we trust that we have been able to borrow what we needed from the neighboring discipline of psychology. At the same time we do have a feeling that mass communications studies have actually been dominated by a psychologizing perspective, sometimes unreflectively applied at the expense of an equally important sociological perspective. We would feel content if our book would do its part to help redress the balance.

Another controversial area in which we have taken a stand is the classical question of whether a quantitative or qualitative approach is to be preferred. In our opinion the dichotomy is rather meaningless. All serious social studies must use both approaches, starting with qualitative experiences which, systematized and ordered in various ways, prepare the ground for quantitative studies, which in their turn may lead up to new and more precise qualitative observations, and so on. This is the way we have been working, at least, and we believe this is the way most good research is actually being done. While most of the results presented in this book are couched in quantitative terms, our work started with qualitative studies of children and their media use (the use made of mass media by our own children, for instance). In addition, in later phases of our research program, qualitative moments have been a recurrent theme (for instance qualitative interviews with adolescents, their parents, and teachers). The distinction between quantitative and qualitative studies is often wrongly presented as an either/ or problem. We firmly believe that in reality the obvious solution is: *Both ways!*

Much the same goes for two other basic dichotomies which have been subjected to much heated debate: the anthropological problem about the nature of man, and the sociological problem about the nature of society. "Is man basically an acting and willing subject or a passive object of strong inside and outside forces?" "Is society basically characterized by conflict or consensus?" We firmly believe that human beings are both subject and object, and we also firmly believe that all societies are characterized by both conflict and consensus. Indeed, the interesting problem is the dialectics between the elements of the two dichotomies.

How do willing and acting subjects become degraded into an existence as passive objects, and how do passive objects raise themselves, turning again into acting and willing subjects? How is consensus reached in a society characterized by basic conflicts, and how is conflict kept alive in a society built upon consensus? These, rather than the false either/ or dichotomies, are the really interesting problems, and in both cases, mass media and mass communication play very important roles:

- As carriers of society's overall culture and also of specific subcultures;
- As political arenas of conflict and consensus;
- As evermore ubiquitous and powerful agents of socialization;
- As a means to express group identity and group affiliation, and,
- As individual instruments of knowledge and pleasure, power and subjugation.

More than once, therefore, and in more ways than one, we will have occasion to return to the classical problems of subject vs. object, consensus vs. conflict. As we present the results of our panel studies of the use made of mass media by Swedish children and adolescents, we shall try to be as general as possible, not dealing just with this or that specific, more or less time-honored problem in mass communication research. Rather, we shall also try to approach very general questions and problems central to children and adolescents of all modern societies (and to their parents): children's development, their relationships with family, peers, school, and the mass media; their pictures of themselves, their society, and the world at large.

Our main perspective has been framed within the sociology of communication. We are interested in the role played by mass media, especially television, in the lives of children and adolescents living in a television-saturated society on the verge of a new communications revolution. Media matter to kids, and kids matter to us. That is what our book is all about.

Acknowledgments

This book is based on a decade's research carried out within the Media Panel Program at the University of Lund and the University College of Vaxjoe. Before the start of the program, the two senior authors worked together for about 5 or 6 years on related problems. The book is thus the product of teamwork stretching over more than 15 years and closely involving about a dozen persons.

Over the years, a division of labor has established itself within the group. Ulla Johnsson–Smaragdi and Inga Sonesson have been responsible for each of the two panels forming the backbone of our studies. Along with Elias Hedinsson, Ingrid Höjerback, Annelis Jönsson, and Keith Roe they also supervised the data collection and themselves did a lot of interviewing.

The first sifting of the data was presented in the many technical and preliminary reports produced by everyone in the group. Further data cultivation was undertaken in the six doctoral theses up until now submitted within the program, by Inga Sonesson, Elias Hedinsson, Keith Roe, Ulla Johnsson–Smaragdi, Annelis Jönsson, and Bertil Flodin. Without these theses, of course, this book could not have been written. In the production of the additional data necessary for the book, Ingrid Höjerback and Gunilla Jarlbro were indispensable.

The book itself was written mainly by Karl Erik Rosengren and Sven Windahl, in close cooperation with the rest of the group. Windahl wrote first drafts of chaps. 1 through 4; Rosengren, the prefatory observations, parts of chaps. 1 through 4, and first drafts of chaps. 5 and 6. Rosengren was responsible for rewriting and for the final editorial work. Keith Roe revised the English. Authors and co-authors share the responsibility for the book in its entirety, although, of course, all of us do not subscribe to every single statement in it.

The data of the Media Panel program have been stored and processed according to the general rules and specific prescriptions of the Swedish Data Inspection Board. We thank the Board for comments and advice.

Gunnel Norén was our secretary. Without her patient help and kind efficiency, the group would probably have broken down long ago, from fatigue and desperation.

From outside the group, additional resources were willingly provided by a number of people and institutions.

Already at the planning stage, and often later, Jay Blumler, Ray Brown, Hilde Himmelweit, Denis McQuail, and Anita Werner generously shared with us their own experiences from similar undertakings. Together with Inga Sonesson and Erik Allardt the latter three also acted as "Opponents of the Faculty" when the doctoral theses produced within the program were formally presented to the university. Among the many other colleagues with whom we have had the good opportunity to discuss our work, we would like to mention especially David Altheide, Torbjörn Broddason, Cecilia von Feilitzen, George Gerbner. Bradley Greenberg, Robert Hawkins, Gerald Kline, Mark Levy, James Lull, Kjell Nowak, Philip Palmgreen, Alan Rubin, and Lennart Weibull.

Herman Wold and Karl Gustav Jöreskog tutored us in the powerful but difficult techniques of PLS and LISREL, while Agneta Sternerup at the Lund University Computer Center helped us with the many technical data handling problems associated with the complex design of the study.

Various versions of reports and chapters from the group have been discussed at a large number of seminars and conferences in Europe and the United States. At a symposium in Sätra, convened by Allmänna Barnhuset, Stockholm, overall results from the research program were constructively discussed by a number of Swedish researchers, decision makers and practitioners in the field. At a final seminar in Lund, members of the research group at the Unit of Mass Communications Research, University of Göteborg, in a very productive way criticized the next to last version of the book. Two additional readers provided most helpful suggestions about deletions, additions, and rewriting.

A number of teachers, directors of study, headmasters, and school directors very kindly let us interfere time and again with their work for hours and days on end, so that we could get our bulky questionnaires properly marked by their students. Many teachers also helped us with various ratings of children and adolescents. A number of schoolchildren and adolescents helped by generously taking part in long, qualitative interviews, and essays' writing.

The financial basis for the Media Panel Program has been generously provided by the Swedish Council for Research into the Humanities and the Social Sciences, the Bank of Sweden Tercentenary Foundation, and the Swedish National Board of Education. The University of Lund provided six graduate students' grants. The universities of Lund, Vaxjoe, and Göteborg have offered excellent working facilities and generous leaves of absence for research.

We would like to thank all these friends and colleagues, institutions, and authorities warmly for their assistance and support. What merits our work may have to a large extent are due to them. The remaining weaknesses are our own. We could not bring ourselves to kill all our darlings, much as our friends asked us to do so. We are grateful for what they made us do, though.

Our main gratitude, however, is to 1,768 children and adolescents from Malmoe and Vaxjoe, and to their parents. With much patience and almost complete confidence they told us a lot about themselves and their lives, again and again, as many times as we asked. We hope we have understood the essence of their story, although for technical reasons they were forced to tell it mainly by ticking off items in questionnaires. We also hope we have been able to retell it faithfully, for it is a story worth telling.

Lund and Vaxjoe, in May, 1987

K. E. R., S. W.

1

Introduction

1.1. GENERAL BACKGROUND

The Media Panel Program is the framework of the study presented in this book. The research program is carried out jointly at the Department of Sociology, the University of Lund, and the Department of Information Techniques at the University College of Vaxjoe, Sweden. The aim of the program is to study media habits and the causes and effects of television use among children and adolescents. The directors of the program are Professor Karl Erik Rosengren and Dr. Sven Windahl.

The first work of the Media Panel Program dates back to 1969, when two of the members started a series of studies within the uses and gratifications tradition. This early work resulted in a number of reports and articles published in the 1970s (e.g., Rosengren 1974; Rosengren & Windahl 1972, 1977; Rosengren et al. 1976). A focus of interest at that time was the relation between the audience and media content, termed parasocial interaction, in which members of the public established quasipersonal relationships with people they meet on the screen (Horton & Wohl, 1956). As will be seen later in this book, our interest in this type of relationship persists, at the same time as our scope has broadened.

During our work within the uses and gratifications tradition in the early 1970s, a growing interest emerged for applying this approach in a large study of media use among children and adolescents. There were several reasons for this, one being that we wanted to study the origins of individuals' mass media use, and we found that it would be suitable to concentrate on younger members of the audience, comparing the mass media use of Swedish children and adolescents, its causes and effects, with phenomena in other countries.

Processes of media use and media effects are sometimes naïvely conceived of as occurring in a social and cultural vacuum. Very often we automatically accept results of communication research in other countries and cultures as valid for the context in which we find ourselves, forgetting to ask whether the many differences that undoubtedly exist between the two settings have any importance. For many years this

1

has been the case for Europeans, many of whom have willingly adopted American frames of reference, only to be subsequently surprised when perceiving that results obtained by U.S. researchers have been difficult, if not impossible, to trace in European replications. It could possibly be argued that the Media Panel Program, too, has uncritically accepted views and frameworks with origins elsewhere. We hope that we have not. At least we have been aware of the problem and, throughout the book, we shall occasionally discuss this matter when we find it relevant.

Studies aimed at finding the impact of cultural differences on communication between societies are too few (for exceptions, cf., e.g., Melischek, 1984; Miyazaki, 1981; Melischek, Rosengren, & Stappers, 1984). One reason for the scarcity of such studies may be the dilemma they have to face: They must use comparable concepts and operationalizations at the same time as they are required to heed the idiosyncrasies of the particular country and culture under study. That dilemma, however, should be regarded as a challenge rather than as a reason for evading such studies. The Media Panel Program, at least, is aware of the challenge.

This is a Swedish study, and the results we present reflect a Swedish reality. At the same time we maintain that what we have to say possesses a more universal applicability.

In order to give the reader some flavor of the Swedish cultural context, we shall provide a short description of two contemporary aspects of it, that of the Swedish media structure and that of the Swedish school system. Between them, and in interaction with the family and the peer group, mass media and school dominate the lives of Swedish children and adolescents, just as in all other modern societies.

1.2. SWEDISH MEDIA AND SWEDISH SCHOOLS

1.2.1. The Media Scene

The prevailing Swedish media ideology is best characterized as one of social responsibility (Gustafsson, 1983; Hadenius & Weibull, 1980; Siebert et al., 1956). Radio and television are of a "public service" type, and state intervention into the press is minimal and positive (cf. Gustafsson & Hadenius, 1976; Hultén, 1984a). Controversies in the media sector (for example, complaints about media content by the public) are regulated mostly outside the regular judicial system by press and radio-television councils and "ombudspersons." Media professionals seem to enjoy relatively high autonomy compared with their counterparts in many other countries (Windahl & Rosengren, 1976, 1978).

The Swedish Broadcasting Corporation, Sveriges Radio AB, has a monopoly status but is not governmentally owned. The owners include labor and adult education organizations, churches, the press, the Church of Sweden, representatives of the business sector, and so forth. Basically, broadcasting is regulated by the Broadcast Act, which states that permission to broadcast in Sweden is given exclusively by the government. There is no precensorship, but complaints may be raised before the Radio Council, which controls how the broadcasting company performs with regard to the Broadcast Act and other regulations.

It is important to note that in principle there is no (and in reality very little) direct governmental intervention into programming. Within the given structure of the broadcasting system, Sveriges Radio is an independent body with considerable freedom to act within the frames of "impartiality and factuality." Sveriges Radio is mainly supported by licence monies (only educational programs are paid for by the state). There is no commercial programming in radio or TV and no commercials. The question of whether commercials should be allowed or not has been discussed for at least the last 20 years. This debate has recently received fresh stimulus as a result of the foreign satellites which have started carrying commercial content into Sweden, often redistributed by way of cable (Roe, 1985b; Severinsson, 1985; Svärd, 1985).

The Swedish radio contains three channels, one for information and culture, one for (mostly classical) music, and a third that carries light music and local programming.

Television offerings comprise two channels which are supposed to be competitive within certain limits. Television started on a regular basis in the late 1950s. In 1969 the second channel was added to the first, and in 1970 color TV became the norm. Each channel is on the air for about 50 hours a week. Typical weekday programming starts at 4:30/P.M. on one channel and 1 hour later on the other, both with children's programs. (Daytime educational TV is transmitted for the benefit of the schools.) Both channels close down between 10 and 11 at night. Weekend programming starts earlier and ends later.

In Sweden, just as in most other industrialized countries, TV is the most important mass medium (cf. McCain, 1986). The average daily viewing time for the whole population aged 9–79 is about 2 hours (Mediebarometern). Amount of time spent viewing peaks in late childhood and early adolescence, and again shortly before and after retirement. The former time period is the object of study of the Media Panel Program.

Between 50% and 60% of the content broadcast is of Swedish origin. An idea of the content structure of Swedish TV is presented in Figure 1.1 where the relative time of different categories of content is contrasted to the relative time the public devotes to these types of programs during an average day. From the figure it is evident that for the categories "facts and documentaries", "music," and "children" output is relatively larger than consumption. The relatively higher output of these categories may be said to reflect the ambition to offer, not only entertainment, but also information and culture, as well as programming especially designed for the younger viewers. With news, fiction, and sports it is the other way around. Here, the viewers' interest exceeds the output. It is possible to uphold the difference between output and public preferences because of the monopoly (today increasingly threatened by satellite broadcasting in combination with new cable systems). With the print media the situation is different.

The Swedes are heavy consumers of print media. This holds true especially for the daily and weekly press. Few, if any, other countries evidence a higher consumption of daily papers per capita (Gustafsson, 1983; Gustafsson & Hadenius, 1976; Weibull, 1983a, 1983b). The output is also relatively large. Some 110 dailies (papers issued 3–7 days a week) are published, and there is still competition between papers even in smaller towns and cities. This competition to a large extent has been sustained by a system of subsidies to the press, aimed at giving the

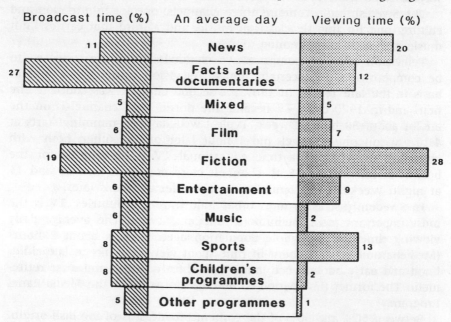

Figure 1.1. Types of TV Content Broadcast and Consumed on an Average Day (From Wigren & Gahlin, 1981)

weakest paper in a competitive situation sufficient resources to enable it to carry on (Gustafsson & Hadenius, 1976; Hultén, 1984). The circulation figures for the daily press have been fairly stable during the last few years; only the evening papers have shown a decreasing circulation.

There is also a fairly large market for popular weeklies. It is estimated that the Swedish population of some 8.3 million consumes about 200 million copies of popular weekly magazines a year. These are mostly read by women. Most of these magazines also draw the main part of their readership from the working and lower-middle classes (Mediapocket).

During the last decade the circulation of specialized magazines (hobbies, technology, etc.) has increased substantially. These types of magazines draw their readership mainly from the upper echelons of society.

Closely related to the weeklies are the comics. In 1979 the comics market held some 55 different publications totaling some 42 million copies a year. The bulk of the market is imported and translated, even if many efforts have been made to produce more Swedish material. The single largest comics publication is Walt Disney's "Donald Duck." The market has been shrinking in terms of the number of publications, but the number of copies is relatively stable (TS-boken). Most comics are read by youngsters in the age brackets studied by the Media Panel Program.

Another medium appealing to youth is film. Just as in most other comparable countries the cinema market in Sweden contracted more or less continuously during the 1970s and 1980s. One obvious reason for this is the increasing use of TV and, recently, video recording. The yearly number of visits to the movie theatre is approximately 26 millions (1979). Of special interest to us is the fact that, on average, the cinema public is quite young. On a normal night some 55% of moviegoers are under the age of 25 (of these, 64% are males; Mediapocket; Svennning & Svennning, 1983). Most of what Swedish movie houses offer is imported (and subtitled). In 1979, 6% of what was shown was of Swedish origin (Svenning & Svenning, 1982).

During the period of study both cinemas and broadcast television got a new competitor. A new medium entered the market and was intensively debated, namely, the videocasette recorder. Sales increased steadily during these years, with the figure of 0.14% of all households having such recorders in 1977 rising to 3.2% in 1980 and 20% in 1984. (Hultén 1986; Orvesto 1985; Video Committee, 1981).

Recent special studies of video indicate that children and adolescents use video recordings much more than do adults. In 1981 about 43% of the adolescents in Malmoe had access to video, at home or with friends etc. In 1984, 42% of the Malmoe adolescents had access to video at home (Höjerback, 1985; Hultén, 1984b; Roe, 1981; cf. Wall & Stigbrand, 1983). When published, these results were widely debated, as was the video medium as such, actually so much so that it seems appropriate to talk of a "moral panic" (Lindell, 1984; Roe, 1985a; Svärd, 1985). The main reason for the debate about video was that films on video could now reach the public, especially the youngest part of it, without passing through the regular official "censorship" channels of the Swedish government operating for cinema film. There are reasons to believe, however, that the rapid expansion of VCRs in the early 1980s is now flattening out. After the hectic introductory phase that so often occurs when new media are being introduced, video recordings seem to be entering calmer waters.

After this short presentation of the Swedish media scene, we turn to a presentation of the Swedish school system.

1.2.2. The Swedish School System

The interplay between those two important agents of socialization, the school and the mass media, have been analyzed within the Media Panel Program by Sonesson (1982), Jönsson (1985), and Flodin (1986). Roe (1983a, p. 107) offers a short description of the Swedish school system which may help to understand some of the results presented in other parts of our book:

> There is not scope here to describe the Swedish school system in detail. Descriptions of both the history of reform and the present system may be obtained, in English, from Andersson (1969), Stenholm (1970) and Lundgren (1979). Briefly we may remark that all children must attend school for at least nine years. Practically all children attend state comprehensive schools, although a miniscule private sector does exist. The minimum leaving age is 16, and all state schools are mixed according to sex. The great majority (84% in 1980) continue to the high school (gymnasiet) for periods of 1–4 years depending on the courses taken.

In essence (especially in comparison with the British and American systems) the system is centrally organized. There exists a "teaching plan" for each subject taught in each year which is centrally determined and meant to be followed by every child within the system reading those subjects. This plan deals with general aims, content, standards, and so forth. Considerably leeway exists, however, within the general plan for teachers to organize and conduct their lessons in the way they wish.

All pupils follow the same courses of study up to the end of the sixth year. After this specialization may begin with choices available in a number of subjects. Obviously choices made at this time later on may affect the student's choice of line of study at the high school, although formally, the early choice should not affect later choices.

During the period of this study an end-of-year mark was awarded in grade 3, and from the sixth year onwards. The end-of-year mark is based on a 5-degree scale, (1 low to 5 high; average 3). The concepts of pass and fail are no longer formally used. The 5-degree scale is meant to be applied relatively. It is intended that the marks of all Swedish pupils reading a given subject at a given age are to be distributed over the scale in accordance with the Gauss curve. 40% of students should receive 3, a little over 20% at 2 and 4, and only a few with 1 or 5. The distribution is thus not based on the course but on how the performance of each student reading the subject concerned relates to all other students reading the subject. It is important to note that theoretically the curve is meant to be achieved over Sweden as a whole and not in each individual class (taken from Stenholm, 1970). The system of mark giving has not been without controversy. The notion of a normal curve over the entire country tends to be unfulfilled as teachers are more reluctant to mark down than up. Consequently the curve tends to be skewed toward the upper end of the scale.

After these presentations of the Swedish media scene and the Swedish school system, we turn to a presentation of the Media Panel Program.

1.3. THE ORGANIZATION OF THE MEDIA PANEL PROGRAM

1.3.1 General Background

The Media Panel Program is a large venture. Between 1975 and 1981, some 1,800 children and adolescents and their parents were questioned about their media habits and a number of related phenomena. This report is based on only a part of the material thus gathered.

The children and adolescents whose media habits are dealt with in this book live in two Swedish cities. The larger one, Malmoe with some 230,000 inhabitants, lies in the center of a metropolitan area right across the Öresund straits to Copenhagen. The other one, the southern Sweden inland city of Vaxjoe, with about 65,000 inhabitants, was chosen because it stands out as something of a Swedish Middletown. With this, we cannot claim to have covered, for example, the rural parts of Sweden, but we do have an opportunity to compare the middle-sized and the larger city.

The media scene in these two cities can be summarized as follows: For Vaxjoe the TV options were at the time of the study confined to the two channels of Sveriges Radio, but in Malmoe people had and have the additional opportunity of watching a Danish TV channel regularly. As for radio, both cities had their public service local radio station in addition to the three Sveriges Radio channels. The fact that Sweden is a newspaper-reading country, is mirrored in Vaxjoe (two morning papers) as well as Malmoe (three morning and one afternoon paper). As for movie theaters, Vaxjoe had four in 1980, Malmoe some 20. Movies are also regularly shown to young people in the municipal leisure centers.

Our major aim has been to study media habits and their origins, effects, and consequences during childhood and adolescence. This is done in two studies, designed to be treated as independent from each other but comparable. The Malmoe study concerns the younger media users and the Vaxjoe study covers the older. The Malmoe study is based on a three-wave panel, the "preschool panel." The Vaxjoe study has a combined cross-sectional and longitudinal design, where the backbone is a three-wave panel—the "Main (Vaxjoe) Panel"—of some 500 students attending primary school.

Dr. Inga Sonesson was responsible for the Malmoe study, whereas for the Vaxjoe part the responsibility has been mainly with Dr. Ulla Johnsson–Smaragdi. Other contributing members of the group are Dr. Bertil Flodin, Dr. Elias Hedinsson, Ms. Ingrid Höjerback, Dr. Gunilla Jarlbro, Dr. Annelis Jönsson, and Dr. Keith Roe.

1.3.2. Theoretical Points of Departure

The theoretical approach in this book is broad. We want to show that childrens' and adolescents' media use and what comes out from that can be approached from a number of different vantage points. That conviction is manifested in our basic conceptual model and in the way we have structured the book.

Two major traditions in communication research are the uses and gratifications approach and the effects tradition (Rosengren, Wenner, & Palmgreen, 1985; Bryant & Zillmann, 1986). On several occasions over the years, we have advocated a merger of the two traditions into a "uses and effects approach" (Rosengren & Windahl, 1972, 1978; Windahl, 1981). This idea is not new, but only too seldom has it been carried out in empirical work (cf. Palmgreen, Wenner, & Rosengren, 1985).

With the uses and effects approach we cover a full process: a causal chain starting with sociological and psychological conditions for media use, going from there to media use itself (our main interest being TV), and ending up with the consequences and effects of media use. The aim to cover the entire process is present in the conceptual scheme that has guided our efforts as an organizing, heuristic device from the very beginning (Figure 1.2). This is not to say that our theoretical thinking has not developed under the period of study. It has, as will be evident from the discussions in this book.

In the scheme, the main hypothesized relationships between six bundles of variables are marked out with arrows. (Others are, of course, possible.) Much of the theories, models, hypotheses, concepts, and operationalizations are offsprings of the thinking and work of the research group itself; more is humbly borrowed from other sources.

The scheme offers an opportunity for an overview of our main variables. The main variables contained in the different boxes are listed in Table 1.1. The actual number of variables used in the program is larger—several thousand.

In the overall disposition of the book we have wanted to point at the possibility to use different perspectives when looking at media uses and effects among young people. After a basic description of television use, our focus is on three perspectives: development, social class, and socialization as these phenomena affect and are affected by media use, especially television. Media use, as well as its effects and consequences, are different at different developmental stages, in different social classes, and types of socialization.

Common to these three "perspective" chapters is an effort to elaborate on two basic insights. First that, far from being a homogeneous phe-

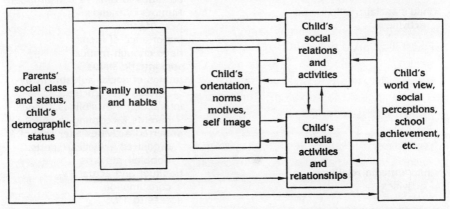

Figure 1.2. Conceptual Scheme of the Media Panel Study (From Rosengren & Windahl, 1978)

Table 1.1.   List of Main Variables in the Media Panel Study

Variable Area	Variables	
Parents' SES, child's demographic status	Parents'	Age, education, marital status, occupation, social class, place of birth
	Child's	Gender, age, grade birth order
Family norms and habits	Parents'	TV habits and preferences, dependency on TV, selectivity in TV use, attitudes to TV and to child's TV use (Brown & Linné, 1976; Sonesson, 1979), perception of parental TV control, interaction with children (according to parents), family communication pattern (Chaffee et al., 1973)
Child's orientation, motivation, interests, norms		Orientation toward parents/ friends (Bowerman & Kinch, 1959), self-image (Rosenberg 1965), attitudes to school (Murdock & Phelps, 1973), attitudes to own TV consumption
Child's social relations and activities		Number of friends, best friend, importance of friends, have enough friends, sociometric status, ratings of social adjustment by parents and teachers, interaction with siblings, friends, parents (according to child), preferred activities after school, organized activities (sports, hobbies, clubs)
Child's media relations and activities		Habitual and actual TV consumption, access to TV, TV preferences (type of content preferred and actually viewed),

Table 1.1.   List of Main Variables in the Media Panel Study

Variable Area	Variables
	TV viewing situation, control of TV viewing by parents, dependency on TV, motives for watching TV (Greenberg, 1974), selectivity in TV use, TV relations (parasocial interaction, capture, long-time identification), parents' estimate of child's TV viewing and preferences, consumption of radio, newspapers, comics, weeklies, books, cinema, popular music, video recordings motives for listening to music, types of music preferred
Child's school achievements, world-view, social perceptions, etc.	School tests and grades, educational plans, dream job, anticipated future job, perception of sex roles, perception of occupational structure (Gerbner et al., 1980), perception of amount of crime (Gerbner et al., 1980), mean world index (Gerbner et al., 1980), locus of control (Rotter, 1966, 1975), important events in Sweden and the world, perferred country for emigration, new year's wishes, attitudes to politics, political activities

nomenon, the media use of children and adolescents is highly heterogeneous, not only differentiated along the basic structural dimensions of age, gender, and social class but also along a number of intervening variables such as attitudes and values held by the child and its family. Second, that the media use of children and adolescents is part and parcel of those two very basic processes of development and socialization. We believe that the character of childrens' and adolescents' mass media use, as well as its causes and consequences, can be properly understood only in the light of these two insights.

This is not meant to be a book specifically on Swedish youth and their media world. We believe that much of what we try to show applies in many other countries, and we do not believe that our methodological and theoretical approach is specifically Swedish. Rather, what we have tried to do is to combine a European and an American tradition in communication research, bringing some theoretical perspectives from sociology and social psychology to bear on empirical communication research.

1.3.3. The Design of the Malmoe and Vaxjoe Studies

Data for the *Malmoe study* build on a representative sample, originally 303 children born in 1969 and in the fall of 1975 attending the Malmoe municipal preschools (a voluntary year preceding the compulsory school system and attended by 98% of the children). The children were approached in the fall of 1975, and during the spring semesters of 1979 and 1981, that is, in preschool, grade 3 and grade 5. (In the rest of the book, these childrens' age will be given as 6, 9, and 11, not taking individual variations into account.)

In preschool, data were collected by Dr. Sonesson in long personal interviews; in grades 3 and 5, by means of questionnaires administered and completed at school. Teachers rated the children along a number of dimensions in preschool and in grade 5, and survey data were also completed with various types of register data. The mothers of the preschool children were approached by means of personal interviews and with mail questionnaires when their children were in grades 3 and 5. (The reason for approaching the mothers rather than both parents is because the parents seemed to want it that way. In a pretest we explicitly asked 50% of the fathers, 50% of the mothers to respond. But as it turned out, even in the majority of the cases where we asked the father, the mother was given the task—an indicator, perhaps, of still-existing sex roles in the division of labor between Swedish parents.)

In this situation, we decided to approach only the mothers (unless the child was living with a single, divorced, or widowed father). This goes also for the Vaxjoe study. In some 80%–85% of the cases, the parent responding turned out to be the mother. In many of the remaining cases, the mother was not a member of the child's household at the time of the investigation (ill, divorced, dead, etc.). All the same we will often refer to data obtained from the mothers as pertaining to "parents" or "families", since they do often refer to the family as a unit. Figures for panel mortality, response rates, and so forth, for the Malmoe study are given in Appendix A.1. They are all quite satisfactory, given the circumstances of a 6-year, three-wave panel study of small children and their parents.

The *Vaxjoe study* is more complex, having a combined longitudinal and cross-sectional design. Data were collected in three research waves: in the falls of 1976, 1978, and 1980. The design of the study is shown in Figure 1.3. In each wave some 1,000 children and adolescents from grades 5, 7, and 9 were questioned. In the first and the third wave the parents (mothers) of all the students were also included; in the second wave we only gathered data from the parents of those entering the scheme.

The adolescents born in 1965 constitute the main panel and are the only ones studied in all three waves of the Vaxjoe study (see Figure 1.3a). For the main panel we sampled some 500 adolescents; the other samples contain about 250 adolescents. The adolescents born in 1963, 1967, and 1969 constitute three "side panels" and appear in only two waves. The aim of the design was to ensure a combination of a longitudinal and a cross-sectional approach. With such a design, even better than with a panel alone, we could come to grips with the time dimension, so often overlooked by mass media researchers (Kline, 1977). Since our project deals with people in age groups where things change rapidly over time, this possibility has been of great value.

Changes and differences over time can be due to three main types of effects: age (or maturational) effects, generational (or cohort) effects, and situational (or contextual) effects. (In addition we may have effects due to first-order or higher interactions between age, generation, and situation.)

Our mixed approach enables us to describe and analyze the data in the following three ways:

1. *Panel analyses* demonstrate differences between the same group (cohort) of individuals as they move through time. Such differences and similarities may be due to maturational or situational effects (Figure 1.3a).
2. *Cross-sectional analyses* demonstrate differences and similarities between different age-groups at the same time. These differences and similarities may be due to maturational or generational effects (Figure 1.3b).
3. *Diagonal analyses* demonstrate differences and similarities between individuals of the same age at different periods of time. Such differences and similarities may be due to situational or generational effects (Figure 1.3c).

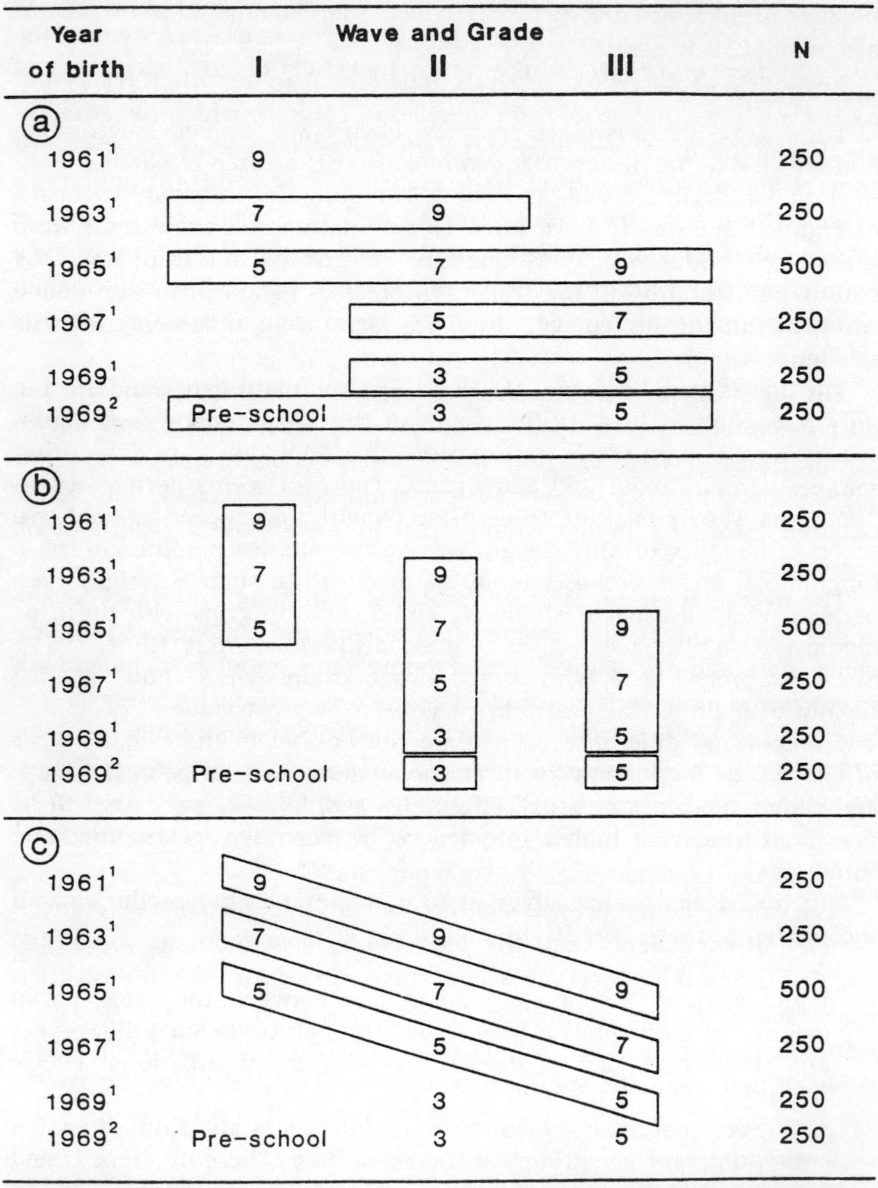

Year of birth	Wave and Grade			N
	I	II	III	
(a)				
1961[1]	9			250
1963[1]	7	9		250
1965[1]	5	7	9	500
1967[1]		5	7	250
1969[1]		3	5	250
1969[2]	Pre-school	3	5	250
(b)				
1961[1]	9			250
1963[1]	7	9		250
1965[1]	5	7	9	500
1967[1]		5	7	250
1969[1]		3	5	250
1969[2]	Pre-school	3	5	250
(c)				
1961[1]	9			250
1963[1]	7	9		250
1965[1]	5	7	9	500
1967[1]		5	7	250
1969[1]		3	5	250
1969[2]	Pre-school	3	5	250

[1] Data gathering for the Vaxjoe study. [2] Data gathering for the Malmoe study.

Figure 1.3.   Three types of Analysis in a Combined Cross-Sectional and Longitudinal Design

As each type of analysis offers its own combination of possibilities and limitations, combinations will often be advisable. Sometimes we shall point to the complexities of the phenomena under study by simultaneously presenting cross-sectional, panel, and diagonal data, or various averages of such data.

Regardless of the type of analysis undertaken, an important restriction on the analyses, of course, is the number of cases on which the analyses are based. Each of our three research waves comprised a sample of some 1,000 children and adolescents of the fifth, seventh, and ninth grades. (Note also the anomaly in the design, namely, the 250 extra third graders included in the second wave of the Vaxjoe study as a counterpart to the third graders in the Malmoe study.) The main panel, starting with the fifth graders in 1976, has a sample twice as large as the other samples.

For logistical reasons, the Vaxjoe samples could not be random, but all possible efforts were made to ensure that the school classes drawn for the sample taken together would be as representative as possible for the city of Vaxjoe. The main panel includes practically all Vaxjoe children belonging to the cohort born in 1965, which ensures good representativeness.

The overall response rates are satisfactory although they are considerably lower among the parents than among the children and adolescents. Data and discussion about response rates, number of individuals in subgroups often used in our analyses, missing data due to nonresponse, and missing items in indexes can be found in Appendix A.1.

Besides the more common types of statistical analysis, three statistical techniques used in this book (MCA, PLS, and LISREL) may need to be presented somewhat more closely to the reader not versed with them. This is done in some detail in Appendix A.2.

As a rule we do not present significance tests of percentage differences, correlation coefficients, and the like. We believe more in combining the size of the difference and the strength of the correlation with their theoretical relevance or intuitive plausibility, than with the statistical significance, which often reflects only the size of the subgroup under study. When used, the significance is symbolized the following way:

$P \leq .05$ *
$P \leq .01$ **
$P \leq .001$ ***

For further details on data collection, see Appendix A.1, as well as Johnsson–Smaragdi (1978, 1983), Sonesson (1979), Hedinsson (1981), Roe (1983a), Jönsson (1985), and Flodin (1986).

1.4. PLAN OF THE BOOK

The overall plan of the book is simple. Having in this chapter presented the general background of the Media Panel Program, as well as its theoretical and methodological points of departure, the following chapter will provide some descriptive data about the media use of the children and adolescents in the Malmoe and Vaxjoe studies. As a rule, the description is differentiated with respect to age, gender, and social class, but basically it is given in common-sense terms, as far as possible avoiding any specific theoretical perspective, explanations or interpretations. The aim of the chapter is twofold: firstly, to make the reader familiar with the way mass media in general, and television in particular, are used by Swedish children and adolescents, and, secondly, to give the reader a general feeling of the nature of our data and the opportunities they offer for various types of analysis.

The descriptive chapter is followed by the three main chapters of the book, each of which is guided by a different theoretical perspective. The lives of children and adolescents are always formed by two basic processes, development and socialization, which take place within a social structure differentiating individuals along the three very basic dimensions of age, gender, and social class. Our three main chapters represent three different orientations to the interplay between the social structure and the processes taking place within it.

Chapter 3 centers on the processes of biological, cognitive, and social development and the way that media use by children and adolescents may be understood in developmental terms. Chap. 4 deals with social class and the way that dimension of the social structure affects the media use of children and adolescents, as well as the effects and consequences of that use. Chap. 5 regards childrens' and adolescents' media use as a specific case of the general process of socialization, stressing the fact that socialization to a large extent is differential with respect to the age, gender, and social class of the individual being socialized.

Common to the three chapters is an effort to elaborate on two basic insights. *First* that, far from being a homogeneous phenomenon, the use made of mass media by children is highly heterogeneous, differentiated both along the basic structural dimensions of age, gender, and social class and along a number of intervening variables such as attitudes and values held by the child and its family. *Second,* that the media use of children is part and parcel of those two very basic processes of development and socialization. We believe that the character of childrens' mass media use, as well as its causes and consequences, can properly be understood only in the light of these two insights. That belief is further discussed in the sixth and concluding chapter of our book.

2

Use Of TV: Some Descriptive Data

Television use has been a main focus for this research program. It may well be said that during the last few years, other media than TV have gained in importance among children and adolescents. In spite of this, we maintain that television is a major, perhaps *the* major, medium, occupying a large part of young people's free time. Therefore, understanding the many facets of television use helps us to understand media use as such. It will also help to understand the future use to be made of the so-called new media.

2.1. THE CONCEPTS OF MEDIA USE: HABITUAL AND ACTUAL CONSUMPTION

The task of describing media use may appear simple enough. However, in media research the term "use" has a variety of meanings, ranging from sheer "exposure" to a more or less well-motivated use of mass media content for fulfilling certain needs, as in most uses and gratifications studies (Windahl, 1981). We believe that in order to tap the notion of media use properly, something more than the often-used one-dimensional measurements is needed. Our own conceptualization is four-dimensional (Rosengren & Windahl, 1978; Sonesson, 1979; Windahl, 1981):

1. *Amount of consumption, in terms of time or media content:* That is, how much time is dedicated to the medium, how much media content is consumed.
2. *Type of content preferred and consumed:* That is, what kind of media fare is preferred and consumed.
3. *Type of relation to the content consumed:* That is, whether the user identifies with, or pseudointeracts with, the actors appearing in the media content—in the moment of consumption, and in the

18

long run (cf. Horton & Wohl, 1956; Rosengren & Windahl, 1972, 1977; Rosengren et al., 1976).

4. *Type of consumption situation (context):* That is, whether television content is consumed alone or in the company of others, if it is a primary or secondary activity, and so forth.

Other aspects could have been included as well. Degree of activity (Levy & Windahl, 1984, 1985) and dependency (Ball–Rokeach, 1985) would appear to be good candidates for inclusion as well as motives and gratifications, two major ingredients in uses and gratifications theory (Palmgreen & Rayburn, 1985). For "activity" we lack data that fit into this context. "Dependence" we regard as coming before and after use, and something similar goes for "motives" and "gratifications."

The first aspect of use to be discussed is the amount of media consumption. It can be measured in a number of ways, and we have used two. One operationalization is in terms of habits of consumption (which will here be called "habitual consumption"). Here, respondents are asked how much TV they generally watch. The other is in terms of actual consumption during a given time period ("actual consumption"). Researchers often fail to distinguish between these forms, but there is a profound difference (cf. Weibull, 1983a, 1985).

Habitual viewing stands for a pattern and depends on stable factors such as life situation, social position, general needs and interests, and general media output. A weakness with this type of measure is that we do not know the respondents' time frames—does an "average week", for example, mean the last week or an average of the last 4 weeks?

"Actual consumption" is, of course, more situationally bound. Both specific situation and specific media output are determinants, while general life situation and social position exert only an indirect influence. The relationship between the two aspects is presented in Figure 2.1.

For the Vaxjoe study the results on habitual viewing emerge from an index based on a series of six questions by means of which the respondents were asked to estimate their daily viewing on weekdays and at weekends.

Number of viewing weekdays per week;
Number of viewing hours per weekday;

Number of viewing Saturdays per month;
Number of viewing hours per Saturday;

Number of viewing Sundays per month;
Number of viewing hours per Sunday.

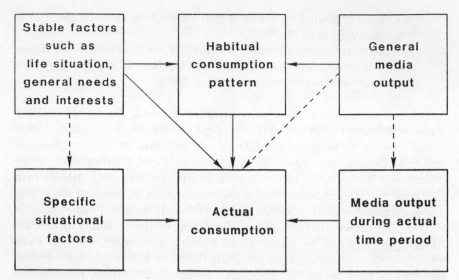

Figure 2.1. Relations Between, and Determinants of, Habitual Consumption and Actual Consumption of Media Content (Adapted from Weibull, 1983)

Weekly television viewing was then obtained by multiplying viewing days with viewing hours and adding the weekday, Saturday, and Sunday figures.

The parents (mothers) were also asked to rate their children's amount of TV consumption in the same way in which the children themselves did. This double set of data offers insights which either technique alone could not offer. (On parents' reports of children's viewing, cf. also Anderson et al. 1985, although these authors do not clearly make the distinction between habitual and actual viewing.)

The same techniques were used in the third wave of the Malmoe panel. In the first wave of this panel, however, we used a picture test to measure amount of consumption, since estimates made by 6-year-old children could not be expected to be very reliable (cf. below). Similarly, in the second wave of the Malmoe panel—when the children were about 9 years old—we used a somewhat simplified set of questions to measure their habitual consumption.

In the first wave of the Malmoe panel parents were asked to estimate their children's TV consumption in the same way as the parents of the Vaxjoe panel (but with only two questions instead of six). In the third Malmoe wave the estimates were done in exactly the same way in the two panels.

In both panels actual consumption was measured by means of a "diary" for 1 week during March, 1981. For the Malmoe panel this was just after the regular third data gathering wave; for the Vaxjoe panel it was about 4 months after that wave.

2.2. HABITUAL VIEWING

2.2.1. Habitual Viewing: The Malmoe Study

On the average Swedish children and adolescents watch less TV than do, for example, their American counterparts, who are reported to watch between 3 and 5 hours a day (Lawrence et al., 1986; Lyle & Hoffman, 1972; Morgan, 1980). On the other hand Swedish children and adolescents watch more than, for example, Norwegian ones, for whom Werner (1982) reports 1 to 1.5 hours a day. These differences to a large extent reflect the amount of TV output (and, perhaps, to some extent, the way consumption was measured in the different studies). Swedish figures tend to average between 2 and 2.5 hours a day (Filipson & Schyller, 1982; Johnsson–Smaragdi, 1981, 1983; Sonesson, 1982; Wigren, 1980, 1982).

Our Malmoe study offers data covering the age span from 6 to 11, differentiated for gender.[1] The results are presented in Table 2.1. They show that viewing increases considerably between these ages. In grade 5, at the age of 11, both boys and girls estimate their habitual viewing to be at least 2 hours a day.

Table 2.1. Habitual TV Consumption by Schoolyear and Gender. (Minutes/Day. Malmoe Panel, Parents' Ratings)

Wave and Gender					
I		II		III	
Preschool Boys	(6 years) Girls	Grade 3 Boys	(9 years) Girls	Grade 5 Boys	(11 years) Girls
97	86	106	97	105 143*	102 123*

* Children's Ratings

---

[1] We use the term "gender" when referring to the social meaning of being a male or a female, a young woman or a young man (cf. Game & Pringle, 1984, p. 15). The term "sex" is used when our arguments have somewhat closer connections with the biological bases of gender, for instance, in arguments about biological development. In some cases both terms may be used and in such cases we have as a rule preferred the term gender.

However, it should be noted that, except for grade 5, the data are based on parents' estimates (usually by the mother). The parental estimates differ markedly from the self-estimates that we have for the 11-year-olds. What creates the difference between parental and self-estimates is a methodologically interesting question (cf. Anderson et al., 1985). Is parental control perhaps most extensive in the early years of childhood? In any case, as the child grows older it is rather probably that more and more TV viewing will be done away from parental control, with the result that parental estimates will be increasingly less reliable. On the other hand, we may also assume that during the earlier stages of children's development the ability to estimate time is less developed.

An additional complication is that there may be a difference in parental perceptions of girls' vs. boys' viewing. Girls are usually more closely supervised by their parents, which may mean that the estimates of their viewing are more accurate than those for the boys. This may explain why the gap between boys' and girls' figures is smaller in the parental estimates than in their own. It is possible that the differential supervision of boys and girls may also explain the somewhat anomalous finding that girls' TV viewing seems to peak later than that of boys. (Otherwise, of course, girls are about 2 years before boys in reaching the transition phase between childhood and adolescence. For a more detailed discussion of related matters, cf. sec. 3.3.1).

2.2.2. Habitual Viewing: The Vaxjoe Study

Table 2.2 presents an overview of the habitual consumption figures from the three waves of the Vaxjoe study. The table contains average daily viewing by age and gender, as rated by the adolescents themselves, and by their parents (usually mother). The highest self-reported figure in the material (2 hours and 28 minutes) is found among boys aged 11 in 1976; the lowest (1 hour and 13 minutes) for 15-year-old girls in 1976 and 1980. The highest parental ratings in the table (1 hour and 34 minutes) are found for 11-year-old boys in 1978, and 13-year-old boys in 1980 (actually the same boys). The lowest parental rating (1 hour and 10 minutes) is found for 15-year-old girls in 1980.

There is an interesting pattern to be found in the differences between parents' estimates and the self-reported figures: a large gap for the 11-year-olds, especially for the girls, whereas the differences for the 15-year-olds are typically small, especially for the boys. A possible reason for this pattern was discussed in the previous section.

The table provides an opportunity for looking at television viewing in relation to age and gender. As for age, it is obvious that children

Table 2.2. Habitual TV Consumption by Schoolyear and Gender. (Minutes/Day, Vaxjoe Study, Parents' Estimates Within Parentheses)

Grade and Age	Wave and Gender					
	I		II		III	
	Boys	Girls	Boys	Girls	Boys	Girls
Grade 5, 11 years	148 (87)	124 (89)	139 (94)	128 (86)	136 (92)	103 (74)
Grade 7, 13 years	131 (86)	97 (81)	120 (—)	97 (—)	118 (94)	108 (76)
Grade 9, 15 years	100 (84)	73 (74)	100 (—)	76 (—)	91 (81)	73 (70)

in the fifth grade watch considerably more than adolescents of the ninth grade. Similar results have been found in several other studies (see, e.g., Comstock, Chaffee, Katzman, McCombs, & Roberts, 1978; Feilitzen, 1976; Lyle & Hoffman, 1972; Robinson, 1972; Werner, 1982). Usually, however, the claim that TV viewing declines during adolescence has been based on cross-sectional data. Table 2.2 and Figure 2.2 offer additional support by giving not only cross-sectional data, but also data from the main Vaxjoe panel and two side panels. From both cross-sectional and panel data, the same conclusion is to be drawn: a marked decrease in viewing during the age period under study. For the main panel this decrease goes from about 135 minutes on an average day in the fifth grade (11 years old) to about 85 minutes a day in the ninth grade (15).

From what we know from many other studies and from Tables 2.1 and 2.2 above, boys and girls tend to have different TV habits. Typically, boys are heavier viewers than girls of the same age, a pattern which proves its stability in spite of the dramatic changes occurring in the average amount consumed during different periods of childhood and adolescence.

Another important factor in explaining television use is social class. Usually working-class individuals watch more TV than do their middle-class counterparts. In Figure 2.3 these two background factors are combined, using data (means) from all three waves of the Vaxjoe study.

Social class was operationalized by means of an additive 5-point scale built on the occupational status of both parents (1-high status, 5-low). This class dimension was then dichotomized into middle class (values 1–3) and working class (4–5). The coding of the occupations was done on the basis of widely used Swedish lists of occupations ranked according to status. (Cf., for instance, Carlsson, 1958; Flodin, 1986; SCB, 1980, 1982. For a detailed discussion of the notions of class and status, see

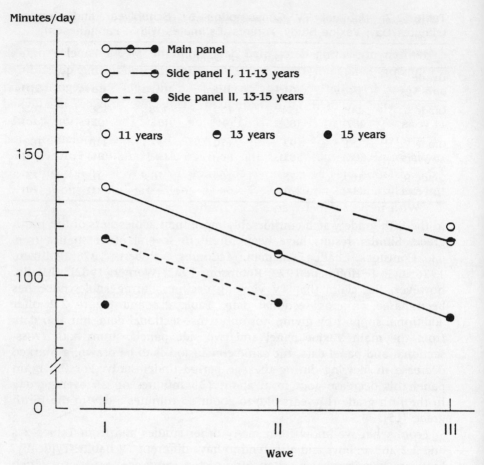

Figure 2.2.   Habitual TV Viewing by Age. Three Cross-sections, Main Panel and 2 Side-Panels (Minutes/Day), Vaxjoe Study. (From Johnsson-Smaragdi, 1983)

chap. 4 in this volume. For more details of the operationalization as such, see sec. 4.5.1)

The data of Figure 2.3 demonstrate the expected tendencies with great clarity. (By averaging over waves, situational and generational effects are controlled for as much as possible, allowing "pure" age effects to stand out more clearly; cf. sec. 1.3.3) The heaviest viewers are working-class boys, while the lightest viewers are middle-class girls. Middle-class boys and working-class girls come in between. In grade 5 (age 11), social class and gender interact, in grade 9 (age 15) the pattern is more clearly additive, gender differences being more important than class differences. Class differences diminish over time, while gender differences decrease in the middle class and increase in the working class.

When presenting descriptive data from the Media Panel Program, Johnsson–Smaragdi (1983, pp. 92ff) raises the interesting question of whether, over the years, adolescents from different subcategories tend to homogenize their TV consumption. (The same problem is touched on by Jönsson in her thesis (1985, pp. 69ff.) This question can be answered in at least three different ways: for whole populations, and with respect to within-class and between-class variation. Furthermore, the variation may be measured absolutely or relatively, that is, in terms of coefficients of standard deviation or coefficients of variation.

With respect to between-class variation in absolute terms, Figure 2.3

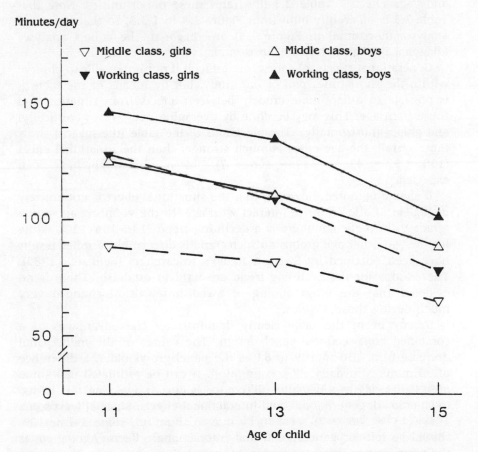

Figure 2.3. Habitual TV Consumption by Age, Gender and Social Class. Average of 3 Waves. Vaxjoe Study.

above provides a clear-cut answer: considerable homogenization occurs over time between the different gender and social class categories. This is also confirmed in Table A.6 in Appendix 3, where we find a considerable homogenization in absolute terms (linearly decreasing standard deviations). This is in line with earlier results reported by Morgan (1980), who maintains that this homogenization is a typical feature of television viewing in the years of adolescence. As can be seen in a second look at the same table, there is, however, at the same time a *decrease* in relative homogeneity—a paradoxical result of interaction between structural restraints and developmental changes. Such complicated interactions appear in other areas as well.

In an earlier section (1.3.3) we discussed the opportunities our design offers to distinguish between "generational effects," "situational effects," and "age effects." Table 2.3 illustrates these opportunities. Note that Table 2.3 is differently built from Figure 1.3 in 1.3.3, so that the panel analyses (horizontal in Figure 1.3) are diagonal; the cohort analyses (diagonal in Figure 1.3) are horizontal.

Generational effects, of course, are difficult if not impossible to observe within the short time span of our study, but by means of the table it is possible to differentiate crudely between effects from situation and those from age. This may be done by averaging over waves (vertically) and grades (horizontally). The marginals of the table (the means) show that, overall, the age effect is much stronger than the situational effect $(130 - 87 = 43, \text{vs.} 113 - 106 = 7)$. This is what might have been expected.

It should be noted, however, that the situational effect is not entirely negligible. It also seems to interact with age. In the youngest age-group (grade 5) in particular there is a declining trend (136–134–120), while for the two other age groups no such trend is discernible. Similar results have been obtained by Swedish Radio's researchers (Feilitzen, 1985). The reasons for the declining trend are hard to establish. There is no evidence that the programming of Swedish television changed very much during those 4 years.

In any event the table clearly demonstrates the advantages of a combined cross-sectional/panel design. The values of the main panel decrease from 136 to 109 to 83 as the panel grows older, a difference of 53 minutes in daily TV consumption. It can be estimated that some 80% $(130 - 87 = 43)$ of this difference is due to age. The rest is due to situational, generational, and interactional effects. Since at least some 10% $(113 - 106 = 7)$ seem to be due to situation, some 5% or 10% should be left for generational and interactional effects. Age, then, is the prime mover, but even within as short a time as 4 years, situational and generational factors are not entirely negligible. This is an important

Table 2.3. Average Habitual Consumption of TV in 3 Age-groups and 3 Waves. (Minutes/Day, Overall Means Controlled for Differential Size of Subgroups, Vaxjoe Study)

| | Wave | | | |
Grade	I	II	III	Mean
5	136	134	120	130
7	115	109	114	113
9	88	89	83	87
Mean	113	111	106	110

finding, for it encourages caution in drawing age-related conclusions from cross-sectional data, or even from panel data alone. The combination of the two types of data admits much stronger conclusions than each of the two types of data alone. Another way of strenghtening our conclusions is to use more advanced techniques of statistical analysis. An example of this will be given in the following section.

2.2.3. LISREL Analysis of Habitual TV Viewing

In this section we shall present the first LISREL model to appear in the book. In later sections, the reader will find a number of similar LISREL and PLS models, offering a wealth of information not otherwise available. We have tried to present the models in such a way as to make them understandable to the reader not previously familiar with the techniques of analysis on which the models are built. However, the interested reader unfamiliar with the techniques will probably do well in consulting Appendix A.2 before reading this section.

The model presented here is a relatively simple LISREL model of habitual TV viewing in our main Vaxjoe panel. The example is borrowed from Johnsson–Smaragdi (1983, pp. 88ff).

In the model the six measurements of TV viewing are combined into three manifest variables—amount of TV viewing on weekdays, Saturdays and Sundays, respectively—and thereafter used as indicators of the latent variable "amount of habitual TV viewing per week."

Manifest and latent variables constitute the measurement model in which it is also possible to estimate measurement errors. The relationships between the latent variables in their turn make up the structural model (see Figure 2.4).

From the coefficients linking the observed variables with the latent constructs in the model it appears that it is TV viewing on weekdays that is most heavily loaded on total viewing during a week, while TV viewing on Saturdays is the weakest of the indicators throughout the model. These coefficients also represent reliabilities of the measure, showing that the weekday indicator is the most reliable, and the Saturday indicator the least. The factor structure is fairly consistent over time. The coefficients on the arrows leading to the indicators from above represent measurement errors, while the coefficients on the double-headed arrows indicate correlated measurement errors. Apparently TV viewing at the weekend is not exactly the same thing as TV viewing on weekdays. Considering the age of the respondents and the differential programming, this is not very remarkable.

The stability of the TV measure is also moderately strong in the LISREL model, about .65 for each of the two 2-year periods. These coefficients, linking TV viewing at 11 years with TV viewing at 13 years and this in its turn with TV viewing at 15 years, also express the magnitude of the direct and indirect effects of earlier on later TV viewing. No direct path between TV viewing at 11 and at 15 is to be found, which means that TV viewing at 11 affects viewing at 15 only indirectly, since in this model the influence is transmitted exclusively through viewing at 13 years. The proportion of unexplained variance

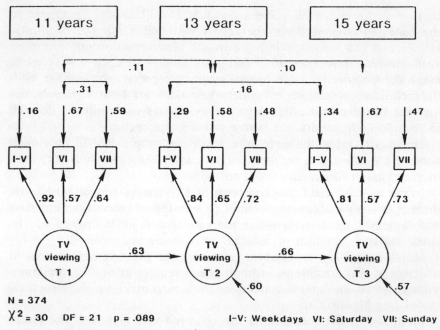

Figure 2.4. LISREL Model of the Stability in TV Viewing Over Time. Vaxjoe Main Panel. (Standardized Solution. From Johnsson-Smaragdi, 1983).

(due to disturbances or errors in the equations) in TV viewing at 13 and 15 is fairly high (.60 and .57), indicating that earlier TV viewing is able to explain less than half of the variation in later TV viewing.

The real strength of the LISREL technique comes to the fore in complex causal models rather than in relatively simple discriptive models like the one just presented. Nevertheless, it is interesting to compare the model with the graphic presentations offered in the previous section. They present a picture of drastic change in the television habits of children and adolescents in the age brackets under study. What the descriptive LISREL model just presented tells us is that in spite of these drastic changes, there is considerable stability in television habits. The amount of television viewed is drastically reduced for most or all of the children. Nevertheless, those who were high on television when 11 years old, also tend to be high when they are 15. That is the main message of our model. In later sections, we shall have occasion to modify this overall message somewhat, and also to compare it with the stability of television viewing of the parents (cf. secs. 2.7 and 5.3.2).

2.3. ACTUAL TV CONSUMPTION

2.3.1. Actual and Habitual TV Viewing Compared

In a previous discussion (sect. 2.1) about actual and habitual viewing, we noted that the terms of habitual and actual viewing stand for quite different phenomena. In order to supplement our results on habitual viewing with data on actual viewing we made an extra data collection in March, 1981, after the third wave of the Malmoe panel had been collected. At that time we requested the respondents to fill in a questionnaire, a diary of a detailed program schedule presenting the transmission times of all the TV programs of the previous week (two Swedish channels in Vaxjoe; in Malmoe, additionally, the Danish channel). We wanted to have data about actual TV viewing, data that would provide both specific and detailed information. (Anxious not to strain our relations with the respondents and the school authorities, we had refrained from asking for time-consuming diary data in the first two waves.)

Habitual and actual viewing are two distinctly different phenomena. Therefore, it would be wrong to expect a perfect correlation between them. In fact, the correlations between actual and habitual viewing in the Vaxjoe study are fairly low, as may be seen in Table 2.4, which presents the zero-order correlations between the habitual viewing measure and the diary data (weekly viewing).

Table 2.4. Zero-order Correlations Between Habitual and Actual TV Consumption During 1 Week. (Vaxjoe Study, Third Wave)

	Grade		
	5	7	9
Boys	.33	.24	.39
Girls	.52	.39	.52
All	.47	.30	.47

For a perfect fit to occur between the two phenomena at least three conditions must be met:

1. The information from the respondents should be accurate on both levels;
2. The actual time period should be an "average" time period;
3. Viewing behavior itself should be "average" for that particular time period.

It is hard to say anything about accuracy. But the measure of habitual consumption builds on six questions, and that of actual consumption on a detailed TV diary, so some efforts have been made to ensure accuracy.

Strictly speaking, of course, there is no such thing as an "average period." The choice of the week for the diary was largely determined by external considerations. For school (and other technical) reasons we were forced to choose a particular week in March. As it turned out, this was anything but an average week, if indeed such a thing exists at all. Two nights were dominated by lengthy sports events, and we can see that the boys—some of whom are great sports fans—show lower correlations than the girls. (The fact that the week we had to choose was a rather atypical one, may appear a disadvantage to our comparisons. However, it may also be used to show some theoretical arguments in sharper relief; cf. sec. 2.4.2)

As for viewing behavior, we know that it may vary considerably between seasons (see, e.g., Greenberg, 1976; Wigren & Gahlin, 1981). Our habitual consumption and actual viewing questions were posed at different times of the year (November, 1980–March, 1981); nevertheless, both occasions lie safely within the main "TV season."

Feilitzen (1976) maintains that questions about habitual viewing usually yield higher figures than corresponding diary data. But this was not the case in our study, as may be seen in Table 2.5.

It is noteworthy, however, that in spite of the fact that we measure

Table 2.5.   TV Consumption According to Questions About Habitual Viewing and TV Diary. (Minutes/Day, Vaxjoe Study, Third Wave)

	Grade		
	5	7	9
Habitual consumption	120	114	82
Consumption according to the diary	166	147	128
Habitual viewing in percentage of actual viewing	72	78	64

two different phenomena, there is the same tendency in both data sets, namely, the declining figures over age. The differences in mean consumption time may, to some little extent, be explained by the overlapping in reported viewing in the diary. But more important is the fact that Swedish TV aired some 4 hours of ice hockey that particular week. That "deviant" output illustrates in an effective way the difference between the two phenomena of habitual and actual media consumption. Actual viewing is to a large extent caused by very specific factors. More general and stable factors are more important to habitual viewing. But as we shall see in the following section, they also play their role for actual viewing.

2.3.2. Actual Viewing, Gender, and Social Class

Figure 2.5 illustrates the role played by social class, gender, and age for actual viewing.

As for gender, again it is clear that—controlling for social class—in every age-group boys watch more than do their female counterparts (although working-class girls watch slightly more than middle-class boys). For the boys, the age differences follow the main trend, with figures declining over age. Among the girls, seventh graders watched more than did fifth graders. We do not know which of these two categories it is that really deviates from the pattern, but, interestingly, we do find much the same anomaly in our radio data (Flodin et al., 1982). Figure 2.5 suggests that it may be the fifth graders that for various reasons were "too low", and additional data from Höjerback (1985) support this assumption.

Two other tendencies are suggested in our data. One is that—

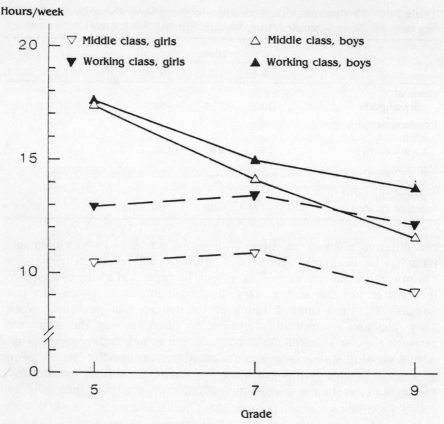

Figure 2.5. TV Diary. Actual Viewing Time by Social Class, Gender, and Grade. Hours/Week. Vaxjoe Study, Third Wave.

controlling for social class—gender differences tend to decrease over time. The gender differences in the fifth grade are almost twice as large as in the ninth grade. In contrast—controlling for gender—class differences tend to increase over time. This is especially visible among the boys (whereas among the girls the difference is very small). That gender differences in TV viewing tend to decrease over time has been reported elsewhere (cf., e.g., Filipson & Schyller, 1982; Greenberg, 1976). Earlier in this chapter we found that class differences in habitual viewing seemed to narrow over time, while gender differences increased in the working class and decreased in the middle class (Figure 2.3). It is intriguing to see that the class differences develop differentially for habitual and actual viewing. In the literature it has been suggested both that class differences in TV viewing increase (Greenberg & Dervin, 1970; Hedinsson, 1981, p. 107; Lyle & Hoffman, 1972) and that they decrease (Morgan, 1980).

The combined result of the various tendencies in our material is that the between-group range diminishes, with working-class boys clearly leading, middle-class girls clearly trailing, and the two other categories close to each other in the middle. One specific cause of the complicated pattern of Figure 2.5 may be the specific program mix of the diary week, with its heavy sports element.

We shall have reason to return to these and related problems in subsequent sections and chapters.

2.4 TV PROGRAM PREFERENCES AND ACTUAL VIEWING OF DIFFERENT TYPES OF CONTENT

TV consumption figures tell us only part of the truth about people's TV habits. We also need to examine their attitudes toward what they actually watch. This leads us into the content aspect of media use. This aspect in turn will be divided into two subaspects: preferences and actual viewing of different types of television content.

2.4.1. Preferences

Both as preschoolers and as third graders, the children of the Malmoe study were asked in an open question to state their favorite program(s). The answers were categorized in two ways: children's programs vs. general, adult programs on the one hand, and educational, entertainment and exciting programs on the other (cf. Soneson, 1979). Table 2.6 shows the results for boys and girls at the ages 6 (preschool) and 9 (third grade).

In this table, the changes are quite dramatic. Most striking, perhaps, is the change in preferences from childrens' programs at the age of 6

Table 2.6. Type of Favorite Programs by Gender and Age. (Malmoe Study. From Sonesson, 1982)

| | Preschool | | Grade 3 | |
	Boys %	Girls %	Boys %	Girls %
General Programs	13	7	87	80
Children's programs	87	93	13	20
Total	100	100	100	100
Educational programs	16	16	6	8
Entertainment	55	80	29	42
Exciting programs	29	4	65	50
Total	100	100	100	100

to general, adult programs as favorites at the 9, a tendency earlier noted by Feilitzen (1976). Another marked shift in preferences between preschool and the third grade is from entertainment programs to exciting ones.

Both sexes demonstrate the same pattern for the shift from children's programs to general programs. Gender differences, on the other hand, are visible when it comes to the distinction excitement/entertainment. In preschool, both boys and girls prefer entertainment to exciting programs, although the balance is much more even for the boys. In the third grade both boys and girls prefer exciting programs, but here the balance of excitement/entertainment is much more even for the girls. In both cases, boys prefer exciting programs much more than do girls.

In spite of the gender differences there is also some tendency toward convergence over time. In the lower part of the table in particular the differences are, on the whole, less dramatic in the third grade than in preschool. This tendency returns even more strongly among the older children.

In order to tap the TV preferences of the older children we asked them to state their preferences among 13 types of programs. This was done in all three waves of the Vaxjoe study and in the third wave of the Malmoe study. In the 1976 and 1978 waves the respondents were asked to name the 3 types of programs they like best (out of 13). In the third wave respondents were asked to rate all 13 types on a 5-point scale. This change gave us more information but a loss of comparability. Consequently, the preference data presented in Figure 2.6 are taken from the third wave only.

The average attitude toward most content types is positive. Only two types of content, social/documentaries and debate/interview, show values less than 2 (which corresponds to the response alternative "neither like nor dislike"). The respondents are not strongly negative toward any type of TV content—a fact which tells us something about the role of TV in the lives of children. Yet there are some differences within this generally positive outlook.

The most popular content categories are detective/crime stories, films, serials, and sports programs. This preference structure—very positive evaluations of entertaining and fictional content and less positive for informational content—is similar to results from other studies of media preferences among children and adolescents (Comstock et al. 1978; Feilitzen, 1976; Lyle & Hoffman, 1972; McLeod & Brown, 1976; Rubin, 1977; Wigren, 1982). It is also in agreement with the results just presented for the preschool panel in Malmoe.

In a previous section we noted that gender and social class are

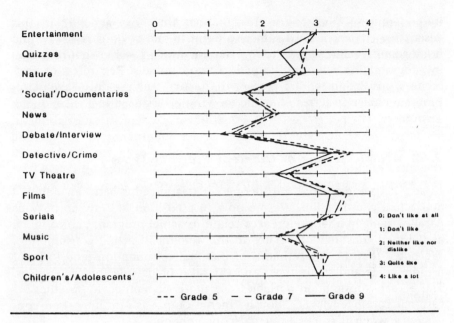

Figure 2.6.   TV Program Preferences by Grade. Vaxjoe Study, Third Wave. (From Flodin et al., 1982)

variables that strongly affect adolescent TV consumption. In the case of preferences their impact is less powerful. Actually, in preferences, there is a considerable homogeneity. Differences are small. Gender differences are somewhat greater than those caused by social class. Detective stories, films, and serials are preferred by one and all. After that boys tend to prefer nature programs and sports; girls, music and programs designed for young people.

McLeod and Brown (1976) report increasing gender differences over age but in this respect, too, there are only marginal differences in our data between the different age groups (cf. Johnsson–Smaragdi, 1983, p. 107). The homogeneity found *in nascendi* among the third graders now has become almost complete. In the Malmoe study of 11-year-olds (fifth grade), too, we have found almost identical preference profiles (cf. Sonesson, 1982). These results lead us discuss two problems.

First we have the problem of whether people tend to differ more in terms of the amount of mass media content they use than in their preferences. This question has been answered in different ways (Comstock et al., 1978; Wilensky, 1964). Our results show the former type of tendency, with greater variance between age, gender, and class categories for amount of viewing than for preferences.

Our second question concerns the possible causes of the homogeneity in preferences. What factors bring about this homogeneity? In this descriptive chapter it must suffice to point to one obvious factor behind homogeneity; namely, Swedish TV output, which is somewhat restricted by programming rules and limited to two channels. Regardless of preferences it is within this framework that actual viewing must take place. Program choice in terms of actual viewing is discussed in the following section.

2.4.2. Actual Viewing of Different Program Types

In sec. 2.1 we discussed the theoretical relationships between habitual and actual consumption. We are now in a position to draw an obvious parallel, namely, that preferences relate to actual program choice much as habitual consumption relates to the amount of actual consumption. We noted that the determinants of habitual consumption tend to be of a more basic and stable type, and this also holds true for preferences. The actual consumption variables are more susceptible to specific, occasional contingencies. Obviously, media output is one important contingency when it comes to actual consumption.

This case is similar to the relationship in social psychology between attitudes and actual behavior, where attitudes often fail to predict behavior. With this type of relationship we can never expect preferences to be perfect predictors of actual choice of media contents. Furthermore, the relationship is probably different for different media. Baranowski (1971) refers to results suggesting that preferences are poor predictors of TV viewing.

By means of the diary we are able to study preferences manifested in actual viewing behavior. Some TV programs, of course, stand out as more popular than others during the diary week. Indeed, one or two programs gathered an almost incredible public: 83% of the fifth graders in Malmoe watched "Dallas", 86% in Vaxjoe. Such figures should be compared with what, in Sweden, are otherwise considered large audiences. At the time of our data collection, some 40% of the population watched the first prime time news program, "Rapport" (cf. Findahl & Gaspar, 1981).

In Figure 2.7 diary data are presented, showing what types of programs the respondents really watched during the week of observation. If we compare the diary data with the data about preferences in the previous section, we find that, to a large degree, the discrepancies have to do with supply and demand. For instance, it will be recalled that one of the favorite program types was detective/crime stories. This category is totally absent in Figure 2.7, owing to the simple fact that there were no such programs on Swedish TV during the diary week. On the other hand, the final matches of the Swedish championships in ice hockey were played during that week, helping sports to appear as the generally most viewed program type during the diary period.

The high figures for films, serials, and entertainment are all to be expected in the light of the preference results. Similarly, but conversely, the category of debate and interview was seldom viewed and received correspondingly low ratings in the preference results. News was extensively viewed—about half an hour a day—in spite of quite modest preference ratings. Possibly we have an influence here from the viewing habits of the parents, an influence which may not yet have reached the level of appreciation and preferences.

Surprisingly popular was the category of documentaries and social reports which was noted as not very popular in earlier data. This discrepancy, however, may be at least partly accounted for by the fact

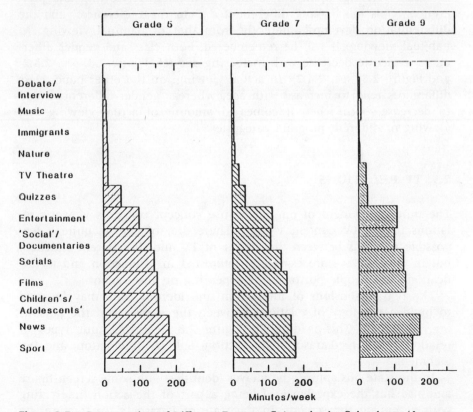

Figure 2.7. Consumption of Different Program Categories by Schoolyear (Average Minutes/Week). Vaxjoe Study. (Adapted from Flodin et al., 1982)

that in the coding of the diary this category was used as something of a catch-all category including, for example, film review programs. Possibly parental viewing habits may have an influence on this category, too.

In Flodin et al. (1982) the full results from the Vaxjoe diary are found with actual viewing by age, gender, and social class. The homogeneity in preferences is not to be found in actual viewing. Age, gender, and class exert their influence, with gender differences decreasing and class differences increasing with age (as suggested by the cross-sectional diary data).

Class differences were most marked for the ninth graders, among whom the working-class children watch most; this holds true for all content types of some popularity. Gender differences were most prevalent in grade 5, where the boys are the heaviest viewers in all the more popular content categories.

Actual viewing, then, differs from both habitual viewing and preferences. It is much more differentiated than the preferences, and the differentiation develops differently from that of habitual viewing. In habitual viewing, it will be remembered, both class and gender differences tended to decrease with increasing age (cf. Figure 2.3, sec. 2.3.2, and Figure 2.5, sec. 2.4.2). In actual viewing, on the other hand, class differences tend to increase with age, whereas gender differences tend to decrease, both when it comes to amount of actual viewing and viewing of different program categories.

2.5. TV RELATIONS

The third component of our media use concept concerns viewer's relations to the TV content viewed. There are, of course, quite a few possible relations between the viewer of TV and the content watched, but in our case we are especially interested in interaction and identification with people portrayed or appearing on the screen.

The two dimensions of interaction and identification may be used to build a typology of relations between the viewer and the persons on the screen. This is done in Figure 2.8, featuring four types of relations: Capture, Parasocial Interaction, Solitary Interaction, and Detachment.

In the state of Capture, the viewer identifies with some screen figure and also has the experience of being a part of the action (interacting with others on the screen). In the state of Parasocial Interaction, he or she does not identify but interacts with some person on the screen.

INTERACTION

	Yes	No
Yes	**Capture**	**Solitary interaction**
No	**Parasocial interaction**	**Detachment**

IDENTIFICATION (row label spanning left of the table)

Figure 2.8.   A Typology for Relations Between Viewer and Contents Viewed. (From Rosengren & Windahl, 1972)

In Solitary Interaction one identifies without interacting. Detachment signifies the absence of both interaction and identification.

The concept of parasocial interaction was introduced by Horton and Wohl (1956), was systematically related to other TV relations by Rosengren and Windahl (1972), and was subsequently operationalized by Rosengren et al. (1976), also offering operationalizations of the concepts of Capture and Long-term Identification' (the latter term denoting a state of identification reaching beyond the fleeting moments of identification occurring during the very act of viewing). Identification has been dealt with by, among many others, Furhammar (1965), Feilitzen and Linné (1974), Lyle and Hoffman (1976), Noble (1975), Nordlund (1978).

Recently, McQuail (1985, p. 135) has presented a powerful plea for including into models of media use "a generalized process of involvement, arousal or 'capture'." This "general sensation" is said to "free the spectator/reader/listener mentally from the immediate constraints and/or dullness of daily life and enable him or her to enter into new experiences (vicariously) which would not otherwise be available (except by use of imagination)." It is obvious that this general sensation is pretty close to (but does not differentiate between) the notions of parasocial interaction and capture as presented above. (The notion of "arousal" is a different matter altogether.)

Within the Media Panel Program parasocial interaction, identification, and capture have been studied by Sonesson (1979), Hedinsson (1981),

Johnsson–Smaragdi (1983), Hedinsson and Windahl (1984), and Windahl et al. (1986). We regard relations as part of media use. We are not unaware, however, of the possibility of regarding identification and parasocial interaction as gratifications. Even so, we feel that these gratifications are such an integral part of media use that they are indeed best conceived of as an aspect of media use rather than as a motive or an effect. (Motives for, and effects of, TV viewing are discussed in other parts of the book; sections 3.3.5 and 4.5.3)

In the Malmoe panel, two types of identification were studied in preschool and in grade 3: "identification of similarity", and "wished-for-similarity". Both types were measured by a single question. The level of identification was more or less the same between the two waves, but an interesting development was observed in the gender relations. While in preschool, boys showed a higher level of identification of similarity than girls (54% vs. 43% feeling themselves to be similar to children of the screen), it was the other way around in grade 3 (59% vs. 66%).

Otherwise, we found no significant relationship between, on one hand, identification of either type, and on the other, gender and social class. In a follow-up study of the Malmoe panel, however, Sonesson (forthcoming) is able to show that—contrary to much conventional wisdom—children's TV relations are indeed positively related to real relations and interactions of children and adolescents (cf. also sec. 5.2).

It is no easy thing to study these subtle relationships between young children and the TV content they consume in quantitative terms. By the age of 11, it becomes somewhat easier, and even more so among the more developed adolescents. In order to study the relations established by the viewer to the content consumed in the age brackets 11–15, we used a composite scale tapping capture (interaction and identification at the moment of viewing), and also long-term identification (cf. Rosengren et al., 1976). The reliability of the scale in terms of internal consistency is quite satisfactory (alpha coefficients of about .85 in all three waves). The scale consists of two fillers and seven items such as:

> "Sometimes when I watch something exciting on TV, I feel as though I were part of the action."

> "I often feel as if I were one of the persons I see on TV."

> "It happens that I feel like being somebody I have seen on TV for a long time afterwards."

When looking at the amount of TV consumed we have found that it varied quite dramatically during adolescence, a fact that we discussed in the light of the generally low stability characterizing the period of adolescence: a period of upheavals rather than stability. What about TV relations in this respect?

Figure 2.9 based on data from the Vaxjoe study main panel, demonstrates a clear tendency for TV relations to decrease with age. This holds true for both boys and girls and after control for social class. The variables of age, gender, and social class influence TV relations in an intricate pattern of interaction. In grade 5, there are no gender differences, and moderate differences for social class. In grade 9, the girls are more involved than the boys. Most of the difference is due to age (and amount of TV consumption; cf. Figs. 2.10 and 4.3). The highest mean score (11.0) is found for working-class boys and girls in grade 5; the lowest (7.0), for middle-class boys in grade 9.

The age and social class differentiation is more or less similar to that found for amount of TV consumption, while the difference between the sexes is turned around. Girls consistently watch less television, but in

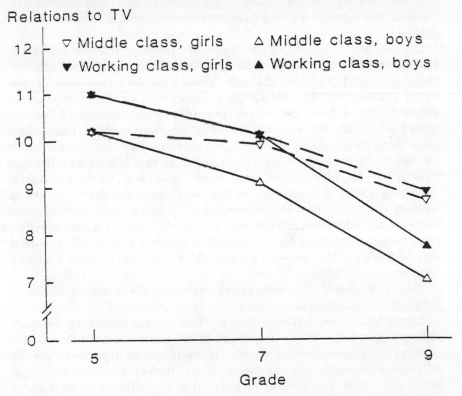

Figure 2.9.   Relations to TV by Grade, Gender, and Social Class. Vaxjoe Main Panel.

grade 9, they are clearly more involved. (Measured in a different way, we found a similar tendency among the girls of the Malmoe panel who, already in grade 3, have stronger relations to TV content consumed.)

In sec. 2.8 we shall find that the consumption and relation aspects of TV use are rather independent. In sec. 4.5.2, we shall see that, in contrast to TV consumption, TV relations are only weakly related to sex and social class. In sec. 3.3.4 it will be shown that TV relations exerts an influence of its own, over and above that of amount of consumption, gender and social class on the important variable of "TV dependency." These are good reasons for regarding TV relations as an important aspect of TV use.

2.6. THE CONTEXT OF MEDIA USE

The fourth, and last, aspect of media use (as we have conceived it) is the context: the situation surrounding use. Situation here is rather narrowly defined: the proximate environment of the child's media use. (In secs. 4.4.1 and 4.6.2 quite another context of TV viewing will be studied.)

Obviously, the context of the proximate situation may be defined in any number of ways. In her thesis on television use and school achievement, Jönsson (1985), for example, focuses on the importance of maternal attitudes toward, and participation in, the child's media use. In this section, we have singled out one of a large number of possible aspects of media use contexts, namely, whether viewing takes place alone or in the company of others. In the case of children in particular (as well as in connection with adult viewing) this is a heavily debated aspect, and for many good reasons (cf. Sonesson, 1979; Webster & Wakshlag, 1982). For example, it may be maintained that TV viewing without company may have greater and more harmful effects since there are no individuals around who may mediate, explain, and interpret what is said and shown on TV; and since children who watch TV alone may be more easily frightened than children who watch in the company of others.

Table 2.7 shows to which extent watching TV alone is found in different subgroups of our sample.

Contrary to expectations there is virtually no difference between different age-groups in the proportion of programs watched alone. Also contrary to expectations, a parallel analysis shows that there are no differences between different social classes. However, within each age-group and social class there is a consistent gender difference. Boys spend a greater proportion of their total viewing time alone than do girls. Why is that so?

Table 2.7. Number of Programs Watched Alone, Total Number of Programs Watched, and Proportion of Programs Watched Alone, By Gender and Grade. (TV Diary, Vaxjoe Study, Third Wave)

| | Grade | | | | | |
| | 5 | | 7 | | 9 | |
	Boys	Girls	Boys	Girls	Boys	Girls
Number of programs a week watched alone	9.3	4.8	6.1	4.2	5.4	3.1
Total number of programs watched	26.2	22.0	19.4	19.8	16.4	14.4
Ratio programs watched alone/ total number of programs watched	.35	.21	.31	.21	.32	.21

The reason which comes first to mind is the simple fact that boys watch more TV than girls (secs. 2.3.1 and 2.4.1). If parents of boys and girls watch about the same amount of TV (which they do; cf. sec. 3.3.4), the simple arithmetical consequence could very well be that boys would watch more TV alone than girls.

Unfortunately, this explanation only puts the question one step backwards in the causal chain. Why do boys watch more TV than girls? There may be a host of answers to that question, of course. Girls may give more time to their homework, to household work, to interaction with peers and parents, and so forth. And boys may be less tightly controlled by their parents than are girls. Actually, Swedish parents do not seem to control their children's TV viewing very much (Hedinsson 1981, p. 90), but what control there is, is somewhat unevenly distributed: girls' TV viewing seems to be more often supervised (Sonesson 1979, p. 86).

But why, then, is girls' TV viewing more closely supervised than that of boys? The answer to that question obviously must be made with reference to the current gender roles in Swedish society. The primary context of TV use is the family, but the widest context is society itself. The same goes for all media use, of course. We will soon present some data about the use of another medium than broadcast TV. Before turning to that task, however, we will take an overall look at the interplay between the various aspects of TV use as we have conceived them.

2.7 A STRUCTURAL EQUATION MODEL OF TV USE

In the previous sections of this chapter we discussed various aspects of TV use, one by one. In this section we shall relate three such aspects to each other. Our instrument for doing this is a PLS structural equation model (see Appendix). The three aspects of TV use included in the model are: amount of consumption, preferences, and relations to TV. Included in the model are also the social-class and gender variables. The model draws on data from all three waves of the Vaxjoe panel study.

Before turning to the model itself, we need to say something about the preference variable as used here. It is based on our question about what type of content the respondents prefer on TV. In the first two waves the respondents were given a list of 13 program types and asked to pick the 3 they liked best. In the third wave they had to mark for each of the 13 program types how much they liked it. However, we saw the need to construct an index tapping one important aspect of the preferences. We chose "informativity of contents preferred."

The 13 program types were rank ordered on a scale from the least informative (crime/detective) to the most informative (social reports/ documentary). The rank order was based on multidimensional ratings by a dozen experts (graduate students and faculty of mass communication research, cf. Hedinsson, 1981, p. 75). On the basis of their content preferences the respondents could now be given a value on the "in-formativity index."

TV consumption in the model is the measure of "habitual consumption" earlier described; TV relations is the operationalization of capture and long-term identification presented in sec. 2.5 above.

The PLS model is presented in Figure 2.10. Note that the figure renders only the structural, inner model. The outer measurement model is not included in the figure, although, of course, it was part and parcel of the statistical model. (See Appendix for further information about PLS and LISREL models.)

We shall discuss three aspects of the model: the notion of stability, the implications for our "use" concept, and the role of social class and gender.

The stability of the three use variables varies. It is lowest with the preference index and highest with TV consumption. On the whole it must be considered low, but it should be borne in mind that in most respects the period of adolescence is anything but stable, characterized, indeed, more by upheavals than by stability. A natural point of reference here is the stability of the parents' amount of TV viewing. As expected, this stability is much higher than that of the adolescents (a Pearson coefficient of correlation of .62 over a 4-year period, as compared with .35 for the adolescents during the same period).

Another point of reference is the longitudinal data of TV consumption, preferences, and relations offered in secs. 2.2, 2.5, and 2.6. Here we

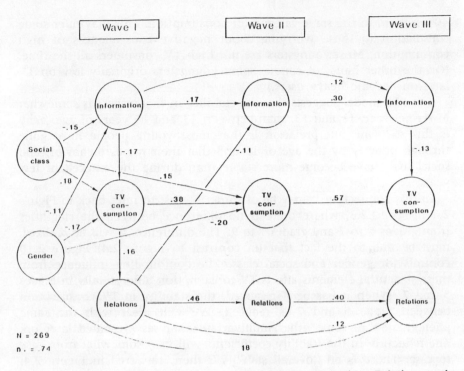

Figure 2.10. Longitudinal PLS Model of TV Use: Consumption, Relations and Informativity

found dramatic changes in amount of consumption, less change in TV relations, and high stability in preferences. The order of stability in our present model is almost completely reversed. Informativity has the lowest scores throughout, while amount of consumption shows the highest value (.57) and relations the next highest (.46). This shows that level stability (measured by comparisons between group averages, as in previous sections) and individual stability (measured by correlations or related measures) are two different things. TV consumption is drastically reduced during adolescence, but those relatively high or low on TV in grade 5 tend to be relatively high or low also in grade 9. Conversely, TV preferences may be stable for the group of adolescents as a whole, but at the individual level, stability may be much less pronounced. (For a more detailed discussion of these phenomena, cf. Johnsson–Smaragdi 1983, pp. 83ff. Cf. also Figs. 2.9 and 4.3.)

In order better to concretize these arguments, Figure 2.11 is offered. It expresses individual stability in terms of transition frequencies between high and low TV consumption. It will be seen that the abstract stability coefficients of the structural model mean that, in reality, only some

40% remain in the same category of consumption. This may offer some consolation to those worrying about negative consequences of high consumption. Most youngsters are not high TV consumers all the time. (On the other hand, of course, some youngsters originally low on TV later on become heavy users.)

The PLS model suggests that the stability in this respect is somewhat lower between 11 and 13, than between 13 and 15 years of age. Why is this so? One interpretation is that most young people have gone through puberty by the age of 13 and that their minds, behavior, and social lives have become more stable than during the antecedent few years.

In this connection it may be of some interest to refer back to Figure 2.4 in sec. 2.2.3, where there is no difference between the stabilities from grades 5 to 7 and grades 7 to 9. The difference, it will be realized, must be due to the fact that (in contrast to Figure 2.4) Figure 2.10 controls for gender and social class. The confounding influence from these structural elements affects TV consumption differentially in grades 5 and 7. When it has been removed, the stability in TV consumption between grade 5 and 7 is reduced. We will meet with the same phenomenon in some other multivariate analyses presented later on. The reduction in the stability coefficients will vary somewhat from case to case. There is an "overall stability", then, rendered in Figure 2.4, and one "specific stability," rendered in Figure 2.10. The strength of the specific stability depends on the variables controlled for in the analysis.

It is interesting to note that this argument does not seem to be applicable to the relations variable. Does this mean that puberty has less impact on the inclination to interact and identify with the content of TV than on the amount of TV consumption as such? The answer to that question cannot be provided here, but we shall look at it more closely in the chapter on media use and development (sec. 3.3). For the moment, it may be sufficient to note that we regard the stability of the relations variable as being comparatively high. It is a subtle phenomenon, hard to measure, and we regard the coefficients of .46 and .40 as indications that "there is something there," and that the concept constitutes a line worth pursuing. This belief is strengthened by the fact that TV relations have been found to exert a unique influence on some dependent variables over and above that of TV consumption (cf. secs. 3.3.3 and 3.3.4; Hedinsson, 1981; Hedinsson & Windahl, 1984; Windahl et al., 1986).

Since preferences, amount of consumption, and relations to content are all parts of our media use concept, the relationships between them are of great interest. One would have expected a more or less complex

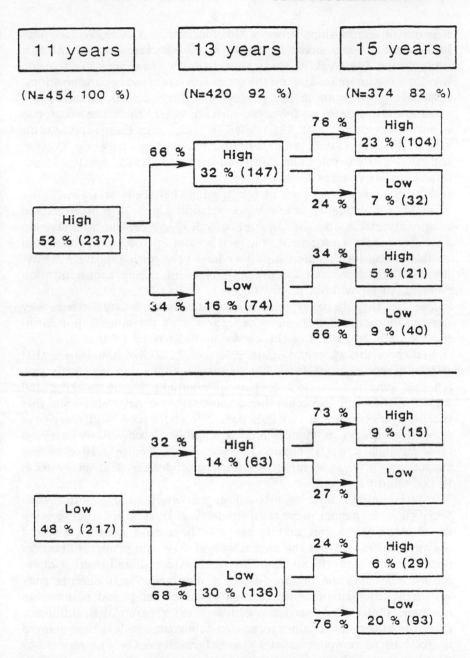

Figure 2.11. Stability and Change in TV Viewing Over Time (Based on Median-Splits of the Age Groups)

network of relationships between the concepts over time. We see very little of that in the model of Figure 2.10, however. Only in the first wave do we find weak to moderate relationships between, on the one hand, TV consumption and, on the other hand, preferences and relations, respectively. Later on in the process the three aspects of media use seem to exert little or no influence on each other. The three subaspects of media use seem to be less related to each other than expected. (In several different LISREL models of the relationships between TV consumption and identification, Johnsson–Smaragdi [1983, pp. 139ff.] obtained similar results.)

Why is there no network of relationships between the waves? Why is there, for example, but a weak relationship (−.11) between the relations variable and the preference index? At present we have no answers to these questions. It may well be that for subgroups one would be able to find such relationships. (We have been testing separate models for boys and girls, and for different types of family communication patterns, so far without much success.)

The fact that the three aspects of media use to a large extent may develop independently of one other makes it all the more important to include them in studies of the causes and effects of TV use.

Earlier in this chapter (Figure 2.3, sec. 2.2.2) we have noted that class differences in habitual TV viewing tend to decrease with age, whereas gender differences develop differentially in the working and middle classes. On the other hand, however, we have also seen that when it comes to actual viewing, class differences tend to increase over time while gender differences tend to diminish (observations based on cross-sectional data; cf. Figure 2.5, sec. 2.3.2). Figure 2.10 does not support any of these seemingly conflicting tendencies. Instead we seem to get a third answer.

Whether diminishing or increasing, we would have expected both social class and gender to exert an influence at least on habitual viewing in all three waves, but that is not so. The reason for this apparent anomaly is the fact that the appearance of class and gender differences does not necessarily mean that class and gender should exert a direct influence at the time of the difference observed. The difference may well stem from an influence exerted at an earlier period of time. In our case, both social class and gender seem to exert their influence primarily at the start of the process, an influence which is then relayed by the various components of TV use themselves. The PLS model has thereby reminded us of the important distinction between observed differences and actual influence. (In sec. 4.5.2 we will further develop this argument with respect to social class and habitual viewing.)

We note with special interest that gender independently influences relations to TV at the age of 15, but not before. At the age of 15, of course, the two genders are definitely established as such, whereas before that age differential individual development and incomplete gender role socialization may tend to blur some differences between them.

On the whole, the model gives us the impression that stability is not very high for any of the three components of television use. This is far from unexpected, bearing in mind that we are dealing with one of the most dramatically changing periods of life. The interaction between the three aspects is lower than expected, and the influence exerted by gender and social class does not confirm our earlier results of increasing social-class influence and a decreasing impact from gender. In the chapters on social class and development we shall have occasion to return to these questions.

2.8. VIEWING OF VIDEO RECORDINGS

Even if TV is at present the most important medium for most people, demanding more direct attention than any other medium, we all know that mass media use is by no means confined to television viewing. Within the Media Panel Program, TV is in focus, but we have also collected data about the use of some other media: newspapers, cinema, books, and comics.

Some of these data will be presented in later chapters on media use as related to development, social class, and socialization. In this section, some attention will be given to the medium which is closest to television, namely, video recordings, coming to the screen not by way of broadcasting or cable, but via the videocassetts.

In sec. 1.2.1 on the Swedish media scene, we offered a first glimpse of video's introductory phase in Sweden. The originally rapid expansion of the VCR seems now to be flattening out. In 1985, about a quarter of the Swedish household had a VCR, but there is heavy geographical class and age differentiation. Children and adolescents have shown a lively interest in video. We have already seen that in 1984 more than 40% of adolescents in Malmoe had access to video at home (cf. Höjerback 1985, 1986; Johnsson–Smaragdi & Roe, 1986; Sonesson 1984).

VCR use was only studied at one point in the research program as here reported, namely, in the third wave in connection with the TV diary question (March, 1981). Our rather crude question about the amount of video use was "Do you often watch video (Yes/No)?" The response to the question, broken down by age, sex, and social class, is shown in Figure 2.12 (Vaxjoe study).

The results are not completely unequivocal, but there seems to be a

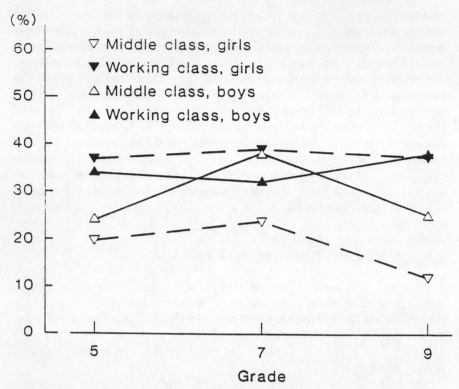

Figure 2.12.   VCR Viewing by Grade, Social Class, and Gender (From Flodin et al., 1982)

peak in viewing in the seventh grade. Gender and social class interact. Controlling for age, middle-class boys tend to watch more than middle-class girls, working-class boys less than working-class girls (except in grade 9). The peak in grade 7 is supported by results from Sveriges Radio, which show that these in the age bracket 15–24 watch somewhat fewer videos than do youngster between 9 and 14 years old (Mediebarometern, 1985).

Figure 2.13 shows what is watched on video recordings in the three age-groups of the Vaxjoe study. Both for boys and girls the viewing of feature films increases with age. Horror films are watched mostly by boys in the youngest age category. The highest figure for violence is found for 13-year-old boys.

The types of videos (violence and pornography) which triggered a moral panic in Sweden (cf. sec. 1.2.1), are still richly represented on the market. But what has increased is the category of more ordinary films earlier shown in movie theaters. Thus, even if many adolescents

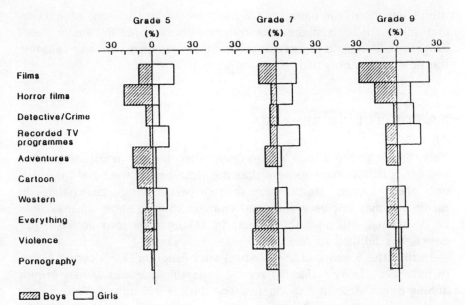

Figure 2.13. VCR Preferences by Grade and Gender. Vaxjoe Study, Wave 3.

still prefer action-oriented content, the altered output on the video market has probably resulted in a rise in the quality of the video content watched by them. In contrast to broadcast television (cf. Figure 1.1), the large market admits a high concordance between preferences and actual viewing.

At present, Swedish adolescents use video mostly for watching rented recorded cassettes. However, there is a tendency that with the increasing normalization of the phenomenon of video, the VCRs are increasingly being used for home recording, especially by girls. This tendency will probably be strengthened when in a couple of years foreign satellite television will reach the adolescents by way of cable (a process which is already on its way). With more channels to choose among, the need for rented videocassettes will be reduced (a tendency which may already be on its way).

When our diary study was undertaken in 1981, VCR viewing was only in its infancy in Sweden. Several years later, the use of video has not yet found its final shape. No doubt, however, the flurry around videos during the late 1970s and early 1980s is being gradually replaced by more normal conditions, much as 30 years ago the new medium of television gradually found its form and its place in society.

Frequent studies will be necessary to achieve a better understanding of the VCR phenomenon. These studies, of course, have to include the use of television, radio, and other mass media by children, adolescents and adults. In such studies the results presented in the Media Panel Program will be able to serve as a benchmark against which to calibrate the new results obtained.

2.9. CONCLUDING REMARKS

This chapter has to a large extent dealt with changes over time. In that context it is important to note that the time period we have studied is only about 5 years. During such short a period, long-term changes in media use may not be visible, and changes that do show up may only be occasional. Still, we think that, in taking time into account, our design has fulfilled its function.

During the 5 years of the Media Panel Program, TV viewing seems to have been fairly stable between comparable age and gender groups among our adolescent respondents. The data reveal only a slight overall decrease in viewing. While the trend in viewing is next to negligible, the age differences are considerable. We have demonstrated that television consumption increases until the age of 9 to 11; then, it drops continuously. This is in line with most other research in the field; granted that the peak may be somewhat differently located from time to time, in different countries, and in different parts of the same country (cf. Greenberg, 1976; Himmelweit, Oppenheim, & Vince, 1958; cf. also sec. 3.3.1).

Gender differences are also considerable, as has been shown many times. Boys consistently watch more than girls. Their developmental curve lags behind that of girls by about 2 years.

There are also clear differences between the viewing patterns of different social classes. Working-class children watch more than do middle-class children, in some cases much more.

All these generalizations refer to one aspect of television use: what we call habitual viewing. Actual viewing on a specific day or during a specific week shows a similar but not identical pattern. In addition, amount of viewing is only one component of what we call television use. Other components are TV preferences, relations, and context of viewing. It appears that these other aspects of TV use are not as closely related to amount of viewing as one would have expected. This is a strong reason to include them in future studies of television use.

Above all, our data clearly demonstrate that at any specific point in time the use of TV is by no means a homogeneous phenomenon. On the contrary. Being embedded in a complex matrix of age, gender, and social class, affected by and affecting in its turn a host of social circumstances, it shows a highly differentiated pattern. In the three following chapters we will try to describe and explain, some of the intricacies of that pattern in the light of development, social class, and socialization.

3
Development and Media Use

3.1. INTRODUCTORY REMARKS

Kurt Lewin (1951) maintained that the best occasion to study a phenomenon is when it is in a state of change. We take his advice. The young people we study are at a turbulent age. At no other time in life does so much change occur so fast as in childhood and adolescence. Young people develop differentially along several dimensions simultaneously, and their relations to the media are more or less continuously changing. In this chapter, we will study media use and media effects from a developmental perspective. It is our belief that the observations we make in looking at this age-defined population will help us to a better general understanding of some media uses and effects processes.

We shall first discuss and relate to each other three different types of development: sexual-biological, cognitive, and social. We will then turn to a discussion of stage theories and stage models in developmental studies. The rest of the chapter will be about development, young people, and media. Drawing on Brown, C. Ramond, & Wilde, (1974) we shall try to present a developmental model of media use (sec. 3.2). In the following sections, empirical results will be offered, which relate developmental variables to media consumption, preferences, media relations, motives, and dependency. The use of a number of mass media will thus be interpreted and understood in terms of our developmental model.

3.1.1. Development and Socialization

It is our impression that when scholars treat the relationships between media use and development, interest is largely confined to either cognitive development or social development. We shall try to escape this one-sidedness by adding also sexual-biological development and trying to integrate and relate these three forms of development. This does not mean, of course, that we are unaware of the fact that different aspects of development influence media use and media effects differentially. We are not. But we do have the notion that there is a rather complex interrelationship between the developmental aspects themselves and, for example, media use. We cannot depict these complex relationships in full detail, but we can hint at them and give some evidence for their existence.

Another chapter in this book deals with socialization, and we have faced a problem in trying to sort out what belongs to the realm of development and what is socialization. It has frequently been pointed out that socialization is a dualistic concept which includes two perspectives: one structural-societal, where the individual finds himself in a process of cultural transmission, and one more individualistic, where the individual "becomes human" (Wrong, 1961) and where development plays a decisive role. Several researchers have proposed an integration of these two points of view (e.g., Johnsson–Smaragdi, 1983; Younniss, 1980; Zigler & Seitz, 1978; cf. also sec. 5.1.3). Suffice it to say here that we are sympathetic to this integration but that, all the same, we have chosen to treat developmental aspects separately from socialization. There is a tradition in communications research dealing with development, and we wish to relate to that tradition.

3.1.2. The Many Faces of Development

There are several developmental dimensions to choose among and to describe. When concentrating our efforts on sexual-biological, cognitive, and social development we are dealing with established, more or less generally acknowledged, traditions. We might also have chosen among more specific points of view, say, the aspects mentioned by Kimmel (1974): (1) The inner-biological, (2) the individual-psychological, (3) the cultural-sociological, and (4) the outer-physical. However, we felt that in an overview of this type it would be better to stay within the safer confines of more generally accepted traditions.

A. Sexual-biological Development. The most widely used theory for describing the sexual stages of early life is still that of Freud (1905). According to Freud, children are at the stage of latency from about the age of 5 to puberty-adolescence. During this psychosexual latent stage boys and girls are mostly separate in their play, and there is an apparent nonsexual orientation (Elkind & Weiner, 1978; Sarnoff, 1976). It is often argued, however, that the term latency is accurate primarily when it comes to heterosexual activities; heterosexual interest, on the other hand, continues to grow during these years.

During early adolescence—approximately ages 11 to 14—marked physiological, physical, and mental changes begin, and sexual maturation starts to take place. The next stage (about 14 to 18) is often called middle adolescence (Elkind & Weiner, 1978). Hence, the individuals studied in our inquiry find themselves in the latency and early and middle adolescence stages.

Adolescence is a period of physical growth. Figure 3.1. shows the adolescent growth spurt which takes place in the early teens. As can be seen, girls have their peak about 2 years earlier than boys. (For further discussions of growth events in boys and girls in adolescent years, see Adelson, 1980; Tanner, 1962.)

A number of factors influence the general pattern of this development. For example, several studies have shown that children from the lower social strata mature physically later than those from the higher strata. This could not be found in the latest Swedish study of the matter, however (Westin–Lindgren, 1979). This finding has been interpreted as a result of the greater equality in Swedish society.

From a communications research point of view it may be noted that sexual development in particular is of great interest, not least because

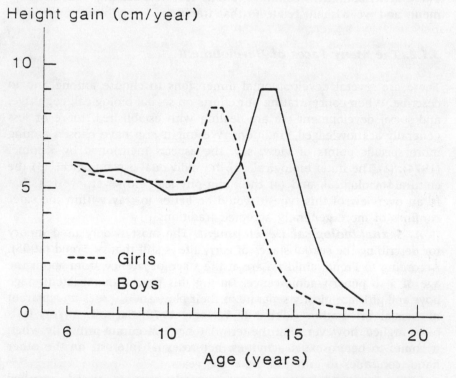

Figure 3.1.   Adolescent Spurt in Height Growth for Boys and Girls (Source: Tanner, 1962; cf. Elkind & Weiner, 1978)

with a changing sexual orientation the need structure of the individual changes. In addition media-related needs emerge, disappear or otherwise change.

B. Cognitive Development. According to Gruber and Voneche (1977, p. ix) a cognitive development theory is a "theory of knowing." It may also be described as a theory of thinking and information processing (Wartella, 1980). The best-known theorist in the field of cognitive development, Jean Piaget, worked for some 60 years with these very significant problems. Piaget (1968) maintains that children from 2 to 6 or 7 are situated in the *pre-operational stage* of cognitive development. During this period the child develops symbolic representations of concrete objects. He or she is perceptually bounded; that is, thoughts are closely tied to perception, but on the other hand mental abilities are no longer restricted to the immediate environment (Wohlwill, 1962).

Around the ages of 6 to 7, children enter the *stage of concrete operations.* This stage generally lasts until age 12. During this period the ability to form concepts of classes, relations, and numbers is learned, thereby greatly expanding the child's conceptual and mental world (Elkind & Weiner, 1978). However, the logical operations mastered apply only to concrete objects and events.

Abstract thinking is developed during the last stage, that of *formal operations.* This stage starts at about age 12. The young adolescent is able to deal with hypothetical reasoning and with many variables simultaneously. He or she is able to understand other cultures and other times, historical as well as future ones. In short, the ability for abstract thinking has increased immensely.

During the course of cognitive development children thus become less dependent on their immediate perception, and their ability to deal with multiple dimensions of phenomena expands. Both these capacities are of great interest when dealing with childrens' media use (Wartella, 1980).

Other scholars have constructed other cognitive stage theories (cf. Bruner et al., 1966; Kohlberg, 1968). In his theory of role taking, Selman (1971) describes how children develop the ability to take the perspective of another person and relate it to their own. During this process the child proceeds through the stages of the egocentric, or undifferentiated, the subjective or differentiated, the self-reflective or reciprocal, the third person or mutual and, finally, the societal or in-depth perspectives. Yet another theory dealing with role taking among children has been proposed by Flavell (1968).

From a media-use point of view, cognitive development is extremely important. We learn from cognitive stage theories how children obtain more and more means and resources for utilizing the media. (See also

Wartella et al., 1979.) The opportunities for using mass media—both the media as such and as functional alternatives to other activities—therefore increase steadily. Aspects of moral development will further be of importance for the effects of mass media use.

Stage theories of cognitive development offer interesting substantive problems to mass communication research. The same theories, however, also point to an intriguing methodological problem.

It is evident that the degree of cognitive development will have an impact on the way in which preschoolers and 15-year-old adolescents perceive and understand, for example, questions about media preferences or time spent with TV in an average week. This implies that differences observed between youngsters of different ages in many cases may be more correctly attributed to the impact exerted by cognitive development on the respondent's way of grasping the question than to other variables. In our study we have tried to cope with this problem as effectively as possible by differentiating our instruments, but we are far from sure that we have been able completely to rule out these kinds of developmental side-effects. One reason is that complete success in this respect would have meant decreased comparability over the panel waves. This is a special case of the well-known problem of objective and subjective standardization (Kinsey et al 1948, p. 51: 1953, p. 60). In general, we have tried to keep to the middle of the road, between the two extremes.

C. Social Development. Some aspects of cognitive development—say, moral reasoning and role taking—are very close to the concept of social development. Both types of development will influence our social lives, for both take place in interaction with others. A major theme when it comes to social development is that of dependence and independence. Most textbooks in developmental psychology describe the declining dependency upon the family, the striving for independence throughout adolescence, and the increasing role of the peer group. During childhood the striving for independence is a means for obtaining other goals, whereas in adolescence it becomes more of an end in itself. McLeod and Brown (1976, p. 201) have described adolescents' development in this respect as follows:

1. The dependence on parental authority will give way to greater freedom and independence;
2. There is an increase in sociability with increasing interest in peer relationships, and
3. Rapid change of the adolescent's time budgeting, with more time spent outside home.

In the lives of adolescents, then, the peer group receives increasing attention. This may be interpreted as increased independence—from the family, that is. But in exchange comes increased dependence on the peer group. Actually, conformity seems to be curvilinear, with a peak in early adolescence (see Figure 3.2).

The ego ideal ("the kind of person I want to be") during these years varies between ages and between cultures. Lutte's (1971) well-known study of this phenomenon shows that in several countries parents are the ideal among younger children whereas friends and celebrities enter as ideals later on. Our own data on parent–peer orientation show a similar pattern (cf. sec. 5.2.2).

From what has been said above it is obvious that social development will be of great importance for the development of media use. The breaking-away from family, the conformity to peers, the adolescent subculture emerging between childhood and adulthood (Elkind & Weiner, 1978) will all contribute to different sets of needs and motives for media use and will also provide frames of reference and perceptions that will undoubtedly influence the nature of media effects.

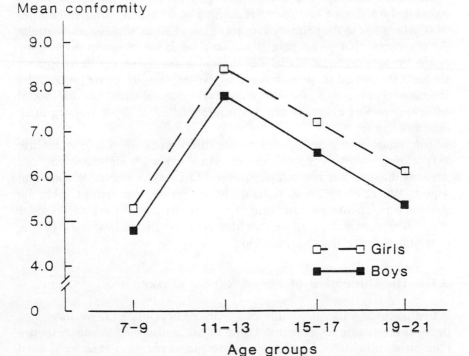

Figure 3.2.   Conformity with Peer Influence as a Function of Age (Source: Constanzo & Shaw, 1966; cf. Elkind & Weiner, 1978)

3.1.3. Relationships Among Different Aspects of Development

We noted earlier that there is a close interrelationship between development and socialization (see also Seltzer, 1982). It is even more clear that the different aspects of development tend to be closely linked to one other. The interrelationships are complex and sometimes very subtle. It is far beyond the scope of this book to explore them fully. A few short remarks will have to suffice.

It is generally taken for granted that sexual-biological development is the most fundamental of the three. It sets the frames for the other two types of development. Through the increase in brain capacity, for example, cognitive development is made possible. Similarly, sexual development will steer the orientation toward peers of one sex or the other, and it is then also responsible for the break with the family. Elkind and Weiner (1978) maintain that adolescents' preoccupation with independence (social development) emerges in part from a feeling of self-confidence, which in its turn depends on the attained stage of biological development.

Cognitive development determines part of the social development. Expanded role taking and moral reasoning abilities will affect the nature of relationships to the primary groups of the child or adolescent. Wartella (1980) argues that social perception to a large extent is determined by cognitive development. Social development affects sexual development through the sexual or pseudosexual activities that are made possible by increased peer group orientation. Developmental strivings for social independence are also assumed to stimulate different aspects of cognitive development.

Our main point, then, is that the three types of development are very closely intertwined. Therefore, when we study development and mass media use, it is not sufficient merely to look at one developmental aspect. We have to assess several. Furthermore, we cannot take the various aspects into account one at a time only. We have to consider their interrelationships as well as the synergy effects that may be the outcome of these interrelationships.

3.1.4. The Dimension of Time: Stage and Age

When discussing the three different types of development, we have also been discussing three different types of stage theories. A stage theory emphasizes qualitative changes assumed to occur in a relatively fixed sequence. The qualitative changes appear at certain critical points in a person's development (Dimmick et al. 1979; Kastenbaum 1975).

Following Riegel (1975), Dimmick et al. (1979) propose a nine-stage life-span model combining biophysical, cognitive, and social aspects of development. For our study the following three stages are of special interest:

Childhood—egocentric stage (1–7 years)
Middle childhood—concrete operational stage (7–12)
Adolescence—formal operations (12–18)

According to this model the preschool children of the Malmoe study (first panel wave) find themselves close to the critical point between the first and second stages. In the two following panel waves the Malmoe children are found at the second level, the middle childhood, concrete operational stage. In the Vaxjoe study, the youngest of the main sample (grade 5, about 11; cf. sec. 1.3.3) are to be found at the second stage, but are close to the critical point that marks the onset of the third stage of adolescence and formal operations. In the second and third panel waves, the adolescents of our main Vaxjoe panel are found at the third stage.

We thereby have the opportunity of assessing media use around at least two critical points in the course of development. There are some problems in this connection, however. One is that although it is rather likely that our Swedish young people have their critical age points at the same time as their counterparts in other countries, we actually have only scant positive evidence that this is really the case. We also know very little about where the secular trends have taken us today. At least in physical terms, young people mature earlier today than they did a century ago (Westin–Lindgren, 1982). It may well be that this trend has moved the critical points somewhat.

The most important problem, though, may be age itself. Several students of developmental processes have unanimously warned against uncritical use of the time concept (Bacen, 1981; Danowski, 1975; Goulet & Baltes, 1970; Wartella et al., 1979; Wohlwill, 1970). Age is not an independent variable. "Age is a vehicle, not a cause in itself", Flavell (1977) maintains. Wartella et al. note that age may only serve to help *locate* developmental aspects of behavior. It cannot *account* for them. Strictly speaking, age is not an explanatory variable. Nevertheless, Wartella et al. maintain that, overall, the age of the child is the best predictor of media use patterns. We may use age as an indicator, then, but we shall always have to look beyond it for explanations. While the indicative efficacy of age may vary there seems to be some agreement that the younger the individual, the closer the correspondence between age and development.

Discussing cognitive development and research on children's understanding of television Wartella (1980), on the other hand, notes that critics of the Piagetian approach in this field warn against drawing inferences too quickly from theoretical work on cognitive development, stressing age-related changes in children's understanding of television instead of stage-related changes. All in all, however, it is probably a sound conclusion that stage is a theoretically more fruitful concept than age. Age, on the other hand, may be used as an indicator of stage. Indeed, it is often the only indicator available.

3.2. A MODEL FOR DEVELOPMENT AND MEDIA USE

There are several ways in which it is possible to observe a correspondence between development and different forms of mass media use and effects. In this section we shall try to construct a uses and development model. The model will then be applied to data stemming from the Malmoe and Vaxjoe studies.

Our model draws upon the work of several scholars, most notably Brown et al. (1974), Dimmick et al. (1979), Faber et al. (1979), and Windahl (1981). These four sources have a uses and gratifications perspective in common. This should come as no surprise, for the uses and gratifications approach lends itself very well to dealing with problems of development and media.

It is a central feature of most developmental theories that at different ages or stages the individual is seen as having more or less different needs, interests, and requirements; these are concepts that are well integrated in the uses and gratifications tradition. On the other hand, human development does not only produce needs, it also creates resources that are instrumental to meet these needs. Need-fulfilling activities and processes constitute an important part of uses and gratifications theory (cf., e.g., Rosengren, 1974). Dimmick et al. (1979) maintain that a crucial task for research is to see how changes in the antecedents of need satisfaction are associated with changes in gratifications at different ages. That will be one of the aims of this chapter.

Brown et al. (1974) have developed a much-used theory or model integrating uses and gratifications research with developmental theory (cf. Wartella, 1979). The process outlined is one of functional reorganization. The basic idea is that media use may be explained by three sets of factors:

1. The types of needs or requirements of the individual,
2. The access and control over content and selection, and

3. The capacity to "read" the medium.

According to Brown et al. (1974) requirements and needs may be of two types. One type consists of continuous needs. During the latency period young people have a *continuous* need for obtaining information and orientation about the environment. At the onset of puberty, however, more volatile needs or requirements become salient. These are termed *cyclical* or *spasmodic* requirements, such as the need for mood control.

Media use is also determined by the degree of access to, and control over, media contents suitable for fulfilling needs. In periods of continuous requirements (such as those presumably dominating during the latency period) it is enough to have access, whereas during puberty (with its onset of cyclical or spasmodic requirements) control over selection is more important. With TV, control is executed by the medium. Therefore, it is argued, TV gradually becomes a less useful medium during the years of adolescence (cf. Roe, 1983a). (With the large-scale advent of various combinations of cable and satellite, of course, this situation may change.)

It does not suffice, however, to have access and control. The child or adolescent must also possess the ability to make use of the medium and its content. Therefore, a third determinant of media use is the degree to which the individual is capable of reading the content, and understanding the grammar and conventions, of the medium. The obvious example is that of the print media, of which the nonreading child can make almost no use at all (cf. Sonesson, 1979, p. 42).

The Brown et al. (1974) theory is the main building block in our uses and developmental model. Like Dimmick et al. (1979) we maintain

The uses and gratifications paradigm implies that changes in the patterns of uses and gratifications could derive from either a) changes in the sociopsychological or biophysical states which result in alterations in the individual's need structure or b) changes in the available media and non-media sources of need satisfaction. (p. 9)

The interplay between needs and supply over time is very important, something which has also been underlined by Faber et al. (1979). The approach of these authors is not exactly a uses and gratifications way of looking at the problem area, but there are some resemblances. They build upon Erikson (1968), and their main idea is that there are different crises or problems connected with each stage of development in the life of the individual. In approaching these crises the individual will use different strategies. The way the crises will be solved is partly influenced by the media use of the individual. The use of media contents will lead to different types of effects, such as knowledge gain, attitudinal, and behavioral change. Frames for the process will be set by different types of constraints: external and internal, as well as media constraints. Rubin (1979) maintains that uses and gratifications research has not tried to link social and psychological origins of media use to each other (cf. Palmgreen et al., 1985). Our model constitutes an effort in that direction.

The uses and development model graphically represented in Figure 3.3 provides a schematic outline of the relationships we hypothesize between development, media use, and media effects.

Developmental events and processes may be cognitive, social or sexual-biological or stem from a combination of these three types of development. Entering a certain developmental period or stage may itself be one such event, becoming able to read or think logically are other, more specific examples.

Resources are of different sorts. Biological development will create physical resources, cognitive development certain mental abilities, and so on. In the course of development the young person will also have access to greater material resources, for example money, enabling the media to be used in a more or less independent way.

Needs and requirements are of the types that are described by Brown et al. (1974). To these could be added, for example, attitudes, interests, and values, which will also lead to differential media use.

We assume that resources interact with needs and requirements in more or less complex ways. In some cases there is a fit between the two, in others there may be resources that do not match a need, or

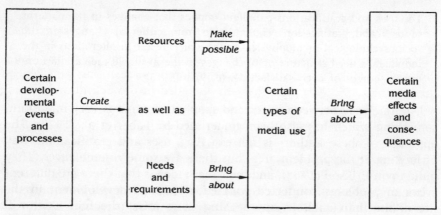

Figure 3.3.   A Uses and Development Model

needs for which there are no resources at hand (cf. Rosengren & Windahl, 1972).

The concept of "use" has been discussed at some length earlier in this book and requires no further explication. Our conception covers consumption as such, as well as various circumstances, and relationships accompanying it.

Following Windahl (1981) we make a distinction between consequences and effects. According to his suggestion, within the uses and gratifications approach the term "consequence" should be used only to denote the outcomes of mass media consumption itself, without taking into account the outcomes of the content consumed. Displacement is just such a consequence of media consumption (cf. sec. 5.2.3). The term "effects" should be reserved to mean the outcomes of consumption of specific media contents under specified circumstances.

We assume that there exist reciprocal relationships between development on the one hand and use-consequences-effects on the other. For example, one effect of mass media use may be to speed up (or delay?) cognitive development. Such relationships presumably are extremely complex (For an example of such complex relationships, see sec. 5.5.3).

The conceptual model presented in Figure 3.3 pieces together several lines of thought about the media–development relationship. It combines three important traditions within mass media research: developmental theory, the uses and gratifications approach, and the effects tradition. The model will now be used as a means to interpret and analyze some of the results obtained in the Media Panel Program. We shall discuss the uses made of various media, drawing upon our model more for organizing, interpreting and understanding our data than for the testing of hypotheses. We turn first to TV use.

3.3. DEVELOPMENT AND TV USE

In this section we shall deal first with different aspects of the use of television, looking at consumption, preferences, relations, and dependency on TV. Motives, not normally included in the definition of media use, are nevertheless of great interest in this context and will also be dealt with in this section.

3.3.1. TV Consumption

Among the descriptive data contained in chap. 2, figures were presented describing habitual and actual TV viewing from preschool age to 15. These results will now be discussed from a developmental perspective.

Rubin (1977) reported that the peak in viewing was reached at 9, whereas Feilitzen (1976) suggested that the highest figures are normally attained at 12. The highest viewing figures for British youngsters were found between 12 and 14 (Greenberg, 1976).

According to our Malmoe material TV viewing increases somewhat between the ages of 6 and 9. Parents' estimates placed the peak of viewing for boys at 9, whereas the girls attained their peak at 11. We would have expected the opposite. From a developmental point of view, the girls should be peaking earlier than the boys, since they reach the transition stage between childhood and adolescence some 2 years before the boys (cf. Figure 3.1).

The self-reported figures from Vaxjoe, both cross-sectional and from the panel, tell a consistent story: TV viewing among adolescents drops dramatically between 11 and 15. The overall tendencies were consistent in all social groups. It was found for habitual viewing and actual viewing alike. This marked decrease in viewing during adolescence has been reported in a number of studies (see, e.g., Comstock et al., 1978; Feilitzen, 1976; Robinson, 1972).

What kind of tentative explanations may be given for these results? Using the terminology of our model, one would say that resources for using television increase throughout the time period. As the child moves through the stages of pre-operation, concrete operations, and formal operations the ability to understand and the ability to analyze constantly improve. From a social developmental point of view, it may also be argued that the ability for role taking, in combination with enlarged social experience, would make TV viewing an ever richer and rewarding activity. The feeling of being at least half grown-up would also enhance the use of the general content of TV.

In spite of this development of resources there is a drastic decrease in viewing after the ages of 9 to 11. We are reminded that greater resources also enable young people to do other things than watch TV. Furthermore, there probably are fewer programs specially designed for young adolescents than for children. Adolescents also are underrepresented and often negatively presented on TV (Larson & Kubey, 1985). However, differential use made of differential resources does not tell the whole story. In order to solve this problem we need to turn to another aspect of our uses and development model, namely, needs and requirements.

Himmelweit et al. (1958, pp. 316ff.) state that, with age, TV viewing becomes less important. This occurs not because of its content as such, but because it fails to meet the specific needs of the adolescent. During the latency and childhood stages we assume that major needs may be fulfilled within the family setting. Although the peer group becomes increasingly important, a large portion of everyday life is spent with the family; and TV viewing is very much an integrated part of family life. Brown et al. (1974) maintain that during this period it is enough for the young person to have *access* to a medium, not necessarily to *control* it.

In early adolescence the need structure changes. There is a striving for independence *vis-à-vis* the family (Avery, 1979). Peer orientation and interest in the opposite sex become much stronger. There is now a need for media contents and uses symbolizing these tendencies of independence and facilitating peer instead of family interaction. There is an increasing need to control media use. Access alone is no longer enough. Therefore TV, with its noncontrollable content, will become less interesting (cf. Larson & Kubey, 1985, p. 395).

According to this uses and development model, then, it is quite natural that, in spite of growing resources, TV consumption decreases during adolescence. It is interesting to note that this tendency holds independently of social class. (The differences in viewing found between social classes will be discussed at some length in the chapter on social class and media use.) It is interesting to note also that when satellite and cable TV is introduced, the age-group most avid in seizing the new opportunities is that between 15 and 25, otherwise notoriously low consumers of TV (Severinsson, 1985). To them, cable and satellite offer new means of control (cf. sec. 3.4).

It has been noted repeatedly that boys lag in various aspects of maturation, sometimes by as much as 2 years (see Figure 3.1 and, e.g., Adelson, 1980; Tanner, 1962). The results from the Vaxjoe main panel relate very well to this lag. In Figure 3.4 it will be seen that fifth-grade girls and seventh-grade boys both watch on the average 120 minutes a day. Similarly, both seventh-grade girls and ninth-grade boys report the same amount of viewing, about 90 minutes a day. It may be argued, however, that this is not a real developmental time lag. If girls start out lower, their lower scores may not reflect development, only an otherwise determined gender difference.

Data from the Malmoe study will add to our understanding of the problem. The youngest children in the Malmoe sample (preschoolers and third graders) were asked to identify a number of pictures of persons appearing frequently on television. The extent to which they could identify these persons was assumed to indicate roughly the amount of television watched (Sonesson 1979, 1982). Because of differences of measurement (cf. secs. 2.2 and 3.1.2) the averages are standardized within each grade, which makes absolute comparisons between the years impossible but allows at least relative comparisons (boys/girls, etc.).

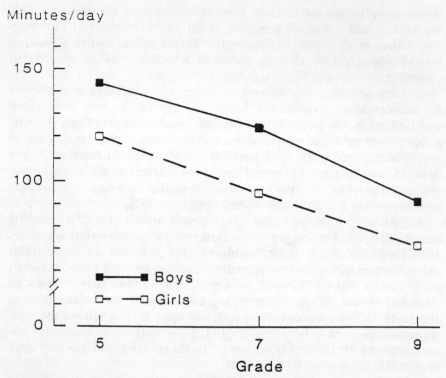

Figure 3.4. TV Consumption by Age and Gender: Vaxjoe Main Panel (Minutes/Day)

Table 3.1. Children's Knowledge of TV Personalities as an Indicator of Amount of Television Watched, Controlled for Gender and Parents' Education. (Malmoe Study, Preschool and Grade 3, Standardized Averages)

| | Parents' Education | | | | | |
| | Low | | Middle | | High | |
	Boys	Girls	Boys	Girls	Boys	Girls
Preschool	103	102	100	97	100	95
Grade 3	105	99	105	93	101	99

With this measurement, girls' TV consumption was found to be lower than that of boys in both age-groups, even when controlling for parents' education. The differences are small indeed, but in no case do the girls have higher scores than the boys.

In grades 3 and 5 in Malmoe the children gave their own estimates of their TV watching (the degree of complexity of the questions being adapted to the age level of the respondents). The results are presented in Table 3.2 (standardized in the same way as in Table 3.1). They show that the girls have a lower consumption than the boys in five cases out of six. Only the category Middle education, fifth grade deviates.

The results suggest that girls consistently watch less TV than boys do. Unfortunately, as we cannot make a comparison between the different age groups, we still do not know whether the girls reach their peak earlier or later than boys. Actually, there are a number of different theoretical models which satisfy our data. Three such models are presented in Figure 3.5. It will be seen that the girls' peak may fall before or after that of the boys. In what ways is it possible to choose among the three models?

Unfortunately, the very development under study makes it difficult to choose among the three models for, as we have seen, the cognitive development of the younger children prevents us from getting exact estimates from them. In this situation the estimates of the parents provide the only solution, even if they may be somewhat biased by prestige factors, and so forth. (It will be remembered that parents' estimates, as a rule, were given by the mother; cf. sec. 1.3.3.)

In the Vaxjoe material, the correlations between parents' and children's estimates of the children's TV viewing vary between .42 and .60 in different categories, with averages of .44, .49, and .58 in grades 5, 7, and 9 respectively. (Estimates given by fathers show somewhat lower correlations than estimates given by the mothers.) In the Malmoe material they correlate between .15 and .40, with averages of .23, .26, and 40 in preschool, grades 3, and 5 respectively. The low values for the preschoolers and third graders, to a large extent, must be due to idiosyncrasies of the children, which again leaves us with the parents' estimates.

Parents of children aged 6, 9, 11 (Malmoe) and 9, 11, 13, and 15 (Vaxjoe) were asked to estimate the amount of TV consumption of their children, the estimates being based on six subquestions on each occasion. In all, we have 22 estimates for various combinations of panel waves,

Table 3.2. Children's Own Estimates of Their TV Viewing Controlled for Gender and Parents' Education. (Malmoe Study, Grades 3 and 5, Standardized Averages)

| | Parents' Education | | | | | |
| | Low | | Middle | | High | |
	Boys	Girls	Boys	Girls	Boys	Girls
Grade 3	118	86	105	102	108	83
Grade 5	123	94	95	111	103	69

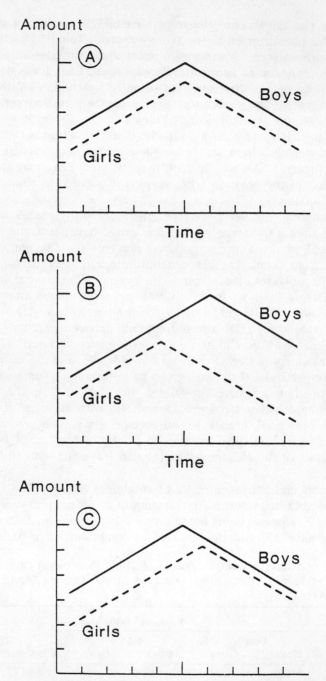

Figure 3.5.   Three Possible Combinations of Curves Indicating Development of TV Viewing among Boys and Girls

gender, and children's age. Where we have more than one measurement for each combination, separate averages were computed for boys and girls, first within Malmoe and Vaxjoe, then between Malmoe and Vaxjoe. The Malmoe data were somewhat higher than those of Vaxjoe, so data based on Malmoe children only (6 years of age) and Vaxjoe children only (13 and 15) were linked to the averages of Malmoe and Vaxjoe obtained for ages 9 and 11.

The result of these operations is Figure 3.6 (based on Table 3.3), which offers an overall view of children's TV viewing at various ages (effects from situation, generation, and place of living have been at least partly adjusted for by means of averaging and linking). The repeated measurements offer some assurance that the data mirror stable tendencies in the children's habitual viewing (as perceived and reported by their parents; cf. sec. 2.2, and Anderson et al., 1985).

Compared with the three models of Figure 3.5, we find that the data of Figure 3.6 point to a fourth possibility. While the girls' TV viewing peaks at around 11, the boys' viewing seems to have a plateau between

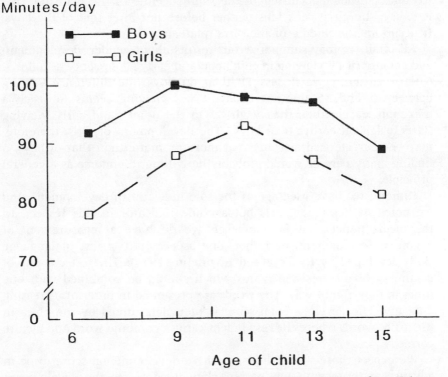

Figure 3.6. TV Consumption by Age and Sex. Combined Averages from Malmoe and Vaxjoe Panels.

Table 3.3. Parents' Estimate of Children's TV Consumption. (Minutes/ Day, Malmoe and Vaxjoe Studies)

	Gender and Wave							
	Boys				**Girls**			
	I	II	III	X̄	I	II	III	X̄
A. VAXJOE								
Grade								
3		94		94		78		78
5	87	94	92	91	89	86	74	83
7	86		94	90	81		76	78
9	84		81	83	74		70	72
B. MALMOE								
	Boys	Girls						
Preschool	97	86						
Grade 3	106	97						
Grade 5	105	102						

9 and 13, rather than any specific peak. (Given the nature of the data, we find it prudent to disregard the slight decline of the plateau.) That is to say, the girls' peak falls neither before nor after that of the boys. It occurs in the middle of the boys' plateau.

All in all we may summarize our results about gender, development, and amount of TV viewing in childhood and early adolescence as follows. Girls consistently watch less TV than do boys, the difference varying between 5 and 15 minutes a day. Boys' viewing seems to reach a maximum earlier than that of girls'. On the other hand, girls' viewing starts to fall off earlier than boys'. The development of girls, therefore, may be characterized as somewhat more dramatic than that of boys, a finding many parents would probably be willing to endorse as a general principle.

Hitherto we have used age as the sole indicator of development, and we noted earlier that age is but a crude indicator in this respect. In the media panel material, however, we do have a measurement of cognitive development, or rather, one aspect of it: a test of language skills developed by Rydberg and Höghielm (1974). The test consists of a number of pictures and words which should be combined with one other in the "right" way. The words are presented in order of increasing difficulty. The developmental score is then determined by the place in the list of words where the respondent cannot combine word and picture correctly.

We expect those with a high cognitive developmental score to be in advance of those with low scores when it comes to the development of media use (cf. Abelman, 1984). Among the Vaxjoe adolescents (who have passed the peak of TV viewing) we would expect those with high scores to be lighter TV viewers. Supposedly they have advanced further in the development toward lesser consumption than we have already met so many times in our data.

The word–picture association test was only administered in the third wave. Consequently we cannot use the main panel but only the cross-sectional material from this wave. The results presented in Figure 3.7 are based on an MCA analysis, dividing the respondents of each grade into three equally large groups with high, medium, and low cognitive development. (Gender and social class were controlled for in the MCA analysis.)

The data of the figure support our hypothesis in an interesting way. Those with high cognitive scores watch more TV in the fifth grade. Yet they are indeed in advance of those with low scores: they start losing interest in TV earlier than the latter. Actually, those with low cognitive

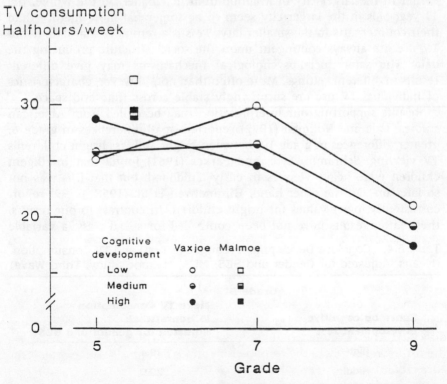

Figure 3.7.   TV Consumption by Grade and Level of Cognitive Development (Based on an MCA Analysis, Adjusted for Gender and Social Class) Malmoe and Vaxjoe Panels, Wave 3

development *increase* their consumption considerably between grades 5 and 7 (while the intermediate group shows a plateau). As a result of this differential development the differences between the three groups are greatest in grade 7 (age 13–14), a phenomenon most teachers and some parents will recognize from other areas of life.

There are some reservations to be made in this context. As we noted above, the data used are not taken from the main panel, and we have thus to make developmental inferences from cross-sectional data. That is often done, but longitudinal data would be more convincing, while a combination of cross-sectional and longitudinal data represents the ideal. In addition, the *n* of the fifth-grade category is low.

Our Malmoe data are of limited value when trying to cross-validate the Vaxjoe data since they cover only the fifth grade. Here we actually find that those with low cognitive scores watch more TV than do those with high scores (Table 3.4; cf. also Figure 3.7). We hypothesize that the development visualized in Figure 3.7 may have occurred somewhat earlier in the larger city of Malmoe than in Vaxjoe. On the whole, the 11-year-olds in the larger city seem to be somewhat more mature than their counterparts in the smaller city. This is a reminder that data about TV use are always contingent upon the social structure producing the data. The same social-psychological mechanisms may give different results in different settings. More often than not, however, characteristics of individual TV use are surprisingly stable across time and space.

Results supporting our interpretation may be culled from American studies. Lyle and Hoffman (1972) reported small differences in grade 6, greater differences in grade 10, between bright and less bright children's TV viewing. Schramm, Lyle, and Parker (1961) found that intelligent children were heavy viewers in early childhood, but that this was not so later on. On the other hand, Himmelweit et al. (1958, p. 99) report consistently lower values for bright children. In contrast to our results, these latter results have not been controlled for social class, a variable

Table 3.4.   Cognitive Development (Language Test) and TV Consumption. (Means, Adjusted for Gender and SES; MCA; Malmoe Study, Third Wave)

Score on cognitive development test	Grade 5 Mean TV Consumption ½ hours/week, adjusted for gender and SES
High	29.4
Middle	29.0
Low	32.3
Beta .10	

which may have a strong confounding influence, possibly more so in England than in Sweden or the United States. We have reason to believe, therefore, that until about 12 cognitively well-developed children watch more TV than do less-developed children. After 12, it is the other way round. That is to say, bright children seem to reach their TV peak a year or two before less bright children.

In terms of our developmental model this implies that after the age of 12, TV is less of a challenge to bright children. To less bright children it may remain a challenge for quite some time, perhaps gradually changing from a challenge into a refuge from other, sometimes only too demanding, challenges created by, say, the school or other socializing agents. In this connection it is interesting to note the observation made by Jönsson (1985, p. 161) to the effect that in preschool, watching children's programs has a positive effect on later school achievement, while in grade 5, watching children's programs has a negative effect on later school achievement (cf. sec. 5.5.3). To less bright children TV may, while for the moment offering a soothing refuge, have detrimental long-term effects.

3.3.2. Development and Preferences

Preferences constitute an important aspect of mass media use. Up to a point preferences determine what one consumes, but one can never, with complete accuracy, predict actual consumption from what people say that they prefer (cf. Baranowski, 1971). In the same way that social scientists have come to be wary about the relationship between attitudes and behavior, we ought to treat the relationship between preference and actual consumption with some caution (cf. secs. 2.1, 2.3, and 2.4).

When it comes to children's TV use we assume that their expressed preferences are, to a large extent, influenced by the opinions of both peers and family members. In the viewing situation other factors will eventually decide to what degree preferences will result in actual viewing. Suffice it here to mention factors such as the sheer existence of a certain type of content, the choice of programs made by the rest of the family, and the time the child has available for watching TV.

On the other hand, one could argue that preferences are very relevant when it comes to development. Preferences are not, we assume, limited in the same way as is actual viewing, but are more an expression of the individual and the stage of development attained. What developmentally related tendencies would one expect to find, when looking at preferences over time?

First, from what was said above, we expect to find variation in preferences during the course of development. Second, we hypothesize that at early ages preferences will be oriented toward obtaining immediate rewards, while later on they will change toward delayed rewards. In other words, one would expect preferences increasingly to deal with information, as opposed to fiction and entertainment. This has also been demonstrated in earlier studies by, among others, Lyle and Hoffman (1972) and Rubin (1977). Let us see whether these expectations are confirmed by our results.

We have already met changes over age in preferences in our preschool panel (Table 2.8, sec. 2.4.1). Between preschool and grade 3 there is a dramatic change in preferences for children's and general, adult programs. In preschool a large majority is oriented toward children's programs as their favorite type of television content: 87% for the boys and 93% for the girls. In grade 3, 87% of the boys and 80% of the girls have adult programs as their main preference. Similarly, exciting programs are chosen only by 29% of the boys and 4% of the girls in preschool. In the third grade, however, the figures are 65% and 50%, respectively.

Changes such as these may be said to mirror the transition from the pre-operational stage to the stage of concrete operations. In the latter stage, the conceptual and mental worlds expand for the child, even if he or she only perceives the concrete events and objects in the environment. Cognitive and social developments make it possible for the child to take a step into the exciting adult world—by way of television. Several studies have reported that children rather early turn to general TV programs instead of, or as a complement to, children's programs (cf., e.g., Feilitzen, 1976; Filipson & Schyller, 1982; Wartella et al., 1979; cf. also Postman, 1982). A developmental perspective offers a plausible explanation for these findings.

There are a number of other factors also leading the child to watch and enjoy adult programs. Firstly, as we have stated many times already, TV viewing takes place in the family group, implying that the norms and preferences of other family members are gradually taken over by the child. Secondly, it is often maintained that programming has little to offer specifically for those who are in the age bracket, say, between 9 and 11. Thirdly, at this age children are striving to orient themselves in the adult world. Television and its general content is certainly most useful for this purpose, and preferences are shaped accordingly, a fact about which opinions may be divided, to say the least (cf. Postman, 1982). Fourthly, as many parents know, watching adult television programs adds to one's status in the peer group. For example, among boys at this age it is considered daring and grown-up to watch exciting programs. Consequently, we find preferences for exciting programs very early among preschool boys, a finding which may tell us more about peer influence and a desire to be like other boys, than about maturation.

In the Vaxjoe study we find very little in TV preferences that may be said to mirror cognitive, social, or biological/sexual development during the age bracket under study in that panel (11–15). Indeed, homogeneity is almost total. The results from the Vaxjoe study presented in sec. 2.4 show almost identical means for the three age-groups (cf. Flodin et al., 1982). In many other aspects of human behavior the years of adolescence are years of unrest and upheaval. We have also seen that during this period the amount of viewing is related to development. With preferences on the other hand, nothing much seems to happen between 11 and 15. This homogeneity is at odds with results from other countries where preference diversification is reported to increase with age (Rubin, 1977; Wartella et al., 1979).

One explanation for our findings could be that preferences are shaped early, perhaps already before 11, only to stay the same for at least the following 4 years. On the other hand, one may argue that, given our way of measuring them, preferences may indeed have changed, without our being able to detect such changes. An individual may say that he or she prefers films in the third grade as much as does another individual in the ninth, but the type of films they like may differ widely. For a boy or girl of 11 music programs are perhaps not the same thing as what a 15-year-old has in mind. But even granted this, our index should be able to register *some* change. It did not. We therefore conclude firstly, that among Swedish children TV preferences seem to be established fairly early and, secondly, that the general pattern of preferences does not seem to be influenced very much by the developmental upheavals associated with adolescence. What about specific preferences?

Let us turn to a central specific preference, the preference for information-oriented content. Table 3.5 presents the means for the index of preferences for information content described in sec. 2.7. (The higher the figure, the more information oriented the preferences.) For technical reasons we cannot use our main panel here. Therefore, the data are cross-sectional, from the third wave.

The differences between the values in the fifth and ninth grades are small. Yet the tendency is the expected one, even if the differences are not large enough to provide strong support for the hypothesis. However, we do find a more marked increase for the girls in the ninth grade. For the boys the difference is almost negligible. In the fifth and seventh grades, however, the boys are clearly above the girls in preference for informative content. (This holds true also after control for social class.) As a result of this gender-differential development, the difference in

Table 3.5.   Information Preference Score (Means) by Grade and Gender.
(Vaxjoe Study, Third Wave)

| | Grade | | | | | |
| | 5 | | 7 | | 9 | |
	Boys	Girls	Boys	Girls	Boys	Girls
Information preference score	4.71	4.34	4.81	4.31	4.85	4.89

Table 3.6.   Relationships Between Cognitive Development (Language Test)
and Information Preference Score, Adjusted for Gender, SES, and Parent-
peer Orientation. Vaxjoe Study, Third Wave.

Grade and Cognitive Development	N	Information preference score (means) adjusted for gender, SES, parent-peer orientation	
Grade 5			
High	2	5.6	
Middle	10	4.4	
Low	96	4.6	Beta .09
Grade 7			
High	14	5.3	
Middle	34	5.4	
Low	98	4.4	Beta .25
Grade 9			
High	76	5.1	
Middle	49	4.5	
Low	63	4.3	Beta .17

preferences for informative content is largest in grade 7, where so many
other differences are also at a maximum.

What about the relationship between cognitive development and
television preferences? As they have greater resources and capabilities
for understanding this type of content one would expect that, at every
age, the more cognitively developed adolescents would show an inclination to prefer more informative material. In Table 3.6 we present
the beta coefficients between the language test scores and the information preference scores, as well as means for the information scores
in different categories of cognitive development. (Again, because the
language test was only given in the third wave, we have to leave the
main panel and confine ourselves to the third wave of the Vaxjoe study.)

As expected, the information preference score tends to increase with
level of cognitive development. The tendency is visible in all three age-

groups, though beta is lowest among the youngest. (Note the extremely low n in two categories of this age bracket, however.) Cognitive development seems to play little or no role at the age of 11, increasing substantially 2 years later. At the age of 15 cognitive development again reduces its impact on television preferences. As was noted above, preferences at the age of 11 are to a large degree the product of family influences. Development is then of less importance in deciding what to see. With the onset of puberty the individual's taste for television programs develops more independently from that of the family. Now, development may play a greater role in determining taste. But the centrality of television viewing decreases during adolescence as other sources of information or other rewards become more important. That may be one reason, we may assume, why the relationship between cognitive development and TV preferences becomes weaker by the age of fifteen.

An argument against such an explanation is the fact that we have found no differences in preferences between the different age-groups, especially no marked shift in over-all preferences between the ages of eleven and thirteen. Nevertheless, our data once more show that developmental effects on TV use and preferences are at their strongest in grade 7, at about the age of 13. The changes occurring at that age are only to be compared with those occurring between 6 and 10 (discussed, for instance, in connection with Table 2.7). The two periods of change, of course, correspond to the transitions between stages discussed in sec. 3.1.

3.3.3. Development and TV Relations

The TV relations that we are dealing with in this section are identification and pseudo-interaction with people on the screen. The operationalization is the capture/long-term identification index, which was discussed earlier (sec. 2.5). What is the expected relationship between, on the one hand, development and on the other, capture and long-term identification?

There may be several answers to this question, and we believe that at least two possible tendencies may be at work here. To begin with, cognitive developmental psychology usually assumes that role-taking ability develops with age (Selman, 1971; Flavell, 1968). If the ability to take someone else's role increases, then we would expect "TV relations" also to increase with age. Note, however, that there is also a contradictory tendency, namely, that with increasing age the child will be better able to distinguish between what is real and unreal on the TV screen (Schramm, Lyle, & Parker 1961; Noble 1975). He or she will also increasingly realize the true relationship between the real world and the media world. This would lead to less identification and interaction with TV content with increasing age.

In the descriptive chapter we have already seen that the latter hypothesis seems to be the most viable. In the Vaxjoe study, our index of "capture" and long-term identification declines with age, from a score of 10.9 in the 5th grade to 8.0 in the 9th, with modest gender differences in grades 5 and 7, but with a larger gap in the 9th grade (cf. Johnsson-Smaragdi, 1983). This result is in line with Rubin (1977). Noble's (1975) finding that males identify more often than females received only limited support in our material. In the third wave boys had higher capture/long-term identification scores in the 5th grade, whereas the opposite was true for the 7th and 9th grades. In our panel data, there was no difference between boys and girls in grade 5, while in grades 7 and 9 the girls were increasingly more involved than the boys. Using another measure of identification, we found in the Malmoe study that girls identified more than boys already in grade 5 (cf. sec. 2.5). For some reason there may be a turning point after which girls identify more than boys. It is an interesting task to look further into this possibility, with more extensive data than we have at hand here.

Cognitive development, as measured by our language test, is negatively related to capture/long-term identification in the 7th and the 9th grades, but weakly positively correlated in the 5th grade. The Beta association between the two variables is almost the same in all three age groups.

We may conclude that, during adolescence, involvement declines with age, at least as we measure it. One explanation is that the perception of reality becomes better the older one becomes, but it is also possible to look at the result from a uses and gratifications point of view. As Noble (1975) noted, identification, or the loss of one's own identity, may be enjoyable to many individuals in the audience. Rosengren and Windahl (1972, 1977) demonstrate that parasocial interaction is often used as a functional alternative in order to obtain gratifications otherwise difficult for the individual to come by. It may be that the loss of one's own identity becomes less rewarding with age and that interaction with "real people" will be more valued by the adolescent as he or she grows older. Cognitive and social developments influence the use made of TV, and also the gratifications derived from that use.

3.3.4. Development of Dependency

When discussing dependency on mass media and their contents, one may have at least two aspects of the phenomenon in mind. In one case, dependency and its origins lie outside the individual's media use; rooted in, say, the social structure, a general need for information, or a need for escape, or something else. This is the form of dependency dealt with in Ball-Rokeach's Dependency model (Ball-Rokeach & DeFleur, 1976; Ball-Rokeach, 1985; cf. Höjerback, 1985, p. 10). In another sense, dependency stems from media use itself. The individual gets used to a certain medium and its content and thereby becomes "addicted" to it. This type of dependency is described by McQuail and Windahl (1981); (cf. also Rubin & Windahl, 1982, 1986; Windahl et al., 1986). Dependency of this kind may be regarded either as a consequence of mass media use, as such, or as an effect of the content consumed.

Etiologically then, the two types of media dependency are quite different. One has its roots in social structures and processes, the other is the outcome of psychological processes of habituation, mild forms of "addiction" to media use itself. In spite of their different origins, the subjective experience of the two types of dependency may be rather similar to each other. Actually, the crude operationalization of dependency used in the Media Panel research program taps both of the two main denotations of the term in one single question. Our question was: "If, for some reason, you suddenly had to do without TV, would you then miss it?" The four reply categories ran from "very much" to "not at all".

In the sense of "addiction", in particular, dependency is a relation that presumably is very much shaped over time. In general, therefore, one would expect dependency to increase with age. As is seen in Table 3.7 this is not the case. The highest dependency score is found in the fifth grade; the lowest, in the ninth grade. This holds for both sexes and for both the working and middle classes.

Looking closer at the determinants of dependency, we find in Table 3.8 that the strongest Eta and Beta relationships are found between dependency and amount of TV consumption. The table also suggests that this relationship increases with age, implying that the relationship

Table 3.7. Dependency Scores by Age, Gender, and Social Class. Vaxjoe Main Panel.

| | Dependency Score | | | | |
| | Gender | | Social Class | | |
	Boys	Girls	High	Low	All
Grade 5	3.1	2.8	2.8	3.1	3.0
Grade 7	2.8	2.6	2.5	2.9	2.7
Grade 9	2.2	2.1	2.0	2.3	2.2

between age and dependency is more complicated than was foreseen. While the general level of dependence decreases with age, the relationship between amount of TV consumption and dependency increases with age. The other media use factor included in the table, degree of involvement—conceptualized as long-term identification and capture—is fairly weakly related to dependency, although in all cases the relationship is linear. Note also that the unique influence of the subtle involvement dimension (as measured by the Beta's) is stronger than that of gender, and about as strong as that of social class.

Although the influence of gender gets weaker with age, the boys consistently show greater dependency than the girls (cf. Table 3.7). The influence from social class is not reduced to the same extent as that of gender. For all three grades the dependency score is higher for working class than for middle class children and adolescents.

How can we account for results such as these in terms of our developmental model and theories?

The decrease in dependency during this period of life may be attributed to aspects of social development, such as a growing independence from the family and an increasing involvement with the peer group. Television becomes less important for attaining the social goals of life, compared to its importance at earlier ages. In the 9th grade new means have become available for the individual to fulfill needs that are more related to the peer group and less related to the family. As a result of this social development, dependency on TV quite naturally decreases—that is, dependency caused and constituted by other factors than media use and media content.

On the other hand, we note that the relationship between the amount of TV consumption and dependency is strengthened with age. This directs our attention to the other aspect of dependency, the habitual

Table 3.8. Eta and Beta Values for Relationships Between Dependency and Four Independent Variables: Gender, Social Class, Amount of TV, and Degree of Involvement. Controlling for Three at a Time. Vaxjoe Main Panel.

| Independent Variable | Grade | | | | | |
| | 5 | | 7 | | 9 | |
	Eta	Beta	Eta	Beta	Eta	Beta
Gender	.16	.12	.15	.06	.06	.01
Social class	.22	.14	.23	.14	.18	.10
Amount of TV	.34	.27	.42	.38	.43	.41
Degree of involvement	.19	.13	.10	.10	.15	.11

dependency as caused by media use itself. It is reasonable to assume that the strengthened relationship between amount of TV and dependency is an indication of habituation. The more TV you watch, the more you will be used to it, habituated to it, or even "addicted" to it. Since this is a cumulative process, the relationship may be expected to become stronger over time.

Our data, then, support the argument for the existence of two basically different types of dependency. The two types have different types of sources. The first is structural, for instance needs (changing with stage of development and with social position, etc.). The other is mass media use which itself may also have developmental origins.

Unfortunately, our crude operationalization of dependency does not differentiate between the two types of dependency. For the parents, however, we have a clearcut case of media dependency caused by social circumstances.

Parents of 6-year-old preschool children have to stay at home much more than parents of 15-year-old ninth-graders. Consequently, they are cut off from many out-of-home activities they would otherwise have liked to indulge in. When staying at home, they are not always masters of their own time. More often than not, more powerful agents are in command. As a consequence, parents of preschool children should tend to be dependent on mass media, primarily TV, as a substitute for other activities. (In addition, of course, many parents of small children watch TV together with their children, often programs they would not otherwise have given much attention to, thus increasing their amount of TV viewing even more.) This, then, is a case of "structural dependency", a more clear-cut phenomenon than the mixed type of dependency we have been able to measure for the children. Do empirical data bear out our theoretical arguments?

In the Malmoe panel, we measured the parents' amount of habitual TV viewing when their children attended preschool and grade 5. In the Vaxjoe main panel we measured it when their children attended grades 5 and 9. Between them, the two main panels of the Media Panel Program thereby allow us to follow the amount of habitual TV viewing of the parents from the time their children attend preschool (age 6) until they have reached the last year of the compulsory school system (grade 9, age 15).

We have seen that children's TV viewing is strongly related to age, gender, and social class. Figure 3.8 presents the amount of habitual TV viewing of the parents, differentiated with respect to social class and to the age and gender of their children. The figures refer to the self-reported TV viewing of the parent responding to our postal survey (usually the mother; cf. sec. 1.3.3). (The difference between the grand means for habitual viewing as reported by mothers and fathers was next to negligible: 94 vs. 93 minutes a day in grade 5 of the main Vaxjoe panel.)

The data for grade 5 are averages of the Malmoe and Vaxjoe figures. Since parental TV viewing was heavier in Vaxjoe than in Malmoe, the data from parents of preschool children (Malmoe panel) and ninth-graders (main Vaxjoe panel) have been linked to this average. In this way we have controlled for the difference between the larger city of Malmoe and the smaller city of Vaxjoe. Thus the results may be said to approximate the TV habits of the parents of urban Swedish school children during the time period under study. Given the somewhat synthetic nature of the data, we should not pay too much attention to the details of the figure. The main tendencies are interesting enough.

The main tendency of the figure is the heavy reduction of the time dedicated to TV by parents as their children pass through the school system. Parents of ninth-graders view TV some three quarters of an

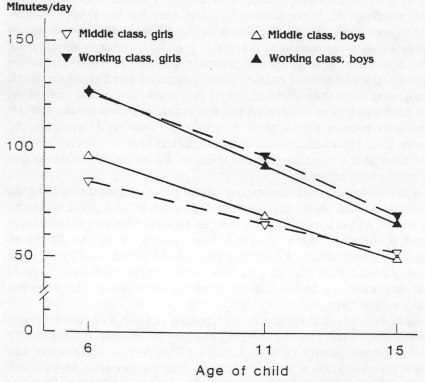

Figure 3.8. Parents' Habitual TV Viewing by Age of Child (Controlling for Gender of Child and Social Class of Parents)

hour less a day than do parents of preschoolers. The difference between parents from different social classes is considerably smaller, but still quite substantial (one or two quarters of an hour). Differences between parents of boys and girls are next to negligible.

The dramatic developments of Figure 3.8 are not found in the usual statistics on TV consumption. They are hidden by the simple fact that audience data are most often presented in terms of means or percentages for age brackets. As a rule, they are not broken down with respect to the situation in the family cycle (although breakdowns with respect to families with and without children do occur). In such terms, most of the parents in our study would have been lumped in the 30–40 age bracket, and at the very best, the striking trend we have just found would have been presented as a standard deviation left unexplained.

The explanation for this striking trend must be sought in the fact that as children grow older, their parents are increasingly less bound to home, hearth, and the TV set. They become less structurally dependent.

It is sometimes said that the media habits of children are influenced by those of their parents (cf. sec. 5.3.2). Here we see that the TV habits of the parents may be heavily determined by the age of their children. (Presumably, the trends of Figure 3.8 would have been similar, but somewhat less drastic, perhaps, had we been able also to approach the fathers. On the other hand, they would probably have been even more drastic, had we based it on parents of one child only, or on those parents having their youngest child in the age brackets under study.)

For the parents then, we may observe a rather clear-cut case of structural dependency. It should be added that the other, more "mixed" type of dependency has also been measured for the parents, these parental results being parallel and giving support to the results obtained for the children. The general level of this subjectively perceived dependency among the Vaxjoe parents diminishes from a mean of 2.4 in grade 5 to 2.1 in grade 9. (In Malmoe it is somewhat lower, and there is no general trend.) Both in the Malmoe and Vaxjoe panels, parental dependency thus measured shows only a week, or non-existent relationship with the gender of the child, and with social class.

More important, however, is the fact that we find moderate to strong MCA betas between amount of parental TV consumption and this type of dependency (controlling for gender and social class), both among Malmoe and Vaxjoe parents. In the Malmoe panel, this relationship is more or less stable from preschool to grade 5 (in the .40s). In the Vaxjoe panel, on the other hand, just as with the Vaxjoe children, the strength of the relationship increases over time: from Beta = .27 to Beta = .37. Structurally induced parental dependency on television diminishes while, as time passes by, amount of viewing seems to keep or even strengthen its hold over parents' subjectively experienced dependency.

Thus, the biological and social development of children makes both children and parents alike less structurally dependent on TV, makes them turn away from TV to less family bound activities, often to activities outside the home. Meanwhile, for those parents and adolescents who stay with TV, continued TV use itself tends to make for increased dependency.

3.3.5. Development and TV-viewing Motives

In uses and gratifications theory, the notion of motives for media use plays an important role (Blumler & Katz, 1974; McQuail & Windahl, 1981; Palmgreen et al., 1985). Differential individual needs manifest themselves in differential motives for differential media use. Several media scholars have investigated the role of motives and have produced various lists or typologies of motives for attending to the mass media (cf. for example, McQuail et al., 1972; Greenberg, 1974; Rubin, 1979). Recently, the term "gratifications sought" has often come to replace the term "motive" (cf. Palmgreen & Rayburn, 1985).

In the Media Panel Program, motives for viewing television were measured with scales borrowed from Greenberg (1974) who presented the most widely used operationalization of motives for media use. In the various different factor analyses undertaken, the following clusters of motives repeatedly emerged (for every motive an example of an item is given):

Recreation: I watch TV because it is good when one wants to rest

Knowledge: . . because I get to know how young persons like myself solve problems that are similar to my own

Talk about: . . because it gives me something to talk about with my friends

Habit: . . because it has become a habit

Pastime: . . because I have nothing better to do

Escape: . . because I can get away from something I don't like doing

The uses and developmental model states that the need structure of the individual is continuously changing as the individual passes through different developmental stages. With age, certain motives will gain in importance as others lose. The preschooler does not approach the screen for the same reasons as does the 15-year-old.

Needs, however, are not alone in determining the structure of motivation. Rubin (1979, 1981) found that most motives correlated with amount of television consumption. This is in line with the basic uses and gratifications model which predicts feedback from media use and gratifications obtained to motives (gratifications sought; cf. Palmgreen et al., 1985). It is logical, therefore, that in a population aged 18 and older, Ostman and Jeffers (1985) found positive relationships between age and the strength of various TV-viewing motives. (TV viewing, it will be remembered, increases monotonously among adults.) Conversely, but equally logically, we would expect motivations to grow weaker among our adolescents, since they show a strong decline in TV viewing.

Motives were measured in all three waves of the Vaxjoe panel, but in the third wave we had to use a somewhat different factor structure. Figure 3.9, therefore, shows the development in motives as measured in the first two waves. In order to reduce situational and cohort effects the data are presented as means of the two measurements available for each gender and age group.

The data clearly show the expected overall tendency to reduction in the strength of TV use motivations. This pattern is especially clearcut for the motives of "talk about" and "habit". As they grow older,

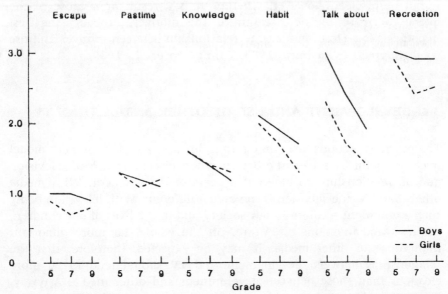

Figure 3.9.   TV Viewing Motives by Grade and Gender. Average of Waves 1 and 2, Vaxjoe Study.

adolescents do not like to see their TV viewing as a habit and they do not use it for the "coin of exchange" function of food for discussions with peers.

The overall pattern is somewhat complicated by the fact that, in this respect, boys and girls differ in at least two ways. In the first place, girls' motivations are weaker than those of boys (excepting the motive of "knowledge"). That is in line with the generally lower TV consumption of girls. Secondly, in three cases ("escape", "recreation", and "pastime"), the girls' curve is clearly U-shaped, while that of the boys is more or less linearly declining.

Speculating on these differences, we interpret them as a result of differential social development in differential opportunity structures. Society offers girls fewer opportunities outside the family to realize the capacities for growth which their development stimulates. As a result, in grade nine they return to the family medium of TV for recreation, passing the time and escaping from a somewhat frustrating situation (social capacity without without social opportunity). They do not seem very happy about the situation either, for they like to see their TV use neither in terms of a habit, nor in terms of food for discussion with others (linearly and steeply decreasing values for the motives of "talk about" and "habit").

Consumption, presumably, is an important factor in this context. It is not quite clear, however, whether it is a result or a cause of the overall decrease in the strength of the motives. Probably the best hypothesis is a close mutual interrelationship between motives and use (cf. Palmgreen & Rayburn, 1985; Palmgreen et al., 1985).

3.4. DEVELOPMENT AND USE OF OTHER MEDIA THAN TV

The previous sections have shown that our uses and development model may be useful as a heuristic device when discussing use of television and its relationships to different aspects of development. With media other than TV, the situation is somewhat different. With television being such a dominant medium in our society and in the lives of our children, the uses and functions of TV are, on the whole, far more important than those of other media. It may be expected, therefore, that the relationships between development and TV should tend to be more clear-cut than those between development and other media. Anyway, let us see what may be said about development and the use of other media than TV, taking radio listening as our first case.

3.4.1. Radio Listening

With the rapid expansion of TV, radio listening decreased considerably in most Western countries. Radio adapted itself to this new situation by trying to fulfill more specific functions for more or less specific groups in society. In Sweden the original one channel system was developed into a three channel system. Later on (1977), in addition, local radio was introduced.

It has been maintained that radio listening increases with age among children and adolescents (cf. von Feilitzen, 1976; Greenberg, 1976; Avery, 1979; Filipson, 1980, 1981). In our data, the picture is more complicated. In 1976, the heaviest radio users were boys in the 9th grade. In 1980, boys in the 5th grade held that position. Flodin et al. (1982) have tried to explain this by the increased availability of transistor radios at low prices which makes it feasible even for younger people to own one of their own.

Figure 3.10, based on the Vaxjoe panel material, suggests that the increase in radio listening is rather small between the ages 11 and 15. The regular pattern of a slight increase is disturbed by the category of working class boys, who constitute the highest consuming group at the ages of 11 and 15 but are about the lowest at the age of 13. The reasons for this development are hard to establish. (Partly, at least, it may have been caused by changes in the radio output, but we cannot point at something specific in that respect.) On the whole the results point to more listening by boys than by girls and more listening among working class than among middle class adolescents. In this respect, the parallel with TV viewing is fairly clear.

How can the application of the conceptual framework of our uses and development model help us better to understand the use made of radio by children and adolescents?

By and large, the output of Swedish radio may be said to consist of three different types of content: rather heavy information programs, music (light and classical), and local news. No doubt it should also be remembered that many of the parents of today's young people do not themselves belong to a generation which listens to radio for all types of content. This may mean that children and adolescents are not encouraged in their homes to use their cognitive skills for radio listening. As a matter of fact, it is quite plausible that a substantial proportion, if not the major part, of adolescents' radio listening goes to Channel 3, the channel consisting of light music interspersed with short news programs and entertainment. Johnsson-Smaragdi and Roe (1986) in a study of over 1,300 Swedish 15-year-olds report that 54% of their respondents never listen to anything but music when they listen to the

Minutes/day

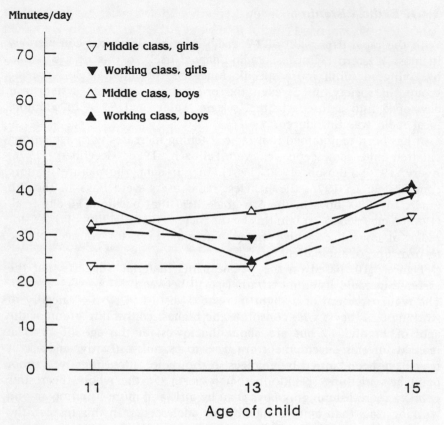

Figure 3.10. Radio Consumption by Age, Gender and Social Class. Vaxjoe Study, Main Panel (From Johnsson-Smaragdi, 1983)

radio, the girls being even more avid music fans than the boys: 58 vs 50%.)

In the last wave of the Vaxjoe study, the 5th graders were the heaviest radio listeners. It has been suggested that this may partly mirror the fact that today even young people have the opportunity to buy radio sets of their own (Flodin et al., 1982). In terms of our model, we may say that material resources for the use of radio are now obtainable at earlier stages of life than was formerly the case.

We have already noted that TV is a medium to which you have access but which you can hardly control. In principle, the same holds true for radio, but the output of radio is more variegated than that of TV. Also, radio content, for example, pop music, is often recorded on cassettes. To a large extent radio is more controllable than TV. This means that—both directly and indirectly—radio could be more functional than TV for the individual entering adolescence. For instance, it could be used for mood control (Brown et al., 1974). Actually we would anticipate much higher figures for radio listening among adolescents, had there been a channel of nothing but pop music which could have been used for mood control. Channel 3 is a step in this direction, but it may be too bland and mainstream for today's adolescents.

The results for radio listening in the media panel material are far from clear-cut and are in some respects contradictory. Probably this is the result of complex patterns of interaction between age, cohort, and situation effects (exemplified by developmental phenomena, economic changes, and more or less time-specific changes in the radio output).

Our main impression of the radio listening data is that the use of radio among adolescents is rather idiosyncratic. It is not as predictable, nor does it have such clear-cut patterns as were found in the case of television. It is also worth noting that there is a considerable gap in the amount of consumption between the two electronic media. Radio may fulfill certain needs, for example, through offering pop music, but our data suggest that its overall importance is small, compared with television. There is no doubt that television is the primary medium. This difference is also the most likely explanation for the difference in stability over time for the consumption data of the two media. TV is more integrated into the lives of adolescents and, consequently, it shows a higher degree of stability.

In order to spread some further light on the complex interaction between gender, age, cohort, and situation effects on radio listening, Figure 3.11 offers data about radio listening somewhat differently organized than in the figure previously presented: cross-sectional data from all three waves of the Vaxjoe study. For all cross-sectional gender subgroups but one there is the same tendency: a higher radio consumption in the ninth than in the fifth grade. The exception is formed by the boys in the 1980 wave, who run contrary to the main tendency. We have interpreted this as a sign of increased ownership of radio sets among boys of 11 (cf. above), but is that the whole truth? And is the main tendency of increased consumption the result solely of a better ability to read the radio medium and better need fulfillment among the adolescents? These are questions difficult to answer with the data we have got, but it would no doubt be worthwhile to gather new and better data in order to look deeper into this specific area. In any case, a follow-up is necessary to reveal whether the 1980 tendency for boys really marks the beginning of a new main trend in radio use by young people in Sweden.

Minutes/day

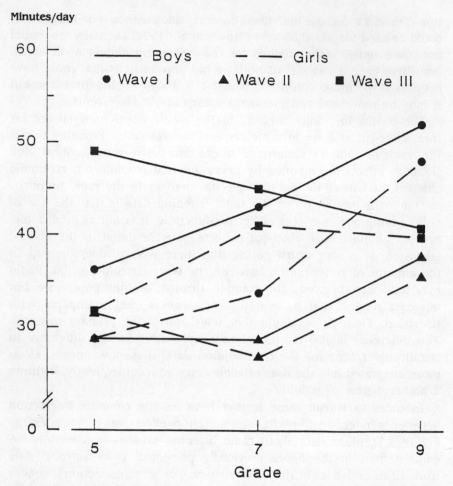

Figure 3.11. Radio Consumption 1976, 1978, 1980, by Grade and Gender (Minutes/Day). (From Flodin et al., 1982)

3.4.2. Newspaper Reading

Swedes are heavy newspaper readers. Readership figures vary, of course, depending on type of measure used and category of reader approached. More than 90% of the Swedish population are regular readers of newspapers. Such figures refer to "habitual reading" (cf. our term "habitual viewing"). If we turn to "actual reading" (cf. our term "actual viewing"), we get somewhat lower figures (some 80%). In the age brackets of interest to us, "actual reading" is much lower. On an average day, some 40% of children aged 9–14 have read a newspaper, usually for less than half an hour (cf. Gustafsson, 1983; Mediebarometern, 1980; Strid, 1983; Weibull, 1983a, 1983b). Most studies show that newspaper reading increases with age, among children and adolescents as well as among adults (Feilitzen 1976; Strid 1983; Weibull 1983a).

If we turn to the conceptual framework of our developmental model we find several reasons for this increase. To begin with, newspapers are more demanding than, for example, TV. As cognitive skills expand it is possible to make greater use of the newspaper. One would also expect that young persons gradually become more inclined to conform with the media use of adults, one significant aspect of which is newspaper reading.

Furthermore, the newspaper is able to fulfill some specific needs which we believe are increasingly felt during adolescence. The newspaper may be used, for example, as a link to the local community outside the family gradually being left by the adolescent. Local newspapers provide information about what to do: dances, clubs, movies, and so forth. Finally, the newspaper is easy to control, in that it may be used anywhere and at any time.

The tendency to increase newspaper reading, then, is easily understood in terms of our developmental theories. At the same time, however, this development-related increase may have been somewhat counteracted by an increasing long-term trend, starting among the young, toward decreasing newspaper reading (cf. McCombs, 1980; Strid & Weibull, 1984; Weibull, 1983).

From a developmental perspective, however, amount of newspaper reading may be less important than what is read, and to what degree different types of contents are appreciated. In looking at these two aspects of newspaper consumption we should bear in mind that we can never expect the correlation between actual consumption and preferences for different types of any media content to be perfect. As was shown in chap. 2 (see also Weibull 1983a, 1983b), several factors such as availability, tradition, and external pressures may bring about a less than perfect fit between the two aspects of media use.

What changes in newspaper reading patterns with age could be expected? As stated earlier in the context of preferences for TV content, we would expect consumption for the delayed, instrumental reward type of content to increase, and for the immediate, expressive reward type of content to decrease (Avery, 1979; Pietilä, 1969; Schramm, 1949). It is easy to conceive of a growing need to obtain material for a judgment of one's own about what is happening in the environment. Consequently, news about what is happening both within and outside of Sweden would be increasingly read as people pass through adolescence. Conversely, the consumption of children's pages and comics will tend to decrease as they become less relevant to the adolescents' needs and resources.

In the Vaxjoe study a combined measure of preference for, and reading of, newspaper content was used in waves 1 and 2, whereas in the third wave the appreciation, as such, of different contents was the focus of interest.

As examples of content that may offer delayed, instrumental rewards to readers we have chosen foreign news, domestic news and news about politics. (Of course this third category is also found in the other two.) As examples of immediate, expressive rewards we have chosen accidents and crime, sports, comics, and contents dealing with radio and television. Figure 3.12 shows the development of news-reading patterns, indicating the percentage of adolescents (boys and girls) who report "liking to read" each of seven categories. (In the questionnaires, there were some additional categories.) The figures are averages of the first two waves. In this way, situational and generational influences are reduced as much as possible, letting age influences stand out more clearly.

There are very few adolescents in our sample who give priority to hard news (first three categories). The percentage for political news is especially low. All the same we find the expected tendency. With increasing age the number of hard news readers increases, especially for the girls.

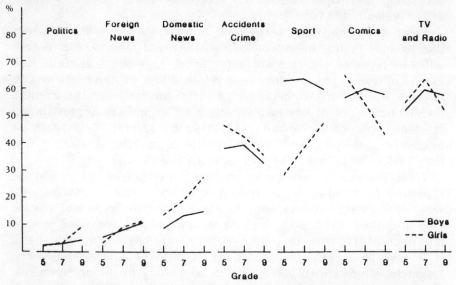

Figure 3.12. Reading Habits and Preferences for Different Types of Newspaper Content, by Grade and Gender. Vaxjoe Study (Percentage Based on Means for First 2 Waves).

All types of content, however, do not have as low values as hard news has. The percentages for accidents and crime, sports, comics, and content dealing with television and radio are considerably higher. The expected tendency of decline is found only for the category of accidents and crime. Later on it will probably rise again, for we know that this kind of content is quite popular among adult men and women of all ages (cf., e.g., Weibull, 1983a).

For categories other than accidents and crime the tendencies are mixed, with boys and girls showing differential developments. Girls have the most dramatic development, with a very strong decline in comics reading, for instance. The curves of the boys tend to be A-shaped, with no clear decline for comics and TV.

The most interesting results, however, concern sports reading. It will be seen that there is a clear tendency toward convergence between boys and girls. The convergence is brought about by a dramatic increase of sports fans among the girls. From a developmental point of view this is of some importance. During this period, from 11 to 15 years of age, girls and boys increasingly interact. Girls come more and more into contact with the topics of the male domain. As a result it seems natural that interest in sports reading will grow. Since the figure is based on averages for the first two waves, the increase cannot be ascribed to situational factors. But it could be that teen-aged girls are more prone than 11-year-olds themselves to practice sports (for instance, girls' soccer, which has become increasingly popular).

In the third wave, respondents were asked about their general appreciation of different newspaper contents. The result is presented in Table 3.9. Two tendencies are noteworthy: The lack of dramatic differences between the age-groups, and the similarities of the scores of girls and boys. We find here the same homogeneity that was found for television preferences. Nevertheless, we do note that, in all three age-groups, the girls are more interested than the boys in ads, entertainment, and family news, while the boys consistently hold the lead when it comes to foreign news, politics, and sports. This is very much in accordance with future gender roles as they manifest themselves in adult newspaper reading (Weibull, 1983a). Once again, however, we must warn readers that we do not really know how respondents of different ages and genders interpret labels such as "domestic news," "politics," "entertainment," and "family news page."

3.4.3. Reading Comics

Previous studies (cf. Feilitzen, 1976) show that the reading of comics tends to go down from the age of about 9. There are several reasons

Table 3.9. Appreciation Scores for Different Types of Newspaper Content. (Vaxjoe Study, Third Wave)

Respondent category	Foreign news	Domestic news	Politics	Accidents and crime	Sports	Advertisements	Entertainment	Family news	Comics	About TV and radio
Grade 5										
Boys	2.3	2.7	1.1	2.9	3.5	2.5	2.9	2.2	3.7	3.5
Girls	2.2	2.6	1.0	2.8	3.2	2.7	3.1	2.7	3.5	3.1
Grade 7										
Boys	2.4	2.7	1.4	3.0	3.4	2.5	3.1	2.2	3.3	3.4
Girls	2.3	2.9	1.0	3.0	3.2	2.7	3.3	2.7	3.5	3.4
Grade 9										
Boys	2.3	2.6	1.6	2.8	3.1	2.3	2.9	1.8	3.2	3.2
Girls	2.4	2.7	1.4	2.8	2.8	2.5	3.1	2.3	3.2	3.2

for this. Cognitive resources for reading comics are generally available at a low age. Although some comics are intended for an older audience, most of the content is tailored for younger categories.

Table 3.10 presents the results for comics reading for the main Vaxjoe panel. Data refer to comics as a medium of its own, that is, weekly and monthly magazines specializing in comics. Comics in other weeklies, and in newspapers are not included. The table shows that girls read comics much less than boys. For both boys and girls the reading of comics declines dramatically after grade 7. The facts that girls in these age brackets consistently read fewer comics than boys, and that the gap between boys and girls widens, may mirror the earlier maturation of girls, the consequences of which we have so often observed in this chapter.

3.4.4. Book Reading

It has often been noted that children read books quite a lot until they reach late childhood. Then the decline in reading is sharp (cf., e.g., Feilitzen, 1976, p. 105). It is intriguing to note that this decrease in book reading takes place at about the same age as the drop in television viewing. Most of our explanations for the TV case, however, do not apply here. Books may be consumed at home, but they are not tied in with the family circle to the same extent as is TV. Books can be read anywhere and at different times. One thus has control over the medium, something which is presumably preferred by adolescents. Reading books written for grown-ups may provide the gratifications of feeling that one is at least half-adult.

On the other hand, reading is an adult-approved activity (Medrich et al., 1982), and it is typically performed at home. Furthermore, it is

Table 3.10. Comics Reading by Grade and Gender. (Percentage; Vaxjoe Main Panel)

| | Grade | | | | | |
| | 5 | | 7 | | 9 | |
Frequency	Boys	Girls	Boys	Girls	Boys	Girls
None	0	6	2	5	9	26
A few a month	19	26	16	29	30	39
One a week	17	19	20	22	19	16
Several a week	64	49	62	44	41	19
	100	100	100	100	99	100

an activity not normally combined with peer interaction, an interaction which during this period of age becomes important, not to say overriding. Social and sexual-biological development is pressing the young boy or girl out of home and hence away from books. In addition, book reading takes time, and in adolescence time is becoming scarcer.

Figure 3.13 shows the development of book reading within the Vaxjoe main panel. For middle-class adolescents, there is a peak in the seventh grade (age 13), which is somewhat later than reported in other studies. For working-class adolescents, however, the decline in book reading is already on its way in the seventh grade. The figure shows two features by now well known from other media panel data: The difference between subgroups is largest in grade 7, and the development of girls is more dramatic than that of boys. These two features seem to be characteristic outcomes of the interaction among biological, cognitive, and social development in adolescence.

3.4.5. The Reading of Weeklies and Magazines

Popular magazines constitute a very heterogeneous category of print media. Most of them are weeklies. A large proportion of them are directed at family audiences, although during the last few decades the relative share for this category has shrunk as more specialized magazines have increased their share of the market, for instance, magazines for boat owners and dog owners, food, sailing, art, and technology. Some specialized magazines try to capture a young public. A large proportion of the popular, weekly magazines, however, are aimed at middle-aged, lower-educated women.

At least some of the weeklies seem to have the function for young people of informing them about the latest fads in different areas and of describing or even prescribing how to dress, what music to listen to, and so on. In this function, magazines and weeklies ought to be increasingly important for young people who want to find an identity and a life-style.

Figure 3.14, based on the Vaxjoe main panel, suggests that the use of weeklies and magazines is greater at the age of 15 (grade 9) than at the age of 11. This result is in line with Avery (1979). The leap upwards comes after 13. Our interpretation is that, with the step into middle adolescence, the young person is able to make use of weeklies and magazines and that at this age there is a felt need to read them in order to be familiar with different life-styles. No doubt a large portion of adolescents' magazine reading is devoted to magazines specializing in popular music.

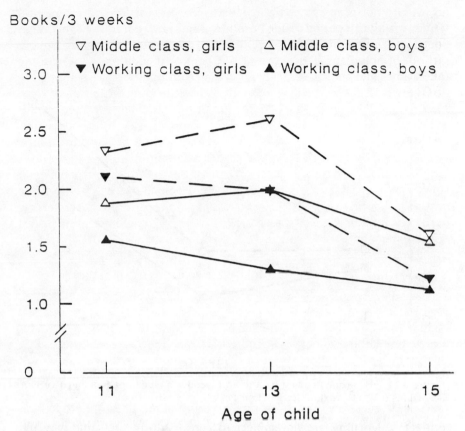

Figure 3.13.   Book Reading by Age, Gender, and Social Class. Vaxjoe Study, Main Panel

The gap between boys and girls seems to increase with age, eventually stabilizing in the gender pattern that is found among adults.

3.4.6. Viewing of Video Recordings

During the last few years the viewing of video recordings has become one of the most debated activities in Sweden. Ownership of video equipment has increased, as in few other countries in the world (probably because VCRs offer an opportunity to bypass the TV monopoly and its restricted fare). The debate has focused on the content of the video-cassettes for sale or rent at a very large number of easily available

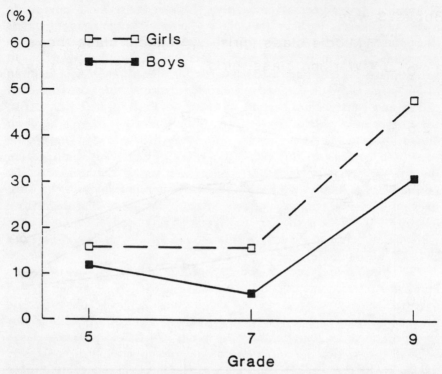

Figure 3.14. Magazine Reading by Age and Gender. Percentage Reading 1 or More Magazines a Week. Vaxjoe Study, Main Panel.

outlets. Video films are not subject to censorship in the same way that movie theater films are, and concern has been aired that such uncontrolled video output is harmful to young people. There is also a potential threat from video to other media (cf. secs. 1.2.1 and 2.8).

From the perspective of our uses and development model, what can be expected of the use of videos among children and adolescents?

The content that one may get out of one's VCR is very varied. In some respects—for example, when it comes to violence and sex—content goes far beyond that of traditional TV. For some types of content—for example cartoons—the cognitive capabilities for using videos are at hand rather early in life. On the other hand, a large proportion of what is offered on the video market consists of films, the full grasp of which demands a rather mature audience.

On the need side, it might be that videos are especially useful in fulfilling adult needs, such as sexual arousal. We have already noted that adult material that is not shown on TV may easily be obtained for video consumption.

From a developmental perspective, however, the most interesting aspect of videos is, perhaps, the degree of control. When trying to assess the nature of video one may ask whether it should be regarded as an extension of TV or whether it is a medium in its own right. As an extension of TV, VCRs are used primarily for time shifting. As a medium of its own, the VCR is used primarily to extend the possibilities of choice and control by means of recorded cassettes for sale or rent. In the former case, videos are seen as a family medium to which, as an adolescent, one may have access but over which one may have only very little control. In the latter, they may be regarded as a medium the use of which one controls, and where use is not primarily the business of the family. We believe that the latter description is the most relevant, a view supported by Roe (1981). He maintains that the central feature of the VCR is the fact that control and choice of content rest with the audience to a much greater extent than is the case with both TV and the movie theater.

The video-viewing pattern among Swedish adolescents—as far as we know it—offers some support for the importance of the notion of control. Adolescents tend to use videos mostly during the weekend (including Friday night). That is the time when videos are at their best as a peer medium for youngsters. A group of adolescents choose one or more cassettes at the outlet (often downtown), sharing the relatively modest costs. The viewing takes place at the home of one of the group, preferably in the absence of parents. This pattern puts almost all the control in the hands of the adolescents themselves: time, location, company, and content (within the frames set by the range of selection provided by the outlet). You can watch the most preferred sequences, or even whole cassettes, more than once. It is obvious that the opportunity for such video evenings in the absence of parents will increase with age, as will so many other opportunities.

This leads us to the hypothesis that VCR use in adolescence ought to increase with age. The tendency toward independence, and the need for control, lead us to the conclusion that the VCR is a useful medium for adolescents. There is, however, also a third answer to our question above. Videos may be both the more TV-like, family medium and a medium that is more independently used. We hypothesize that for the younger children in our panels videos may be more of the first type; for the older adolescents, more of the latter type.

Before we turn to an interpretation of our empirical results, let us just make the additional remark that control and choice are never unlimited. Rental costs of cassettes and the cost of recording may be a very real limitation, especially for younger children. Nevertheless, these costs may be reduced by sharing, which is not the case with, for instance, motion picture theaters.

VCR use was only studied at one point in the research program as here reported, namely, in the third wave in connection with the TV diary questions (March, 1981). The results were presented in sec. 2.8 (Figure 2.13). They do not support the hypothesis predicting increased use of videos with age. Rather, there seems to be a peak in viewing in the seventh grade.

The pattern of video use in the 11–15 age brackets may be confounded, however, by the dualistic use hinted at above. Younger people probably use videos as a family-approved medium; elder adolescents use them as part of their striving for independence. However, our data about *what* is viewed on videos do not really support this view. They do support the hypothesis that girls use videos more as a family medium than do boys. Girls use videos for recorded material more than boys do.

Figure 2.14 in sec. 2.8 showed what is seen on videos in three age-groups of Vaxjoe. Both for boys and girls, the viewing of feature films increases with age. Horror films are watched mostly by boys in the youngest age category. The highest figure for violence is found for 13-year-old boys.

When this study was undertaken, viewing of videos was in its infancy in Sweden. More studies will be necessary to achieve a better understanding of the role of development in use of videos. The first reports from such studies have already been published, by and large confirming the picture given in this section and in secs. 1.2.1 and 2.9 (see, for instance, Höjerback 1985, 1986; Johnsson–Smaragdi & Roe, 1986; Sonesson, 1986). It will be especially interesting in the future to discover more about the two functions of videos hinted at above ("time shifting" vs. "home cinema").

The developmental pattern of video viewing discussed in this section will be strongly influenced by the impending changes in the overall media structure. If satellite and cable television becomes widespread in Sweden (as it probably will), this will probably reduce the adolescents' need for "video evenings" based on rented and recorded cassettes. Also the need for time shifting will be reduced, but probably not to the same extent. The final outcome will be the result of two complex processes of "functional reorganization." As the new media enter the scene, the audience will reorganize their media habits accordingly. For young people, this process of reorganization will take place at the same time as the functional reorganizations caused by the transitions from childhood to adolescence, from adolescence to adulthood.

3.4.7. Moviegoing

In Sweden, as in many other countries, going to the movies has declined during the past few decades. The main reason is often said to be TV. Recently the VCR has emerged as another formidable competitor. In 1984, the rental market for recorded videocassettes surpassed the movie theater market. Already a couple of years before, it had attracted a wider audience (Hultén, 1986).

Despite their decline in popularity, we believe that movies are of great interest from the developmental point of view. The ability to make full use of films grows continuously through the different developmental stages, and it is not fully developed until the stage of formal operations. For the younger children there is also another limitation. The cost of going to the movies is fairly high, and many younger children just do not have enough money for frequent visits.

In sec. 1.2.1 we pointed out that movies are to a large extent a youth medium in Sweden, as in so many other countries. We may assume, therefore that the movies fulfill some important functions for many young people. For example, going alone or with one's peers may be considered a symbol of independence from the family. (Moviegoing as ritualistic dating is not so common in Sweden as it used to be, and still may be in some countries; cf. McLeod & O'Keefe, 1972.) Seeing the movies is, to a large extent, a peer group activity, fitting well into the stages in life when peers are becoming increasingly important.

On the other hand, as Roe (1981) has pointed out, the movies cannot offer very much choice of place, time, or content. From what is said by Brown et al. (1974), movies would then be unsuitable for adolescents, who desire the opportunity of controlling their media use. The truth of all this, however, depends very much on the setting. The larger the city, the greater the movie variety and the greater opportunities for choice and control. In Vaxjoe there are 4 movie theaters, in Malmoe about 20.

What, then, is the profile of moviegoing among boys and girls in our sample? The interplay of situational, generational, gender, and age effects is unusually complicated in this case, so we prefer to present our data as means for the three waves, keeping boys and girls apart. Figure 3.15 offers the resulting data, and we have also included the values for the Malmoe panel. In this way, situational and generational effects are controlled for as far as possible, and the effects of gender and age stand out more clearly.

It will be seen that the increase in moviegoing starts after the age of 13, when adolescents have begun to orient themselves away from their families and toward the peer group. Girls—presumably more under

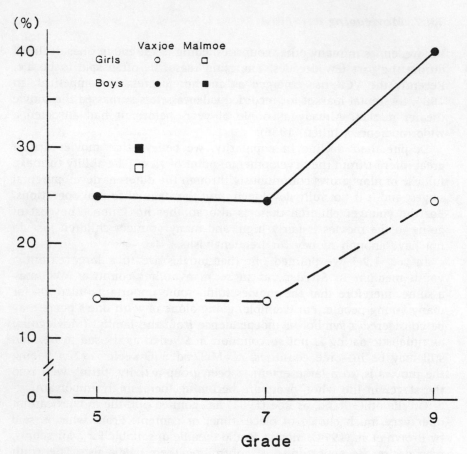

Figure 3.15.   Moviegoing Among Boys and Girls in Vaxjoe and Malmoe. Percentage Going Once a Month or More. (Vaxjoe Data, Means of 3 Waves).

the sway of the family—are less frequent moviegoers than boys. The influence from the need to control the medium may be seen in the higher figures for the Malmoe panel (data available only for grade 5). The differential media structures of Malmoe and Vaxjoe (20 theaters, vs. 4) offer differential opportunities for satisfying the need for control. In spite of the meager output in Vaxjoe, however, the need for peer interaction and family independence is powerful enough to bring about a considerable increase in movie visits. Structural factors probably strengthen this tendency. At 15, Swedish adolescents are allowed to see all movies, whereas before that age they are not allowed to see movies characterized as "forbidden to children."

3.4.8. Listening to Pop Music

Popular music, of course, is no mass medium in itself. It is distributed by a host of media and combinations of media: grammophones, tape decks and cassettes, radio, broadcast TV, and videos. Regardless of its form of distribution, it is extremely popular among adolescents. All this makes it difficult to discuss the media world of children and adolescents without taking into account the uses of popular music.

Popular music is a vague term denoting a very heterogeneous phenomenon. We use the term to designate commercially produced, ephemeral music mainly distributed by radio, records, and cassettes and characterized to a high degree by fads. In this section we use the terms "popular music" and "pop music" synonymously, while in a later section (5.4) "pop" is used to denote a special style of popular music.

As we have noted before, popular music is not in itself a medium. Nevertheless we have decided to treat it by itself, because it fulfills certain needs for the age groups studied and because its use is related in a significant way to the use of other media.

Pop music consumption is a major activity in Sweden, and especially within youth culture. Sales of records were 20 million in 1982, and sales of cassettes (blank and recorded) 25 million (Wallis & Malm, 1984). Filipson (1981) reports that among Swedish adolescents aged 14–17, between 80% and 90% play records and/or cassettes every day. For several reasons it may also be anticipated that pop music listening increases over age in adolescent years.

Figure 3.16 presents data about pop music consumption in three cross-sections and in the main Vaxjoe panel. A decrease in pop music consumption from 1976 to 1980 is clearly visible. However, within all three waves (cross-sectionally) pop music listening increases with age.

Now, if we look at the (dashed) panel curve we see that for this group listening first increases between the ages of 11 and 13 and then decreases between 13 and 15. With our mixed design we are also able to see that the decrease between 13 and 15 results from the fact that the general level of listening to "pop" has markedly decreased. Panel data alone would have presented a quite misleading picture—a caveat toward isolated panels, and a strong argument for mixed designs.

Stated in terms of age and situation, the most plausible interpretation of our data is that there is a main tendency for listening to pop music to increase with age, just as we expected it to do. This overall tendency is then subject to differential influences from situational factors; influences which may change the developmental pattern for single cohorts.

Figure 3.17 demonstrates gender and social-class effects. The largest

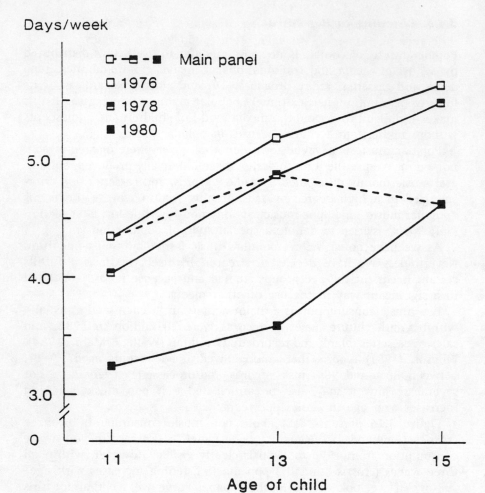

0: **Never listen**   1: **Listen about once a week**   3: **Listen a couple of times a week**   5: **Listen several times a week**   7: **Listen every day**

Figure 3.16. Consumption of Pop Music by Age. Vaxjoe Study, 3 Cross-sections and Main Panel. (From Johnsson-Smaragdi, 1983).

gap seems to be between working-class and middle-class girls, the former being the heaviest consumers of pop music.

Note that Figure 3.17 is based on panel data. Correcting for the situational effect visualized in Figure 3.16, we would have obtained an increase between 13 and 15 for the boys, and approximately no change for the girls between 13 and 15. Thus the boys would have repeated the pattern of the girls, with a lag of about 2 years, a developmental difference phenomenon we have often found in this chapter.

All in all we find that the use of popular music among adolescents differs from the use of TV in two important ways. Pop music use increases during adolescence, while TV use decreases. For pop music, working-class girls are the heaviest consumers: for TV, working-class boys. For both TV and pop music, however, boys' development lags that of girls by some 2 years, and middle-class girls are the least avid consumers.

Days/week

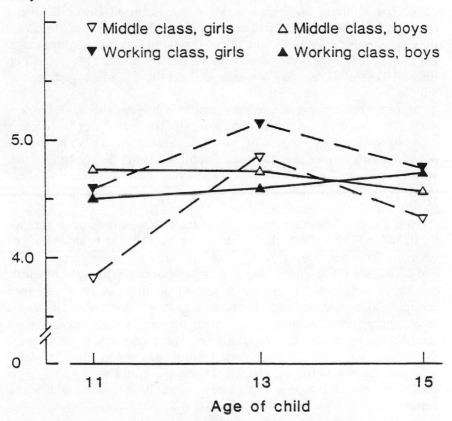

0: Never listen   1: Listen about once a week   3: Listen a couple of times a week   5: Listen several times a week   7: Listen every day

Figure 3.17. Pop Music Consumption by Age, Gender, and Social Class. Vaxjoe Study, Main Panel. (From Johnsson-Smaragdi, 1983).

Why does television viewing decrease from childhood to adolescence, while it is the other way round with listening to pop music? Very probably the reason is that during childhood and early adolescence TV is able to satisfy important needs for integrated family activity. In adolescence the need for doing things on one's own will make young young people turn to playing records and listening to cassettes (cf. Roe, 1983b; Johnsson–Smaragdi & Roe, 1986). Actually, a main function, perhaps *the* main function of pop listening sometimes seems to be protest (Lull, 1983). In many cases, at least, lyrics and volume are an irritant to ordered family life.

In this connection it is important to remember that access to pop music is something that the adolescent may control. He or she need not adapt to the medium in the same way that adaptation to TV is necessary. Music is typically functional for mood control. Another major need in adolescence is the search for identity (Gahlin, 1977), and pop music is useful here, too. For many, the kind of music preferred is almost the nucleus of life-style.

In a number of ways music also relates to biological-sexual development. By means of content analyses of popular song lyrics researchers have shown that the topics of romantic love and courtship are the dominant concerns of popular music (Adorno, 1941; Carey, 1969), and, while preoccupation with these themes may have lessened in recent years, they remain the dominant concern of popular music content (Cristenson, DeBenedittis, & Lindlof, 1985).

This aspect of popular music contents is not surprising when we recall, with Frith (1983), that such music has always been entangled with the experience of growing up, especially in sexual terms. Frith and McRobbie (1978) go as far as to argue that different types of music can be contextualized in terms of sex. Rock music is seen as aimed primarily at a male audience as opposed to "teenybop" which is aimed at a largely female audience and which presents a different model of sexuality in its lyrics, rhythm, and beat. Many researchers have noted that girls in particular have a special relationship to pop which explains why the great majority of pop artists are male and why young girls dominate the teenybopper record-buying public (Denisov & Bridges, 1982).

Puberty, and the onset of the physical and emotional upheavals often associated with it, then, are to be seen as major factors accounting for the upsurge of interest in popular music which occurs almost universally among older children and adolescents. In this respect it has far greater utility than television, which articulates mostly adult concerns. As Larson and Kubey (1985) have summed it up,

Music . . . speaks to adolescent concerns, from heterosexual relations to autonomy and individuation. Rock in particular may be embraced by the young because its very sounds and words mirror the intensity and turbulence of adolescent experience . . . the music reflects the extreme emotional experiences adolescents encounter from moment to moment as part of their daily realities (pp. 407ff.).

3.5. DEVELOPMENT AND MASS MEDIA USE: A CONCLUDING DISCUSSION

In sec. 3.1 we noted that, according to Piaget, the children and adolescents of our two panels move from the preoperational stage, to the stage of concrete operations, to that of formal operations, the transitions between the stages falling roughly between the ages of 6 and 7, and 12 and 13, respectively. In terms of the Swedish school system and our panel waves the transitions come after preschool (first wave of the Malmoe panel) and between grades 5 and 7 (first and second wave of the Vaxjoe panel). The latter passage, of course, coincides roughly with the puberty stage of biological development, marking the transition from childhood to adolescence, a transition which tends to occur some 2 years earlier for girls than for boys.

According to our general model for development and media use, development creates both needs and resources for differential use of the mass media by children and adolescents who find themselves in the midst of these dramatic processes of development. The model was neatly supported by relevant data about media use before and after the two transitions under study. Between preschool and grade 3, there was a dramatic shift from children's programs to adult programs, and from entertaining to exciting programs. From grades 5 to 9, amount of television consumption was heavily reduced, while listening to pop music increased dramatically. For both television and music, girls seem to lead the development by about 2 years, just as they do with biological development, assumed to be a strong determinant of both cognitive and social development.

The coinciding but opposite changes in television and musical habits fit in nicely with well-known developmental changes in qualitative characteristics of needs and resources. The new needs and resources call for, and also make possible, increased control over the media used, and use of peer-oriented rather than family-oriented media (popular music received over transistors, and so forth, rather than television viewed on the family set). The increases in moviegoing and in the reading of weeklies and magazines observed between grades 7 and 9 also fit in very well with the same developmental pattern.

Developmental changes thus affect the transition from one mass medium to another. Taking our analysis one step further, we were able to see how cognitive development may differentially affect the use made of the same medium during different stages of development. In early adolescence, cognitive development seems to lead to increased use of television, while later on it reduced the use of the same medium, a difference to be understood in terms of the different resources made available by differential cognitive development.

It should be remembered, of course, that biological and cognitive development are always accompanied by social development, and that all three types of development are heavily dependent on the social structure in which they occur. For instance, our society offers very different opportunities to boys and girls for realizing the capacities which development provides. That this is so was clearly seen in our data on the differential development of news-reading habits and motives for TV viewing among boys and girls.

In the next decade the media structure offered by society to the public will undergo a drastic change due to new ways of distributing electronic combinations of sound, pictures and written messages: the widespread use of various computer-aided combinations of cable, satellites, and video. According to the theory of functional reorganization, such changes in media structure will have consequences for the way the public will organize their media use. These consequences will no doubt be especially dramatic for children, adolescents and young adults. To the functional reorganizations caused by the structural changes will be added functional reorganizations of the type discussed at some length in this chapter: reorganizations caused by the transitions between early and late childhood, childhood and adolescence, adolescence and adulthood. In such a situation, the need for benchmark data will be great.

In this chapter, data about media use during two developmental transition periods have been presented and interpreted in terms of a uses and development model. Our final conclusion is that while development no doubt has its basis in biology, its results are always realized within the parameters provided by the surrounding society. The mass media structure of society represents an important set of such parameters. The class structure of society represents another set. In the following chapter we turn to the interplay of these two sets of important parameters in the lives of children and adolescents.

4

Social Class And Media Use

4.1. INTRODUCTORY REMARKS

We have seen that development manifests itself in differential media use among boys and girls of different ages. Similarly, socialization manifests itself most clearly in differential media use by adolescents from different social classes. Just as development is a process closely related to gender, socialization is a process closely related to social class (and gender, of course). Differential development and differential socialization, in interaction with each other, create a social space of three dimensions: gender, class, and age. Two values on each of the three dimensions create eight different social worlds. In this chapter we focus on the role of social class in shaping these eight worlds.

The purpose of the chapter is to demonstrate the importance of social class for media use and effects. We also believe that it is fruitful to apply a cultural perspective and to regard class-determined media use as something occurring, to a large degree, in a class-cultural context.

The chapter will begin by discussing our main concepts: class, status, culture, and youth. Three different types of class will be introduced: origin, context, and destination. Then, uses and gratifications research will be approached from a class-cultural perspective.

Just as in the other chapters our main focus is on television, and we shall be examining the relationship between various aspects of social class and various aspects of TV use. Dependency and motives will also be discussed.

Toward the end of the chapter we turn from media use to the effects and consequences of that use. We hypothesize that not only media use in itself is affected by social class. So are the effects of that use. Television tends to hit differently in different social classes.

4.2. TWO BASIC DISTINCTIONS: CLASS AND STATUS; CLASS OF ORIGIN AND OF DESTINATION

The inclusion of the concept of social class into the study of mass communication processes and structures is useful from several points

111

of view. For example, when studying communicator control and ownership aspects of mass communication, one is lead to ask questions about which social values are being transmitted and which interests are being served by the media: whose values, and whose interests? (See, e.g., Golding & Murdock, 1978.) At the receiving end it is usually assumed that the uneven distribution of resources between the different social classes will create different types of media use (cf. Hedinsson, 1981). Furthermore, class-bound interaction will result in class-bound habits, beliefs, and norms. In short, we end up with class-bound culture. The use made of mass media constitutes an important part of that culture.

In spite of the usefulness of the class concept, there is a tendency in some media research not to pay very much attention to the role of social class. This tendency may be regarded as part of a general tendency to study mass communications out of context (Piepe et al., 1978). Yet we all know that mass media use does not occur in a social vacuum. To a large extent, the ways individuals use the media are socially determined, and so are the effects and consequences of that use.

The social-class concept is used in a number of ways, but as a rule it is possible to trace its use to either Marx or Weber. The Marxist definition stems from the assumption that the economic structure of a society creates a class structure, a class being "any aggregate of persons who play the same part in the production mechanism" (Lipset, 1968, p. 298; Parkin, 1979; Therborn, 1978; Wright, 1985).

Max Weber also defines social classes on economic grounds, but while Marx has production relationships as his starting point, Weber bases his definition on market relationships. The class position of an individual is determined by the means that one has at one's disposal to operate on a market. To the notion of social class Weber and his followers add the notion of status, referring to the prestige assigned to a person by others. The class hierarchy is often regarded as more universalistic and achievement-oriented, whereas the status hierarchy tends to be more particularistic and ascriptive (Lipset, 1968; Parsons, 1942/1964; Therborn, 1978; Wright 1985). In spite of this, of course, there is a strong relationship between class and status.

In mass communications research there is no uniform use of the class concept. The Marxist version is found mostly in European research. Weber's work has put its mark on much use of social class on both sides of the Atlantic. In empirical studies, class is often operationalized as income, sometimes, as level of education. More seldom is role in the production process—occupation—taken as the indicator of class.

In the Media Panel Program, occupation is used as the indicator of social class. The young people studied are differentiated according to the occupational positions of both parents, as described in sec. 2.2 and 4.5.1. The use of occupational position brings us closer to a Marxist conceptualization, for the occupations are divided into groups such as blue-collar workers, white-collar workers, and professionals.

While applying a social-class perspective we also have an interest in a resource perspective: The higher up in the class structure, the greater the economic means available for the use of certain cultural products. Included in our perspective is the notion of class cultures and life-styles, built up during generations. Certain types of media use may be considered to be more or less obligatory, based on one's social position. Here a Weberian status perspective, stressing both life chances, rights, and obligations, comes to the fore as much as a Marxian class perspective. While social class may be seen as defining the main framework within which mass media use takes place, social status prescribes the more precise ways in which the media are used by different status groupings (cf. Wilensky, 1964). Education is a good indicator of social status thus conceived.

Besides social class operationalized as parents' occupations, we will use parents' education as a major independent variable for explaining media use and effects, the reason being a conception of media use as largely a product of the cognitive and intellectual resources (and informal obligations) brought about by formal schooling. A common argument for using education as an independent variable is that since media use is a mental and intellectual activity, it will be best predicted by indicators measuring the amount of training received for such activities. In European sociology this simple assumption has been embedded in a rich theoretical structure relating the concepts of class, status, and culture to each other.

The sociocultural foundations of mass media use may to advantage be conceived in terms of the theories developed by Bourdieu (Bourdieu 1977, 1980; Bourdieu & Passeron 1979; cf. Roe, 1983a). A central concept of Bourdieu is that of "academic" or "cultural" capital, defined as "instruments for the appropriation of symbolic wealth socially designated as worthy of being sought and possessed" (Bourdieu, 1977). This cultural capital will affect, for example, the child's success at school. It will thus mediate the relationship between family background and school outcome (DiMaggio, 1982). The notion of cultural capital does not only apply to school progress, however. It will also affect extraschool activities such as mass media use.

Bourdieu's theories seem to be very appropriate to the type of study that we have here: the media use of young people in a family cultural context. Not only may we regard cultural capital as affecting media use; it is also feasible to turn the perspective the other way around, regarding the media habits of the family as part of cultural capital. In both cases the notion of cultural capital goes well together with the use of education as a main independent variable.

Besides parental social class and education, we are going to use yet another background variable in our analyses. Reference group theory and the concept of anticipatory socialization tell us that not only the class one comes from shapes one's activities, beliefs, and attitudes. The social class one is aiming at, the one in which one thinks one will end up may be equally important. We assume that some young people find themselves in the anticipatory socialization process described by Merton (1963), a process during which an individual takes on the behavior and attitudes of a group he or she is aspiring or expecting to become a member of.

In terms of social class, reference group theory tells us that we need to heed not only class of origin, but also class of destination. In many, perhaps even most, cases adolescents will think of their class of destination as being much the same as their class of origin, but in some cases class of origin and class of destination will not coincide. It is one of our tasks in this chapter to study the interplay of class of origin and class of destination (the latter variable being operationalized as the occupation one expects to obtain when grown up).

In this section we have been discussing the concepts of status and social class. We have also made a distinction between two types of social class: class of origin and destination. In the next section our arguments will be related to yet a third type: class of context.

4.3. A THIRD TYPE OF SOCIAL CLASS: CLASS OF CONTEXT

In mass communication research it has been pointed out again and again that the actors of the mass communication process are influenced by their social environment. Riley and Riley (1951) maintained that by isolating the people in the process, and by seeing the process as occurring outside social life and structure, communications scholars left many of their results uninterpreted and unexplained. Because of this basic insight these authors achieved the reputation of having introduced a "new look" into communications research (Mendelsohn, 1964). The theory of the two-step flow of communication (Katz & Lazarsfeld, 1955) also located the receiver within a social context. One would have expected these results to have permeated subsequent mass communications research, but that is hardly so.

The research tradition giving most attention to the social context of the communication process is probably uses and gratifications research

(Rosengren et al., 1985). As research has proceeded along these lines, it has been increasingly recognized that the social environment is a rather complex phenomenon. Most people live in a differentiated sociocultural environment, actually experiencing a welter of influences. Indeed, we believe it would be difficult to find anybody who could be regarded as a product of only one subculture's influence. The objects of our study, children and adolescents, may serve as an example. Through their family they belong to a certain social class. Their peer group may include persons from other social strata. In their school class, several social groupings may be represented, while the school itself may have certain sociocultural traits. For a working-class child, school may represent middle-class culture, preaching middle-class norms and expecting middle-class behavior.

In the subsequent analysis we shall give some attention to the school context. Even in a fairly well-integrated city like Vaxjoe (and certainly in a more segregated city like Malmoe) the schools may be characterized as working class, middle class, or mixed with respect to the composition of their pupils. That is, added to the influence from their own social class, the adolescents on our study will be subject to a differential influence from their school environment—a "Tingsten," contextual effect (Tingsten, 1937; cf. Borgatta & Jackson, 1980).

Thus, besides the two concepts of class discussed in sec. 4.2. (origin and destination), we will have to take yet another concept into consideration: class of context. Especially interesting is the case where class of origin and class of context do not coincide—cases when an adolescent from one social class attends a school characterized as being dominated by another social class—a situation which bears some similarity to phenomena discussed in cross-pressure theory (Lazarsfeld et al., 1944; Pinner, 1968; Powell, 1976). This phenomenon will be discussed at some length in sec. 4.6.

4.4. TOWARD A SOCIAL-CLASS MODEL OF MEDIA USES AND EFFECTS

A constant critique of the uses and gratifications model has been that it seldom specifies and thoroughly discusses the social origins of needs, motives for, and/or gratifications sought from mass media use (Palmgreen et al., 1985). In an earlier section of this book an effort was made to trace these origins within a developmental perspective. We shall now discuss media uses and effects in terms of an emerging model, the basic elements of which are the sociocultural environment, the individual, and the mass media. These elements are related to each other in certain patterns, the relationships of which will be discussed below. But first, let us look at the three basic components.

4.4.1. The Individual

In the Media Panel Program we view the individual in a double perspective. To us, he or she is a willing and acting subject who is at the same time the object of strong societal forces.

On one hand we agree with McQuail and Gurevitch (1974, p. 298) in their structural-cultural version of uses and gratifications research. No doubt, individuals are influenced from outside. Their media use, for example, is constantly being patterned by culture and by social structure and conditioned by past experiences of media content. On the other hand, societal influence manifests itself in, and is also modified by, internal constraints and positive forces; values, norms, and motives are internalized by the individual and affect media use to a considerable extent, over and above the direct and indirect influence coming "from outside."

While we maintain that both these perspectives are equally valid, in this chapter we shall be paying most attention to the class perspective: the individual as an object of strong outside forces. The individual as a subject, purposively acting on the basis of his or her values, norms, and motives, will receive more attention in the following chapter on socialization.

4.4.2. The Mass Media

A mass medium may differ from other media in terms of its psychological and physical availability (Chaney, 1972; Hedinsson, 1981; Johnsson–Smaragdi, 1983). It may also be described as more or less useful in meeting the expectations of an individual or a group, a social class, and so forth (Weibull, 1985). Media are mostly commercial, their main aim being to maximize (or rather optimize) their share of the potential audience. This may be achieved in several ways. For some media the strategy is to widen the range of content in order to please people from as many walks of life as possible. For others the aim is to seek out a carefully defined target audience in order to gain a large enough part of the potential public.

The structure of mass media content varies between countries with different media ideologies (McQuail & Windahl, 1981). In countries with a libertarian type of mass communications ideology (Siebert et al., 1956) the market aspect of mass media production is stressed, and we may assume the media output to be more or less in accordance with the structure of "taste groups" of society. In the social responsibility-type of countries, because of certain societal norms guiding the production and distribution of media content, this fit between public taste and media content presumably tends to become less perfect. Sweden, being a social responsibility-type of country, shows these characteristics in the case of television. The Swedish Broadcasting Corp. seems to be less guided by the aim of maximizing young audiences than of purveying a TV fare which may be considered ideologically and culturally suitable. Swedish TV, therefore, plays another role in youth culture than does TV in some other countries (cf. sec. 1.2.1).

Even within one society, however, we usually find that some mass media are stable, while others are more dynamic and changing, continually seeking to adapt to the audience. A public service-oriented media institution such as Swedish television tends to be less dynamic and volatile in this respect than, for example, the commercial record industry. In Sweden, just as in the U.S., the latter may be described as developing and producing in cycles (Peterson & Berger, 1975). We believe that the cyclical metaphor is especially valid for those sections of the mass culture industry aiming at youth culture consumers. Typically, fads and fashions are first produced at the periphery of the cultural industry and are only later integrated into the production apparatus and mainstream culture. Then a new cycle starts and, after some time, mainstream culture adapts to this new cycle, too. In the following section we will discuss mass culture and youth culture in somewhat greater detail.

4.4.3. The Sociocultural Environment: Youth Culture and Class Culture

The concept of culture has been given a wide range of meanings (Kroeber & Kluckhohn, 1952; Rosengren 1984, 1985b; Singer, 1968; Vermeersch, 1977; cf. also sec. 5.1.2). Within a sociological framework, culture can be approached in a number of ways. Piepe et al. (1978) name some of the possible perspectives:

1. Culture as something shared, consensual, and integrative;
2. Culture as class-divided, systems of meanings associated with class cultures;
3. Culture as something individual, subjective, heroic; for example, youth cultures;

4.   Culture as an autonomous level of symbolic activity and behavior; for example, the symbolic system of television as a cultural system.

The four approaches may be combined in various ways. In the present study we shall touch upon all of them. Approach No. 4 encompasses practically everything mass communication scholars think of when they discuss media content and its effects. Approaches Nos. 1 and 2 are not mutually exclusive, for, within classes, socially divided culture may be shared, consensual and integrative. Obviously, approach No. 3 is highly relevant to the population of our study. Together with approach No. 2 (class culture) it will form our main focus of interest. Class-related youth cultures offer differential resources to different groupings of adolescents. Differential mass media use is one important example of such resources. Different class or status groups use different interpretative systems and cultural patterns. "Culture and social structure (are) inextricably linked. Indeed, culture is social structure in its symbolically organized and meaningful aspect" (Piepe et al., 1975, p. 5).

From what has been said above it may look as though we expect cultural habits closely to follow class boundaries. This is not the case. We know that social class is not at all the only determinant of, say, mass media use. What we wish to stress is that it is an important one.

A common argument against using a class-cultural perspective is that during the last few decades class differences have become small and almost negligible in postindustrial countries such as Sweden. There is considerable evidence, however, that in several societal sectors class differences are as demonstrable today as they were decades ago, in spite of considerable efforts to narrow the gaps. One such area is the school. In spite of great efforts undertaken in Sweden during the last few decades to equalize both preschool and the comprehensive school system (within which our respondents are located) it still contains easily visible, systematic tendencies of class segregation (Arnman & Jönsson, 1983; Svenning & Svenning, 1980).

Such differences no doubt tend to interact in various ways with other differentiating forces in adolescent society, for instance, the various "youth cultures" often assumed to exert considerable influence on the ways of life of today's adolescents. When dealing with the media use of young people the introduction of the concept of youth seems almost unavoidable. But what is youth culture? Indeed, one is sometimes tempted to ask, is there such a thing as an autonomous, classless youth culture?

A number of scholars have answered "yes" to the latter question. Murdock and McCron (1976a, 1976b) trace the notion of youth culture as an autonomous subculture back to Ortega y Gasset, Mannheim, and

Parsons. For several decades Parsons's (1942) ideas dominated the field (Roe, 1983a). Parsons viewed adolescents as passing through something of a social latency period. Compulsory schooling supposedly kept the young away from the stratified sphere of production. Among social scientists the image of youth thus became dominated by aspects of consumption and leisure as ways of life, taking place in isolation from any class-related social context, or within youth regarded as a class in itself (cf. Rosak, 1971).

This view has lately been challenged. Several scholars have maintained that young people are part and parcel of a socially stratified society, not disjunct from it (Cohen, 1955; Murdock & McCron, 1976a, 1976b; Roe, 1983a). Social class and class-bound culture do influence the younger generation in a number of ways, as Bourdieu (1977) and many others have demonstrated (cf. above).

Does this mean that there is no distinctive youth culture? It does not, but as we see it youth culture is primarily a resource, to be drawn upon differentially by youth of different ages and with different social backgrounds. To a large extent, youth culture is a differentiated product of the cultural industry, providing the young with what they may need for the creation, maintenance, and expression of their identity. This cultural production covers a wide range of needs and interests in many kinds of youth groups. A large proportion of this material belongs to the sphere of mass or popular culture.

In sum, our basic standpoint is that, in spite of their disjunction from the process of production, the young people we study are the objects of class-cultural influences. At the same time they are willing and acting subjects who in their activities draw upon what is available within the variegated cultural production of the youth culture industry. Sometimes they definitely and consciously reshape media output to their own purposes.

From this quick description of the basic elements of our emerging model, let us proceed to the relationships between these elements.

4.4.4. The Relationships Among the Individual, the Sociocultural Environment, and the Media

In its most common version the uses and gratifications approach assumes that, to a large extent, more or less basic needs within the individual account for the use people make of media. In addition, use is guided by norms, rules, and tastes acquired through socialization. Finally, material and psychological resources, to no small extent determined by social class, may serve as predictors of media use.

Some media, and some media contents, are more strongly tied to certain social groupings than to others. As McQuail and Gurevitch (1974) underline, certain media patterns are more or less prescribed by the social environment. Certain parts of mass culture address themselves to certain social groups and, conversely, certain social groups get "their" fare from certain mass cultural sources. As noted by Lull (1983) and Roe (1983a), this is especially visible in the realm of pop music, but the principle holds true for most media content, and for most social groupings.

That individuals' media use is thus restricted does not mean that media experience must be an altogether passive affair. Levy and Windahl (1985) show that a structural approach like this does not necessarily prevent us from regarding the media user as both selective and involved in media use. It does imply, however, that the free will of the individual is far from unrestrained by social and cultural structures. Socialization tells the audience member which options in the media flow provide gratifications, thereby confining the selection among available options, as well as other activities.

Although, so far, we have not included media effects in our arguments, they do play an important part in our emerging model. The relationships between uses and effects have been discussed by Windahl (1981). We regard both uses and effects as modified by social class and class culture. As Klapper (1960) pointed out decades ago, the effects of the mass media and their content to a large extent are the outcomes of complex interactions with a host of mediating factors. Social class is one among these.

Mass media effects may be regarded as indirect in other ways, too. In their sociocultural model of media effects, Ball–Rokeach and DeFleur (1976) describe an effects process in which the mass media feed material into culture, and people draw on the surrounding culture for forming opinions, attitudes, and beliefs. With a process of this kind media use in itself will be a less effective predictor of effects on the individual. As Newcomb (1978) has noted, according to this perspective media messages will be more indiscriminately disseminated to people, regardless of how much they themselves watch TV and read newspapers.

While recognizing the value of such perspectives, by and large we tend to stress differences rather than similarities in people's media use and the effects thereof. In discussing the relationships between the elements of our social class and media use model, our main point of departure is that socialization is always differential: people are not socialized in the same way (Hedinsson, 1981; McLeod & O'Keefe, 1972). Furthermore, differential socialization is an exceptionally complex process, with many elements working at different points of time.

In order to illustrate the difficulty of determining the relationship between the sociocultural environment and the individual we shall briefly discuss a question that will be analyzed with empirical data later on. The question is, whether the influence of social background will have its strongest impact on media use in the beginning or at the end of the age period we are studying (cf. sec. 2.7)?

There are several possible answers to this question. Building on the notion of an autonomous youth culture, as suggested by Parsons (1942) and others, one would argue that the impact of social class will be small during these years, increasing as the young person approaches entrance into the sphere of production. Hedinsson (1981, p. 107) presents results about media use which lend some support to the hypothesis that, "The family's social class is a more powerful independent factor in the lives of fifteen year old adolescents, because of more autonomy, than is the case for eleven year old adolescents." Hence, the more mature and independent the adolescent, the stronger the class identification and the more visible the effects on media use.

There are, however, arguments for the opposite opinion, that social class will exert less influence as the young person passes through adolescence. McLeod and Brown (1976, p.225) hypothesize that "the influence of social class on child development should be maximized during the first half of childhood, after which the child will begin to lessen her or his dependence upon her or his parents. . . ." McLeod and Brown find support for their argument in results from studies by Greenberg and Dominick (1969) and Stein et al. (1972). Recently, results pointing in the same direction have also been presented by Roe (1983a) and Johnsson–Smaragdi (1983).

The rationale here is that the main channels for class influence, family ties, loosen as other socializing agents such as peers and school interfere and weaken the power of social class and class culture. We have already noted that the school, as a social environment, may exert a powerful contextual influence on adolescents' media use. To the extent that there is such a contextual influence, the influence from class of origin must weaken, at least in relative terms. On the other hand, the influence from class of destination should grow stronger as the adolescent approaches entrance into the labor market (cf. above).

Thus, the seemingly simple question of whether the influence of social class increases or decreases during adolescence has been answered in two radically different ways in the literature. We have also seen that, in order to provide a really meaningful answer to this simple question, we must reformulate it by distinguishing between at least three types of class: origin, destination and—between the two—class of context. "Where do you come from, where are you going, and where are you right now?"

In terms of these three types of class, we hypothesize that

The influence of origin will decrease as the adolescent grows older;

The influence of destination will increase as the adolescent grows older; while

The influence of context will remain much the same, or, possibly, accumulate, as long as the adolescent remains in school.

Furthermore, the separate influences from class of origin, destination and context will interact, reinforce, and/or counteract each other in various ways under differing circumstances. A strong educational system, for instance, will tend to reduce the influence from both class of origin and destination, while a weaker school system will let these influences stand out more clearly (cf. Himmelweit & Swift, 1969).

According to our arguments, then, the question of changing influence from class during adolescence has not one, but three or more different answers. We believe this holds generally true for the influence of class on all aspects of social life, although naturally, for us, the influence of class in its various manifestations on the nature, causes, and effects of media use is most important. We end this section by a short, empirical subsection illustrating the way in which class may shape the media use of children and adolescents.

4.4.5. An Empirical Example of Class Influence on Media Use

The influence of social class on mass media use may be demonstrated in various ways. The most straightforward way is to show that the amount consumed of this or that mass medium varies systematically among classes. This has been done over and over again by sociologists and researchers of mass communication, and in the following sections we shall add to this growing body of empirical data on differential mass media consumption.

However, sociocultural constraint or influence cannot be restricted to isolated quantities alone. It should also be observable with respect to relations and structures. If we are right in our arguments about the existence of a youth culture partly shaped by the class structure, we should find different relations between the uses of different media in various sociocultural groupings of children and adolescents. Media use should be differentially structured in different social classes. Furthermore, the differential structuring of media use along class lines should be influenced by those other two powerful structuring forces: age and gender. Is this what we find in empirical reality?

Let us first look at media structures in terms of the overall relationships between the uses of different media by the children and adolescents in our study, measured as correlations between the amount of consumption in our main Vaxjoe panel. Disregarding for obvious reasons correlations between the same medium at different times, we find a number of fairly weak correlations between the consumption of the eight media measured in our studies, but only few moderate or strong relationships. Actually, there are only two correlations equal to or stronger than $r = .30$: those between moviegoing and TV consumption in grade 5 (.30) and movies and pop music listening in grade 9 (.32). On the face of it, media use does not appear to be very structured at all. But this is a very deceptive appearance.

What has happened is that social class, interacting with age and gender, functions as a strong depressor variable (Rosenberg, 1968). So, let us control at the same time for gender and social class (measured in the way described in secs. 2.2 and 4.5.1). Doing so, not only do we find structures in media use, we find strong differences in the structures, and in the degree of structuring. Eight media repeated in three waves admit 252 correlations (3 × 28 within waves, 3 × 56 between waves). Sticking to the .01 level of significance, we would expect two or three significant correlations produced by chance alone in each of our four social groupings. But this is not what we find.

At the .01 level of significance, we find the following number of significant correlations:

Working-class boys: 16
Working-class girls: 32
Middle-class boys: 20
Middle-class girls: 45

The degree of structuring of media use is considerable, and highly differential in the four social groupings. The pattern of media use of middle-class girls is about three times as structured as that of working-class boys. The degree of structuring in the pattern of middle-class boys is close to that of working-class boys, while that of working-class girls falls in between. The fact that the influence from gender on the degree of structuring seems to be even stronger than that of social class tells us that social class does not work alone but in conjunction with gender roles. The differences are sociocultural in nature.

Figures 4.1 and 4.2 visualize these differences by contrasting the correlation pattern of middle-class girls to that of working-class boys.

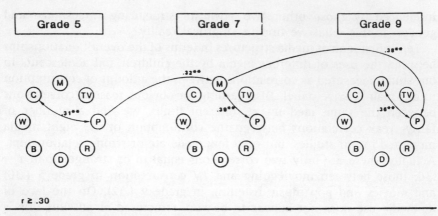

Figure 4.1. Relationships Between Use of Various Mass Media by Working-class Boys. Vaxjoe Main Panel.

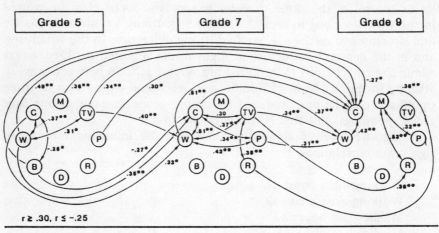

Figure 4.2.   Relationships Between Use of Various Mass Media by Middle-class Girls. Vaxjoe Main Panel.

(No correlations between the same medium are included. For greater clarity, only correlations stronger than .30 have been included in the figures, together with all three negative correlations significant at the level chosen.)

The intricate details of the patterns themselves would form an interesting subject for scrutiny—from which we have to abstain. Suffice it here to note that there are very few negative correlations between the media. Only seldom does the extensive use of one medium negatively influence the use of another. After controls for age, gender, and social class, media use among adolescents seems to be cumulative rather than competitive (cf. sec. 5.2.3 and Johnsson–Smaragdi, 1983, pp. 58, 211).

The important thing in this connection, however, is more simple than that. It concerns the difference in the degree of structuring in the two patterns. The difference is striking. Interacting strongly with age and gender, social class does indeed exert a powerful influence on the pattern of media use by different social groupings. The media culture of youth is structurally differentiated along age, gender and class lines. The process behind the structural differentiation is differential socialization (cf. chap. 5).

Before ending this section, we would like to add a final remark of reservation. Our depiction of the relationship betwen the sociocultural environment and the individual has had a rather deterministic flavor. This does not mean that we deny the possibilities of a more active acceptance and use of surrounding class and culture by individuals seeking to gain and express, perhaps even to transcend, a class identity. This more voluntaristic process may result in a very active media use that is class- or status group-conscious and where media use, as in the case of pop music, serves as an expression of group or class belongingness (Ferrer, 1983; Roe, 1983a; Rosengren, Roe, & Sonesson, 1983). Some such processes will be discussed in sec. 5.3.4.

4.5. CLASS, STATUS, AND TELEVISION USE

In this section we shall discuss social class (based on parental occupational position) and status (based on parental education) as background factors of children's and adolescents' television use. Following Roe (1983a) we shall question the rather mechanistic assumption about linearity in the relationship between social background and media use. We shall take a close look at the influence of social class as it develops over time. We shall finally proceed to show how motives for TV use, as well as TV selectivity and TV dependency, differ in different social groupings in a way suggestive of a cumulative process.

4.5.1. Class, Status, and TV Use: Linearity or Curvilinearity?

When discussing social class as a background variable we have avoided founding the variable exclusively on father's occupational status. Instead we have used a 5-value scale in which both parents' occupation is taken into account. Our basic occupational groupings are the following:

1. Professions, owners of enterprises; self-employed, high-level civil servants.
2a. Upper middle class; middle-level supervisors.
2b. Lower white-collar occupations; lower-level supervisors; highly skilled workers.
3. Blue-collar workers, mostly unskilled.

Our social index builds on the following combinations of the two parents' occupational class:

1. 1 + 1; 1 + 2a
2. 2a + 2a; 1 + 2b
3. 2a + 2b; 1 + 3
4. 2b + 2b; 2a + 3
5. 3 + 3; 2b + 3

It may be argued that categories 1 and 5 are the most homogeneous of the five; category 3 is problematical, allowing for the heterogeneous combination of upper-class and working-class respondents. Nevertheless, we regard our index as better than more conventional SES measurements in which only the class or status of one parent (most frequently that of the father) is taken into account. We often use a dichotomized version of our index: working class (values 4–5 above), and middle class (values 1–3).

The stability of social class measured in this way is very high. The variable refers to measurements taken in the first panel wave (for an exception, see sec. 5.5.5).

Table 4.1 relates to each other two basic variables of our study, habitual TV viewing and the social-class index from above (dichotomized).

The same two variables are found in Table 4.2, but here our social-class variable is expressed in terms of its five original values:

Table 4.1. Habitual TV Consumption and Parents' Social Class (Dichotomized, MCA, Half-hours/week, Vaxjoe Main Panel)

	Grade					
	5		7		9	
	Boys	**Girls**	**Boys**	**Girls**	**Boys**	**Girls**
Middle class	30.9	23.4	25.1	18.0	19.5	14.0
Working class	36.2	32.1	30.5	25.1	22.0	19.0
Eta	.19	.30	.22	.30	.12	.24

When comparing the two tables we find, among other things, that the strict linearity more or less assumed in Table 4.1 is almost absent in Table 4.2. What we can see in the latter table (but not in the former) is that the highest figures for TV viewing tend to be found not in the lowest, but in the next lowest, social class category. A similar curvilinearity has been demonstrated by Roe (1983a), who found that his index of home background (class + education) related to TV consumption in the same way as is the case in Table 4.2 (but only in the ninth grade). Sonesson (1982) found curvilinearity also between status (education) and TV in grades 3 and 5 of the Malmoe panel (cf. below).

These results are at variance with some earlier ones, indicating that the lower the social class, the heavier the television consumption. For instance, Himmelweit and Swift (1976) maintain that heavy use of "on-tap" media is characteristic of those with the fewest resources, such as those in the lower working class. While this may be true it may also be somewhat misleading. Those in the very lowest strata may use TV less than those one level higher up (cf. Roe 1983a, p. 132).

That social classes are not homogeneous in their mass media use has been pointed out by, among others, Morley (1980) and Piepe et al. (1975). The latter note that the increasing differentiation of working-class milieux through rehousing and industrial change has brought about concomitant changes in mass media use. Working-class members living in houses of their own have somewhat different content preferences than those living in multifamily housing.

Let us now return to Table 4.2 and ask: Why this result? There are several, more or less plausible, post hoc explanations:

Table 4.2. Habitual TV Consumption and Parents' Social Class. (MCA, Half-Hours/Week, Vaxjoe Main Panel, Highest Value in Each Column Underlined)

| | Grade | | | | | |
| | 5 | | 7 | | 9 | |
Social Class	Boys	Girls	Boys	Girls	Boys	Girls
High 1	29.0	19.0	24.5	14.5	18.1	10.3
2	30.6	25.3	24.5	19.2	20.8	14.9
3	33.4	25.0	26.9	19.7	18.2	16.6
4	36.2	34.3	31.4	23.1	24.8	20.3
Low 5	36.3	30.9	29.9	26.1	20.0	18.4
Eta	.21	.34	.23	.34	.21	.30

- By tradition, lower-working-class young people enter the labor market earlier than their counterparts in other classes. Since, consequently, the family bonds loosen early there will already be greater freedom for lower-working-class adolescents during the schoolyears to be outside the home and, thus, to do other things than watch TV.
- Parental control is, on the whole, less strict in lower-working-class families. Children may then have greater opportunities to be part of the "street cultures," rather than of a family-oriented culture.
- Working-class and lower-middle-class parents watch TV in a way similar to that of their children. Then the curvilinearity will apply to the class structure in toto, not only to adolescents.

The first explanation is closely related to the second, but of course there may be other reasons for less parental control in the working class than early entry into the labor market.

As for the third explanation, our data give no support for it. In three cases out of four, data on the relationship between social class and parents' television consumption (habitual viewing) show *no* curvilinear pattern such as that found in Table 4.2. This suggests that the pattern is specifically applicable to adolescents, and that we may look for an explanation which includes, for example, differential socialization.

What about the two categories in Table 4.2 that do not conform with the pattern, boys in grade 5 and girls in grade 7? It is difficult to come up with a satisfactory answer, especially for the boys in grade 5, for whom the difference is negligible. We have noted several times already, however, that girls in the seventh grade of the Vaxjoe main panel tend to deviate from the dominant patterns in different respects (Flodin et al., 1982).

We have already mentioned that in grades 3 and 5 of the Malmoe panel, the curvilinearity found for social class and television viewing is also found for the variable of education (Appendix of Sonesson, 1982). In preschool, however, the relationship is linear between mother's education and children's TV consumption. This is also the case in the Vaxjoe panel (where the education index is built in the same way as the social class index—educational status of both parents combined). For the main panel, we get the results presented in Table 4.3. The relationship is linear almost across the board. The higher the parents' education, the lower the TV consumption of their children tends to be.

In spite of the fact that class and status (education) correlate strongly (.68 in the third wave of the Vaxjoe panel), class-determined patterns of culture may differ, then, from patterns determined by status. Social-class behavior is motivated by many different factors inherent in working life, occupational relations, and so forth, whereas educational group

Table 4.3. Habitual TV Consumption and Parents' Education. (Half-Hours/Week, Vaxjoe Main Panel, Highest Values Underlined)

		Grade					
		5		**7**		**9**	
Education		**Boys**	**Girls**	**Boys**	**Girls**	**Boys**	**Girls**
High	1	25.0	20.4	20.7	15.9	15.0	12.5
	2	32.1	22.0	28.1	17.7	18.4	14.9
	3	31.1	26.0	24.2	17.3	20.6	14.0
	4	34.0	31.2	27.5	23.6	22.3	17.8
Low	5	36.9	31.5	31.1	24.8	22.3	17.4
Eta		.27	.31	.27	.30	.20	.18

behavior has its roots within a more confined sphere of society, the sphere in which "cultural capital" is accumulated and used (cf. sec. 4.2). What may confound the social class–media use relationship may be absent in the relationship between status (education) and media.

An additional complication is that cultural capital very probably interacts with economic capital, and interaction which may lead up to increased or decreased curvilinearity. Social class may be regarded as a rough indicator of economic capital available. Table 4.4, featuring habitual TV consumption as jointly affected by parental social class and education, provides some information about such interactions between cultural and economic capital for our main Vaxjoe panel. Due to the close relationship between social class and education, the number of individuals in some cells is small indeed. The results, therefore, should be interpreted with caution. Nevertheless, patterns recurring in all three grades may be given some credit.

One such pattern is the U-shaped curvilinearity appearing in all three grades for those adolescents whose parents have a low education. Similarly but conversely, for those having parents with high education, there is a regularly appearing A-shaped curvilinearity. As a result of these two curvilinearities, adolescents with parents having high social class but low education tend to have relatively high TV consumption, while those having parents with low social class and high education tend to have relatively low TV consumption.

As a matter of fact, in grade 5, the high social class-low education category has the highest consumption of all categories (while in grades 7 and 9 the top figure quite naturally appears among those who are low on both background variables). Equally naturally, the lowest values

Table 4.4.   Social Class, Parental Education, and Habitual TV Consumption. (Half-Hours/Week, Vaxjoe Main Panel, Highest Values Underlined, Lowest Values in Italics, Number of Individuals in Parentheses)

		Social Class		
	Education	Low	Middle	High
A. Grade 5				
	High	28.8	31.1	*24.2*
		(23)	(5)	(93)
	Middle	35.2	29.2	29.1
		(70)	(28)	(32)
	Low	33.5	30.0	<u>41.3</u>
		(117)	(8)	(12)
B. Grade 7				
	High	25.1	25.2	*20.3*
		(19)	(5)	(85)
	Middle	27.3	24.0	24.5
		(67)	(28)	(32)
	Low	28.4	22.1	27.6
		<u>(113)</u>	(7)	(11)
C. Grade 9				
	High	18.1	19.4	*15.0*
		(20)	(5)	(83)
	Middle	19.8	18.2	19.5
		(68)	(24)	(30)
	Low	20.2	18.0	18.8
		<u>(110)</u>	(7)	(6)

in all three grades are found among those high on both background variables.

It will be seen that the combined influence from social class and status on habitual TV consumption is strong indeed, especially in grade 5, where the difference between the highest and lowest values amounts to more than an hour of television a day (close to 3 hours a day vs. 1¾).

The overall interpretation of Table 4.4 would be that there is indeed a complex interaction between economic and cultural capital, between social class and status (operationalized as education). The intricacies of these interactions between the influences exerted by social class and status on adolescents' TV consumption defy any consistent interpretation and certainly deserve continued attention from mass communication research.

As a last word in this section we would like to air our belief that,

on the whole, too little attention has been paid to curvilinear relationships in mass communications research. It is as though we all shunned
results with that type of pattern and always looked for the safe and
simple linear ones. A case in point is the anomaly brought up by Paul
Hirsch in a famous debate with George Gerbner (cf. Gerbner et al.,
1981; Hirsch, 1980), where Gerbner was accused of dropping the category of the extreme nonviewers from his analysis, presumably because
they did not fit the expected pattern. George Gerbner's defense—that
nonviewers represent a very small, and in many ways a deviating
category—is not always applicable. The strength and the type of relationships unveiled are sometimes theoretically much more important
than the size of the deviant group. Furthermore, curvilinearity may be
operating not only for television as a dependent variable, but for
television as an independent variable as well (cf. Fetler, 1985).

Finally, it should be noted that the curvilinearity just observed represents a technical problem in some multivariate analyses assuming
linear relationships (LISREL analyses, for instance). By and large the
assumption of linearity will tend to result in somewhat conservative
estimates of the strength of the relationship under study (cf. sec. 5.4).

Whether linear or curvilinear, the influence exerted by social class
and status on television use must be relayed by a host of intervening
variables such as values and attitudes internalized by parents and children. Some such intervening variables will be treated later on in this
section. But first we will turn to another question. Does the influence
from social background increase or decrease with time?

4.5.2. Increasing or Decreasing Influence?

The tables in the last section do not only reveal patterns in terms of
linearity/curvilinearity. There are some other results that deserve to be
commented upon.

In Tables 4.1 and 4.2 we find an intriguing gender pattern in the
eta values. In all three age groups boys evidence a lower figure than
girls. This result is in accordance with the findings of Johnsson–Smaragdi
(1983), Roe (1983a) and Flodin (1986), in whose LISREL models girls
show more and stronger relationships between home background and
several media variables. It is the same phenomenon visualized in Figures
4.1 and 4.2 of sec. 4.4.5; in particular, the media pattern of middle-
class girls is much more structured than that of other social groupings.

In the case of television consumption, the gender differences are not
surprising. Girls are usually supervised more and given less opportunity

to deviate from family (and thereby class) norms. Boys are allowed greater laxity and may enter into other class contexts than that of their class of origin. Comparing Tables 4.2 and 4.3, we find that this pattern of differential socialization is not so visible for education. In this respect, then, class is a more powerful phenomenon than status.

In addition, let us use the two tables to discuss briefly an issue raised in sec. 4.4.4, namely, the question of whether there is a tendency for the impact of social background (for example, class and education) to increase or decrease with age among adolescents. The two tables give little support to either of the suggested directions. Only for education do we note a marked decrease in Eta values for grade 9. It should be remarked, though, that these values are based on cross-sectional data. The introduction of a longitudinal design may result in another picture. This is done in Figure 4.3, which features a longitudinal LISREL model of the influence of social class and gender on TV viewing and relations. (The interested reader may wish to compare this figure with Figure 2.10, featuring a PLS model of much the same variables. In essence, the two models provide the same answer. Cf. also Fig. 2.9.)

Table 4.5 summarizes the direct, indirect, and total influence of the two background variables on TV viewing and relations in grades 5, 7, and 9, as given in the LISREL model of Figure 4.3. It can be seen that the influence of social class and gender on TV relations is weak and mostly indirect. (Presumably, such relations to a large extent are dependent on more idiosyncratic factors, such as characteristics of personality, and so forth.) The influence of class on TV viewing decreases over time, while that of gender increases between grades 5 and 7 and then is constant at least up to grade 9. These data bear out the hypothesis put forward in section 4.4.4, namely, that the influence from class of origin will tend to decrease over time. Before accepting the result, however, two reservations must be made.

The first reservation concerns the fact that LISREL models build on linear relationships, and we have just shown that the influence from class probably is partly curvilinear. But this discrepancy only means that, for the moment, we have chosen to disregard the curvilinearity and that, as a consequence, the coefficients of Figure 4.4 and Table 4.5 probably are conservative estimates of the strength of the "true" relationships, something which should not influence the decrease or increase over time of these coefficients. (In principle, this conclusion holds true for all the LISREL models presented in this book.)

The second reservation concerns the fact that while social class has been allowed to influence the dependent variables in all three waves, it has not been introduced as a variable in its own right in each of the three waves, something which could have been done and could have been defended on theoretical grounds (cf. Flodin, 1986, p. 173).

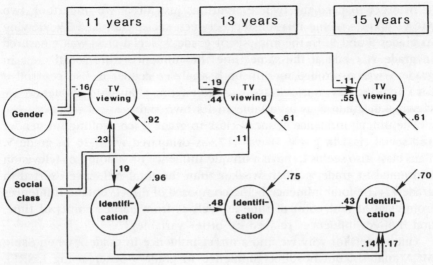

N = 312
χ^2 = 322   DF = 273   p = .023

Figure 4.3. A LISREL Model of TV Use: Viewing and Identification. Vaxjoe Main Panel. (From Johnsson-Smaragdi, 1983).

Table 4.5. Direct, Indirect, and Total Effects of Background Variables on TV Consumption and Identification. (From Johnsson-Smaragdi, 1983)

Casual variable	Dependent variable	Direct effect	Indirect effect	Total effect
	TV consumption at			
Gender	11 years	-.16	.00	-.16
	13 years	-.19	-.07	-.26
	15 years	-.11	-.14	-.25
Social class	11 years	.23	.00	.23
	13 years	.11	.10	.21
	15 years	.00	.12	.12
	Identification at			
Gender	11 years	.00	-.03	-.03
	13 years	.00	-.01	-.01
	15 years	.17	-.01	-.18
Social class	11 years	.00	.04	.04
	13 years	.00	.02	.02
	15 years	.00	.01	.01

It could be argued that doing so would probably have increased the strength of the influence exerted by social class in grades 7 and 9.

In order to heed the two reservations just aired, we undertook two MCA analyses of the relationship between social class and TV viewing in grades 5 and 9. In the analysis of grade 9, social class was measured in grade 9, while at the same time the influence from social class in grade 5 was controlled for. (In both analyses gender is also controlled for.) In this way, social class was given the chance to influence TV viewing in grade 9 as a variable in its own right.

The unique influence of social class in grade 9 (controlling for gender and social class in grade 5) was .17, as compared with .26 in grade 5. Thus class also seems to have a unique influence on amount of television consumed in grade 9, albeit weaker than the total influence exerted in grade 9. (The total influence being composed of direct, unique influences from class at that point of time as well as from earlier points of time, and indirect influences relayed by other variables.)

One reason for why we find a direct influence in grade 9 when using MCA analysis, but no direct influence in grade 9 when using LISREL analysis, may be the fact that the already observed curvilinearity also turned up in these analyses. The negative deviation from the grand mean was greatest in the highest and lowest classes.

The final conclusion to be drawn seems to be that influence from class of origin on habitual TV viewing decreases over time. However, when extreme groups, and curvilinearity in particular, are heeded we may also find a weak to moderate influence in grade 9.

4.5.3. Social Class and Motives

The mass media are not used at random. People go to the media with some ideas in mind about the coming experience. Media use is at least to some extent purposeful. Several times in this report, therefore, we have maintained that the motives for using the media are very central, a statement well in line with the fact that we are working largely within the uses and gratifications tradition.

Within the social-class perspective applied in this chapter we find it quite natural to assume that the ideas, expectations, and motivations for using the media vary considerably between different social groupings. In sec. 3.3.5 above we have seen that the strength of motives decreases with age. We now ask which differences in strength of motives may be found between different classes and educational categories in our material?

Those who expect strong relationships between motives and our background variables may be disappointed. Table 4.6 shows the beta values for the different motives, class, and education when gender is controlled for. They indicate only weak to moderate relationships.

With low betas it is important to look at the pattern of subgroup means (not rendered here). In this case that pattern is clear: In general the lower the class and educational level, the stronger the motivation. The only exception from the pattern is the motive "To get to know about the world around us," where the strongest motivations are found in the upper categories (albeit with small differences).

Our highest betas tend to be found with the habit motive, the strongest relationships being found in the seventh grade. Strength of viewing motivation usually decreases with age among adolescents (Rubin, 1977; cf. sec. 3.3.5). In the data presented here, too, there is a tendency for the background–motive relationships to be lower in the ninth grade than in the seventh, a tendency clearly visible with the habit motivation.

The important remaining question in this context is, why the results of Table 4.6 are not more clear-cut, with larger differences along class and educational lines? It may be that the motives that we are looking at are not the right ones. Others might have proved to be more discriminating and important. It may also be that, in the age brackets we are dealing with here, it is difficult for respondents to report reasons for attending to the media. This latter criticism has been a common

Table 4.6. Viewing Motives as Influenced by SES and Education. (MCA Beta Coefficients, Controlled for Gender, Vaxjoe Main Panel)

| | Beta values for grade | | | | | |
| | 5 | | 7 | | 9 | |
Motive	SES	Educ.	SES	Educ.	SES	Educ.
Habit	.17	.22	.27	.24	.10	.08
Pastime	.15	.15	.19	.21	.15	.13
Escape	.12	.15	.17	.15	.15	.13
Relax	.18	.13	.09	.09	Missing data	
To get something to talk about	.18	.11	.15	.11	.07	.11
To get to know about things	.12	.09	.14	.06	.09	.06
To get to know about the world around us	Missing data				.09	.10
To get to know about myself	Missing data				.17	.16

one in respect of uses and gratifications research (see, e.g., Elliott, 1974; cf. Rosengren, 1985c).

Nevertheless, we think that motives do tell us something about the meaning and nature of the television experience. When we know something about motives we also know something about the role of media use in the life of the individual. The motive dominating television viewing among adolescents in our study, to a large extent, seems to be habit. Social background factors and the habit motive covary.

Generally, there is a positive relationship between strength of motives and the amount of media used. For instance, the relationships between the motive of habit and amount of television consumed are usually quite strong. But is this the case for all social groups, and how does the relationship differ in different social settings, and over time? Part of the answer is found in Table 4.7, where we present the relationships (eta) between habitual motivation and amount of TV in 24 categories based on grade, gender, class, and educational background.

Among working-class children and those with low educational family background there is an increase in the strength of the relationship, whereas there is a tendency towards an (often U-shaped) decrease in the relationship among those from the upper echelons of society. For the former, then, the tendency to television habituation increases over time; for the latter, it decreases.

The fact that television habituation changes differentially over time for adolescents with different social backgrounds may have some con-

Table 4.7. Relationship Between Motive of Habit and Amount of Television Watched. (MCA Eta Coefficients in 24 Categories of Age, Gender, Social Class, and Educational Background; Vaxjoe Main Panel)

| Grade | Social Class | | | |
| | Working class | | Middle class | |
	Boys	Girls	Boys	Girls
5	.24	.26	.43	.43
7	.41	.35	.24	.14
9	.48	.43	.33	.33

| Grade | Educational Background | | | |
| | Low | | High | |
	Boys	Girls	Boys	Girls
5	.25	.28	.38	.49
7	.31	.37	.29	.39
9	.47	.37	.35	.35

sequences for the way they use television. In the following section we will discuss one such consequence.

4.5.4 Social Class and Selectivity

In uses and gratifications theory audience activity is a key concept. The audience member is seen less as a passive, manipulated victim of the media and more as someone who actively attends to the media, seeking gratifications that are related to more or less strongly felt needs (Blumler, 1979; Elliott, 1974; Palmgreen et al., 1985; cf.). Even if this notion of activity is included in most uses and gratification models, very few research efforts to study it empirically have actually been undertaken. Some attempts in this direction have recently been made by Levy and Windahl (1984, 1985). They differentiate between three dimensions of activity: selectivity, involvement, and active use of media content. Of these dimensions, we are here interested in selectivity.

According to theories of selectivity (Klapper, 1960), people discriminate in their use of media fare. This assumption has been contested by, among others, Goodhardt et al. (Goodhardt & Ehrenberg, 1969; Goodhardt, Ehrenberg, & Collins, 1975). In studies of the British television public, these authors found a tendency in parts of the audience to watch indiscriminantly by the clock rather than by program content. In a later study, however, Goodhardt and his colleagues modified their opinion somewhat, maintaining that people tend to be less selective and active when it comes to *when* to watch television and to be more selective when it comes to *what* to watch (Barwise, Ehrenberg, & Goodhardt, 1982; cf. Palmgreen et al., 1985). Levy and Windahl (1984) found that, in the case of watching news on television, a large part of the public could be said to be selective on each of the three dimensions studied by them (cf. above).

In terms of class, Piepe et al. (1978) maintain that working-class viewers tend to be less selective than middle-class viewers. Himmelweit et al. (1958) found the same tendency among a young TV audience.

We have examined two aspects of audience selectivity. To begin with we have looked into selectivity occurring before the actual television exposure. In our diary questionnaire we asked whether the respondents had decided in advance to watch the actual program or not. Secondly, we registered the extent to which audience members saw consecutive programs vs. nonconsecutive.

In order to determine what we may call the preselectivity score we computed the ratio between the programs decided upon in advance and the total number of programs watched during the Wednesday evening of the diary week. If a respondent had seen three programs and had decided in advance to see two of them, whereas the third was reported as watched, for example, just because the set happened to be on, then a score of .67 was recorded. Figure 4.4 gives the result for middle-class and working-class adolescents, respectively.

Among working-class adolescents, selectivity decreases with age. Among middle-class adolescents there is a slight increase. Consequently, in the ninth grade the middle-class adolescents are more selective than their working-class counterparts, whereas the opposite is the case in the fifth grade. According to these data, working-class youngsters are not less selective across the board, but only in grade 9. We are not able to explain why the development runs in different directions for working-class and middle-class adolescents. Also, it should be remembered that these data are cross-sectional, and thus not too well suited to tracing changes over time. All the same, the pattern is intriguing. What about our second aspect of selectivity?

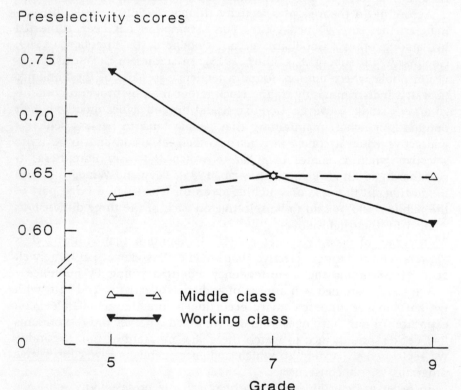

Figure 4.4. Preselectivity Scores for Middle- and Working-class Adolescents in 3 Age-groups. Diary Data. Vaxjoe Study, Third Wave.

In trying to state to what extent respondents had been watching TV "in a row" rather than with pauses between the programs (our second aspect of selectivity), we registered for each respondent in the Vaxjoe third wave the number of TV programs that he or she had watched during 1 night of the television diary week. If the respondent had watched, say, three programs that night, then there were two potential points in time when he or she might have gone directly from watching one program to another. To get the selectivity score the number of actual transitions from program to program was divided by the potential number of program-to-program transitions. If the person in our example above had seen two of the three programs in a row, then he or she would have been assigned a selectivity score of 0.5. Of two potential direct transitions from program to program only one was actually used by this viewer.

Table 4.8 presents the selectivity scores for three age-groups and social categories based on a dichotomization of our social class and education indexes. Again we find that the selectivity of adolescents with a middle-class background increases with age while, on this occasion, for those with a working-class background the pattern is not quite linear. Thus, in the fifth grade, working-class youngsters show a higher selectivity than their middle-class counterparts, while in the ninth grade it is the other way round. This also holds true when background is measured in terms of parental education.

We have no definitive explanation for this unexpected finding of interaction between sociocultural background and selectivity turning up for two different measures of selectivity, and for two different measures of background. At the very least it may be taken as a caveat against any offhand assumptions about the relationship between social back-

Table 4.8. Selectivity by Age, Social Class, and Educational Background. (Dichotomized, Vaxjoe Diary, Third Wave, The Higher the Score, the Lower the Selectivity)

Grade	Working class	Middle class
5	.44	.50
7	.50	.48
9	.49	.37

Grade	Low education	High education
5	.45	.50
7	.53	.49
9	.46	.27

ground and various aspects of mass media use. It is not only that this relationship may change over time and with age. In some cases it may even change direction with age. The variables lying behind such reversals represent a challenging task for future research. So do their consequences. In the next section we will turn to one such potential consequence.

4.5.5. Social Class and Dependency

In sec. 3.3.4 we discussed the notion of dependency on mass media, noting that there are at least two different types of dependency. The term may denote the fact that some individuals, because of structural, positional, and individual characteristics, may have to be content with what the media have to offer, having to refrain from more personal sources of intellectual, social, and affectional gratifications. It may also denote the fact that, as a result of heavy media use, one may gradually become habituated to, and, consequently dependent on such use (an analogue to more serious types of dependency or addiction). It is this latter type of TV dependency that we shall discuss in this section. (This type of dependency, of course, may come about as a consequence of the former.)

There are several possible answers to the question of why people become dependent on a medium. As McQuail and Windahl (1981) have argued, there is a process of growing dependency in which gratifications and repeated use make members of the audience dependent, sometimes almost addicted, to certain media and/or media contents (cf. Windahl et al., 1986). Rubin and Windahl (1982) have pointed to the fact that some people have fewer functional alternatives to certain media than others (cf. Rosengren & Windahl, 1972), and that their dependency on these media in this sense of the word therefore will increase the addictive type of dependency. They also suggest that factors such as perceived instrumentality probably influence the degree to which one becomes dependent. All in all, we may hypothesize that the social groupings experiencing the greatest rewards from using television, having the fewest functional alternatives, and using TV the most, should be those most dependent on TV (cf. Ball–Rokeach, 1985).

It is probable that we shall find these social groupings at the lower, rather than at the upper, end of the class continuum. In this section we have already seen that working-class adolescents gradually grow to be more habituated (and less selective) TV viewers than their middle-class counterparts, and we may assume that they feel more gratified as well. Piepe et al. (1978) support this assumption by maintaining that working-class viewers are relatively more involved with the medium. Taking resources as a point of departure, we may assume that working-class viewers have fewer functional alternatives, while we have seen that lower middle-class and working-class viewers usually consume more television than do upper-middle-class and upper-class viewers.

In the Vaxjoe main panel respondents were asked to estimate their feelings of loss in a situation where they were suddenly deprived of TV. Dependence on television was operationalized by this single question. The relationships between class and dependency can be seen in Table 4.9.

The data in the table invite some observations. First, the relationships are not too strong. They are also reduced when amount of television consumption is controlled for (although gender does not seem to influence the relationship). Secondly, although the differences are rather small, the overall tendency is in accordance with our hypothesis. Dependency is higher at the lower end of the social scale.

The same pattern is also discernible for education and dependency. In this case the relationships are a trifle stronger.

Above were listed some possible reasons for a negative relationship

Table 4.9.   Social Class and Dependency. (MCA, Vaxjoe Main Panel)

Social class category	Unadjusted mean	Adjusted for gender	Adjusted for gender and habitual TV consumption
		Grade 5	
High 1	2.6	2.6	2.8
2	2.8	2.8	2.9
3	2.8	2.8	2.9
4	3.1	3.1	3.0
Low 5	3.1	3.2	3.1
	Eta: .21	Beta: .21	Beta: .13
		Grade 7	
High 1	2.4	2.4	2.5
2	2.6	2.6	2.7
3	2.5	2.5	2.5
4	2.8	2.8	2.8
Low 5	2.9	2.9	2.9
	Eta: .22	Beta: .23	Beta: .14
		Grade 9	
High 1	2.0	2.0	2.2
2	2.1	2.1	2.1
3	2.0	2.0	2.1
4	2.4	2.4	2.3
Low 5	2.3	2.3	2.3
	Eta: .17	Beta: .17	Beta: .11

between social position and dependency. Which of these reasons is the most decisive we do not know. Consequently, it seems to be an important task to discover more about how different social groupings become differentially dependent on the media. Regardless of the "ultimate" causes of such phenomena, it is very plausible that the intervening variables of motives (such as habit) and selectivity, which were discussed in the two previous sections, have their role to play in this process. Similarly, Windahl et al. (1986) found that the communicative climate of the family played an important role in determining the degree of television dependency among Swedish 17-year-olds. In that study it was concluded that media dependency plays a more important role for understanding media use than is usually acknowledged. This section has suggested one way of arriving at dependency. By gradually increasing television habituation, and by decreasing selectivity, low class tends to lead to dependency on television.

4.6. TELEVISION USE AND 3 TYPES OF SOCIAL CLASS

In previous sections of this chapter we have argued that social class can mean at least three different things: class of origin, destination, and context. In this section we shall demonstrate the interrelationships of the three different types of class as factors influencing the television use of adolescents. We start with comparing the influence emanating from class of origin with the one emanating from destination.

4.6.1. Class of Origin, Class of Destination, and TV Use

In this section, we shall discuss the interaction between class of origin and destination in influencing TV use. Anticipatory socialization theory would predict that the media use of an adolescent should be flavored by the media use patterns of the class that he or she expects to end up in.

In the media panel our operationalization of "anticipated class" (class of destination) was first meant to be used as a dependent variable, media use being the independent one. We asked our respondents: "What do you think will be your future occupation?" However, conceptualized as class of destination, this variable may also be regarded as an independent variable. Let us look at the relationships between anticipated social class and habitual viewing as reflected in a simple three-dimensional cross-tabulation (Table 4.10). The data cover grades 5 and 9 of the main panel, the respondents of grade 7 having been given a different formulation of the anticipated class question. As before, occupations were coded into four categories (1, 2a, 2b, 3, with 1 as the highest social class; cf. sec. 4.5.1 above). But this time, of course, there were no conjugal occupations to add. Therefore, the variable of class will have only four values in these analyses.

A familiar pattern emerges; in three cases out of four we find the curvilinearity demonstrated earlier in this chapter. Class of destination does not differ from class of origin in this respect. Further, the eta's are about the same, around .20 to .25.

Given the obvious relationship between class of origin and class of destination, the relationship between class of destination and media use may be spurious. In Table 4.11 therefore, we look more specifically at the impact of class of destination, this time controlling not only for gender but also for class of origin. (For reasons given above, grade 7 is not included.)

Again we find the same relationship. In the fifth and ninth grades, in the working class as well as in the middle class, those who aim at occupations in the highest social class are also the lowest TV viewers. Judging from this table, one might even be tempted to conclude that the influence of class of destination is no less, and perhaps even greater, than that of class of origin.

For working-class adolescents we note the same curvilinearity as has been noted before, even if the differences are small. In the middle-class part of the table we find an interesting difference between the fifth and the ninth grades. In the former the relationship is linear, but in the latter we find that those who believe that their real future job is to be found in the working class watch as little TV as do those who aim at an upper-class occupation. This may be a sign that we are dealing with a deviant group, one that is anticipating downward mobility. It may

Table 4.10. Class of Destination and Habitual TV Viewing Among Boys and Girls. (MCA, Half-hours/Week, Vaxjoe Main Panel, Grades 5 and 9; No Data Available for Grade 7; Highest Value in Each Column in Italics)

| | Grade | | | |
| Class of destination | 5 | | 9 | |
	Boys	Girls	Boys	Girls
High 1	31.1	23.2	19.1	15.2
2	30.1	28.0	18.7	15.5
3	37.1	31.2	25.9	23.0
Low 4	37.5	28.5	22.1	17.6
Eta	.24	.20	.20	.25

Table 4.11.   Class of Destination and Habitual TV Viewing Among Working-class and Middle-class Children. (MCA, Half-hours/Week, Controlled for Gender, Vaxjoe Main Panel, Grades 5 and 9; No Data Available for Grade 7; Highest Value in Each Column in Italics)

Class of destination		Working-class origin			
		Grade 5		Grade 9	
		n		n	
High	1	18	28.5	8	15.6
	2	29	31.9	33	18.6
	3	51	37.6	30	24.8
Low	4	66	34.9	76	21.3
Beta		.20		.21	
		Middle-class origin			
High	1	38	26.3	31	16.4
	2	49	26.6	43	17.2
	3	27	28.3	15	25.3
Low	4	37	31.7	38	16.6
Beta		.16		.27	

be a category of outsiders rebelling against societal norms, some of them, perhaps, because they are doing less well in school. As Roe (1983a) has shown, this category tends to be low on TV consumption. These youngsters are probably more peer- or street culture-oriented than interested in TV viewing within the family setting.

We had expected that the impact of class of destination would increase with age; the closer to occupational life the greater the anticipated socialization effect. There is no sign of that in the working class according to the beta values. However, for the middle class there is a leap from beta .16 in the fifth grade to .27 in the ninth, providing some support for our hypothesis.

From these results we conclude that anticipated social class does indeed influence amount of television viewing (and perhaps media use at large). Media use is determined not only by class of origin, but also by class of destination. What about the influence emanating from class of context?

4.6.2. Class of Origin, Class of Context, and TV Use

The class affiliation of children and adolescents is probably more com-plicated than most communications researchers have acknowledged.

Throughout this study we have talked about working-class and middle-class young people, referring to the social class of their parents. A family with working-class parents is regarded as a working-class family, and the children of the family are seen as working-class children. At the same time we have to realize that for adolescents this feeling of belonging to class is secondary and more or less loosely prescribed. Adolescents are still far from the workplace and occupational life and the class identity that follows from it. This, however, is far from assuming with Parsons (1942) that adolescent life is classless. Our assumption is that adult and adolescent class relations are often quite different. Without contact with any workplace and its different forms of "solidaristic collectivism" the adolescent is more susceptible to classlike influences from the environment. In other words, class as context will be of even greater importance to adolescents than to adults. In this section we shall consider one such context, namely, that of the school. To adolescents, school may represent the most important class of context of all (although there certainly are other types of class of context as well; cf. sec. 4.6.3).

It is widely assumed that in societies such as ours the school as an institution has a middle-class character (Bernstein, 1971–1975; Roe 1983a). For the working-class child, school tends to be a somewhat alien context, saturated with a middle-class type of influence. We may also assume, however, that there is considerable variation both between and within different schools. Some schools and school classes are solidly working class, whereas others are middle class, depending on the home background of the students. This type of variation may be hypothesized to have its consequences. The situation of a working-class child in a class where most classmates have a middle-class background is different from the case where a working-class student is submerged in a solid working-class environment at school. Such differences, it may be assumed, will have some effect on many areas of life, including media use. Class as context, therefore, should not be neglected in studies of adolescent media use.

In our analysis we have defined class of context as the mean for each school class on our combined index of home background (taking into consideration both the social class and the education of both parents, since no doubt class of context is a very sociocultural phenomenon). For technical reasons we have confined ourselves to the ninth grade of the third wave (the Vaxjoe main panel). For each ninth-grade school class the home background mean score has been calculated ranging from 1 to 5 (this time with 1 denoting the *lowest* social class). The highest mean score is 3.53, the lowest 1.71, indicating quite a range of variation in class as context.

The first thing to do is to relate this new variable of class of context to the variable of class of origin (the operationalization of which, on this occasion, is achieved basically in the same way as was that of class of context, that is, by including both the social class and the education of both parents). The relationship between class of origin and class of context is demonstrated in Table 4.12.

It can be seen that there is a strong relationship between the two variables. Adolescents from the upper classes tend to belong to school classes with a high value for class of context; adolescents from the lower classes tend to belong to school classes with a low value for class of context. Given the way that we have constructed our two variables, this result is at least partly tautological, of course. An individual from the upper classes helps to raise the mean of the school class he or she attends, and vice versa. But the important thing is not so much the relationship as such, as the fact that it is far from perfect. In spite of the formally tautological nature of the table, only about 40% of the students have the same class of origin and context. At least half of the students, then, may be subject to differential influence from class of origin and class of context. (In communities of different size and character this figure will vary, both up and down.)

In terms of a generally accepted egalitarian school ideology, though, Table 4.12 may be regarded with mixed feelings. The main problem here would be the range in class of context between school classes. According to the prevailing ideology, there should be no such range at all. This range, however, is a natural outcome of existing geographical segregation, probably reinforced—unwittingly, perhaps—by various measures undertaken by school authorities for various practical reasons

Table 4.12. Relationship Between Class of Context and Class of Origin. (Vaxjoe Main Panel, Grade 9)[a]

		Class of origin				
		Low 1	Middle 2–3	High 4–5	Total	*n*
Class of context (average of class of origin in school class)	High 3.32–3.53	20	32	43	35%	110
	Middle 2.69–3.29	31	30	36	32%	100
	Low 1.71–2.65	49	38	17	33%	104
	Total	100%	100%	101%	100%	
	Total %	27	34	39	100	
	n	86	107	121	314	

[a] For technical reasons (school classes split during time of study) only 62% of the main panel could be included in this analysis.

(cf. Arnman & Jönsson, 1983). From the point of view of the egalitarian school ideology, Table 4.12 may also give rise to some positive feelings, however. After all, school segregation is far from complete. On the contrary. In our terms, a majority of the students have different classes of origin and context. Whether good or bad, this simple fact is what makes our continued analysis possible.

The joint and separate effects of class of origin and class of context on amount of TV consumption are demonstrated in Table 4.13. The influence from class of context does not seem to be any less than that from class of origin, nor does it show any different type of relationship. Comparing the vertical and horizontal marginals, we find in both cases the curvilinearity already observed in sec. 4.5.1 between class and TV use (in spite of the fact that this time the class variable has only three values and parents' occupation and education have now been combined). The curvilinearity of class of context is no less than that of class of origin.

Turning now to the inner cells of the table, we find that when we control for one of the variables, the curvilinear influence of the other one decreases. Only three of the six inner rows and columns show curvilinearity. All the same, the curvilinearity is strongly manifested in the middle cell of the table (the TV consumption of middle-class youngsters in a middle-class context). It is the highest value in the table, almost 3 TV hours a week more than for the inhabitants of the two next highest inner cells of the table, and almost 5 hours more than the lowest values. The combination of middle-class origin and middle-class context constitutes the heartland of TV users. (Note that in this section we use the term "middle class" to denote a middle stratum, not the opposite of the term "working class".)

Breaking down our data yet a step further by also controlling for the variable of gender, we find less curvilinearity in the marginals, and

Table 4.13.   Class of Origin, Class of Context, and Average TV Consumption. (Half-hours/Week, Vaxjoe Main Panel, Grade 9)

		Class of origin				
		Low 1	Middle 2-3	High 4-5	Total	*n*
Class of context (average of class of origin in school class)	High 3.32-3.53	16.0	17.4	16.1	16.5	110
	Middle 2.69-3.29	20.2	25.8	17.4	20.8	100
	Low 1.71-2.65	20.2	19.4	18.1	19.5	104
	Total	20.0	20.7	16.9	19.0	314
	n	86	107	121	314	

about the same curvilinearity in the inner cells of the table (in 8 out of 12 inner rows and columns). The pattern appears to be somewhat irregular, though, no doubt partly because of diminished *n*'s. Another cause of the seeming irregularity of the pattern must be the complex social-psychological processes resulting from the interplay of gender, class of origin, and class of context.

Especially interesting in this interplay are those cases when class of origin and class of context pull in different directions. This is a phenomenon studied in the theory of cross-pressure (Lazarsfeld et al., 1944; Pinner, 1968; Powell, 1976). Cross-pressure theory has been developed mainly on the basis of the categorical variables necessarily used in voting studies. Individuals under cross-pressure to vote for both party X and party Y often show a tendency not to vote at all. Can this line of argument be transferred to the continuous variable of TV consumption?

It is hardly a plausible hypothesis that individuals finding themselves in a class of context different from origin (that is, individuals under cross-pressure with respect to TV viewing) should show a tendency not to view at all. Rather, they could be expected to modify their TV behavior, finding a balance of sorts between the conflicting impulses emanating from class of origin and context. Cross-pressure should not result in withdrawal, but in accommodation. This accommodation is what Table 4.13 shows: Upper-class ninth graders situated in a lower-class context increase their TV consumption (from 8 to 9 hours a week); lower-class ninth graders situated in a hight-class context decrease their TV consumption (from 10 to 8 hours a week). So far, so good. Available data admit a closer view of these social-psychological processes of accommodation, however.

The data of Table 4.13 show the cumulated overall result of a number of microprocesses. What does the process of accommodation look like when we observe it more *in concreto,* at the level of the single individual in the single school class? The process of accommodation could be expected to show up most clearly in clear-cut cases: class-wise clearly deviating individuals in school classes clearly slanted toward the ends of the class continuum. Figure 4.5 illustrates the argument. In terms of this figure we are interested in those individuals who appear in cells 2 and 3, that is to say, individuals who in the class setting belong to the minority.

We have picked school classes which can be classified as significantly above or below the overall average home background score ($\pm$ .10). Eight classes are characterized as lower home background; six, as higher home background. The home background index has got five values. A nonmatching individual is here defined as either belonging to one of

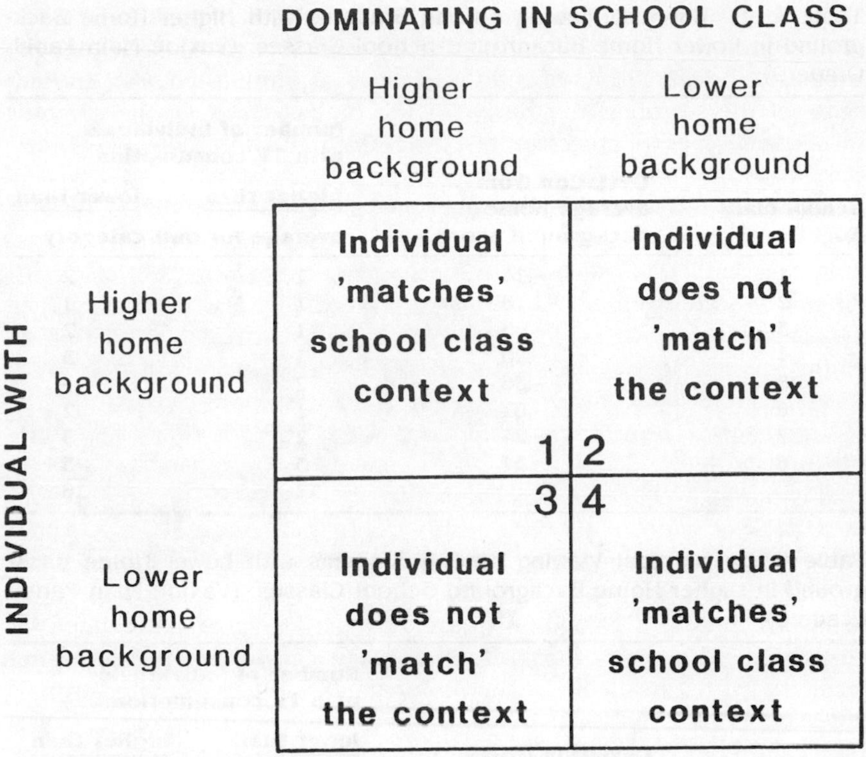

DOMINATING IN SCHOOL CLASS

	Higher home background	Lower home background
Higher home background	Individual 'matches' school class context 1	2 Individual does not 'match' the context
Lower home background	3 Individual does not 'match' the context	4 Individual 'matches' school class context

INDIVIDUAL WITH

Figure 4.5. Relationship Between Individual's Social Background and School Class Context

the two highest categories in a lower home background class, or to one of the two lowest in a higher home background school class. For individuals in these cells we expect a contextual effect of accommodation to occur. In the case of watching television we assume that those in cell 2 will watch more and those in cell 3 will watch less television than the average among youngsters with their home background.

Tables 4.14 and 4.15, in a very rough way, show the impact of the class context. The dependent variable is our usual habitual TV-viewing score. Each deviant individual (significantly lower home background in a higher home background school class and vice versa) has been classified as lying below or above the average TV consumption for his or her class of origin. Table 4.14 refers to individuals in cell 2 of Figure 4.5; Table 4.15, to individuals in cell 3.

First, it will be seen that the number of "class deviants" is small. The variation between school classes is considerable, but each class seems to be rather homogeneous. Secondly, we note that our assumption

Table 4.14. Habitual Viewing Among Students with Higher Home Background in Lower Home Background School Classes. (Vaxjoe Main Panel, Grade 9)

School class No.	Deviation from average home background score	Number of individuals with TV consumption	
		higher than	lower than
		average for own category	
1	-.14	1	2
2	-1.18	1	1
3	-.65	1	2
4	-.20	1	3
5	-.36	2	—
6	-.81	1	2
7	-.24	2	3
8	-.37	3	3
		12	16

Table 4.15. Habitual Viewing Among Students with Lower Home Background in Higher Home Background School Classes. (Vaxjoe Main Panel, Grade 9)

School class No.	Deviation from average home background score	Number of individuals with TV consumption	
		lower than	higher than
		average for own background category	
1	+.44	4	1
2	+.31	3	2
3	+.64	5	1
4	+.53	5	2
5	+.43	1	8
6	+.51	4	3
		22	17

about the contextual influence does not receive any support in Table 4.14. There are more individuals going in the "wrong" direction (less TV than own average) than in the "right" direction (more TV than own average). Adolescents with high social origin and low social context are not influenced as expected by that context.

For students in cell 3 of Figure 4.5 (low social origin and higher social context), the contextual influence, however, seems to be operating more in accordance with our expectation (Table 4.15). In five school classes out of six the distribution is as expected, with more deviants having a lower rather than a higher consumption of television. More individuals are going in the right direction (less TV than own average) than in the wrong direction (more TV than own average). The class forming the exception has as many as nine deviating individuals, probably many enough to form a subgroup of their own, with their own norms and standards for media use.

We should be careful not to draw too far-reaching conclusions from this very crude material. But it is clear that the overall tendency observed in Table 4.13 does not apply without exception across the board when we move to the microlevel of single individuals in single school classes. More specifically, cross-pressure from class of origin and class of context seems to release two basically different ways of reaction: Adolescents in this situation tend to move closer toward either their class of origin or their class of context. The two types of reaction could be termed profilation and accommodation, respectively.

The two classes are different in this respect. More upper-class ninth graders in a low social context (cell 2 of Figure 4.5) move closer toward the ideal of TV consumption prevailing in their class of origin than toward that prevailing in their class of context (16 vs. 12; Table 4.14). With the lower-class youngsters in a high social context (cell 3 of Figure 4.5) it is the other way around. More lower-class ninth graders move closer toward the ideal type of TV consumption prevailing in their class of context than toward that prevailing in their class of origin (22 vs. 17; Table 4.15). In a situation of social-class cross-pressure, lower-class children are more prone to accommodation, upper-class children more prone to profilation.

The net outcome of these contradictory tendencies is the one observed in Table 4.13. Since in this table there is an overall tendency to accommodation rather than to profilation, the upper-class adolescents choosing accommodation must have done so quite substantially, while those choosing profilation must have done so somewhat less wholeheartedly. All the same the overall accommodation of upper-class adolescents is somewhat weaker than that of lower-class adolescents.

Why do lower-class students accommodate more than do upper-class ones? There are at least two answers to that question. It is probably easier to accommodate "upward", toward the viewing pattern of the upper classes. Also, the institution of school itself—teachers and curriculum—is overwhelmingly middle class. Even in a lower-class context, therefore, upper- and middle-class children are encouraged to stay with their class of origin, while lower-class children in an upper-class context are doubly encouraged to accommodate.

In this section we have seen that class of context does indeed exert a considerable influence of its own on the viewing habits of adolescents. Like the influence from class of origin it tends to be curvilinear. The two types of class interact in producing a very high TV consumption among children from the middle of the social-class range, attending school classes also in the middle of the range. In cases where there is cross-pressure from class of origin and class of context, lower-class children are somewhat more prone to be influenced by class of context than are upper-class children. But for both groups, there is an overall influence from both class of context and class of origin. In the next section we will see that this holds true not only for television but also for the use of pop music, the medium which during adolescence gradually supersedes television as the dominant medium (cf. sec. 3.4.8).

4.6.3. Social Class and Popular Music

The relationship between social class and the popular music use of adolescents is a subject upon which much could, and has, been written. We do not have the scope here to deal fully with this subject but we feel that some very brief comments are justified.

Historically, the relationship between social class and adolescents' popular music use has been viewed from at least three major perspectives (cf. sec. 4.3). The early view, following the Parsonian postulation of a "classless" youth culture, was that use of pop was also unrelated to class. Developments in the 1960s led to a respecification of the relationship in terms of youth becoming a class in itself, profoundly antithetical in its cultural expressions to adult culture (e.g., Rosak, 1971). More recently, a growing number of researchers has rejected both of these positions, arguing instead that youth culture(s) and their various expressive forms are indeed class-based in the traditional sense (Murdock & McCron, 1976a, 1976b; Willis, 1978).

Much of this disagreement may well be a result of the lack of refinement of the concept of social class already highlighted in this chapter in connection with TV use. Given the instability and age specificity of much popular music, and the problematical position of youth within the wider social structure of productive relations, the analysis of the relationship between them requires much more differentiated analyses than have generally been employed.

A first step in this direction would be the operationalization of the distinction between class of origin, class of context, and class of destination already presented in previous sections of this chapter. Results presented by Roe (1983a) provide support for such a differentiation in connection with the popular music use of adolescents. Working with the main panel of Vaxjoe respondents, and employing MCA and LISREL analyses, Roe found only very weak relationships between class of origin (measured by parents' education) and amount of use of, and preferences within, popular music. By contrast, moderate to strong relationships were found beetween important indicators of class of context (this time as manifesting itself in peer group orientation, school achievement, and attitude to school) and use of pop, even when controlling for class of origin (cf. Murdock & Phelps, 1973; Sugarman, 1967). Furthermore, there was evidence that a greater early interest in pop among girls in grade 5, and a greater preference for "harder" forms of music, such as punk and hard rock, among boys in grade 9, were negatively related to anticipated occupation (class of destination).

Unfortunately, there is not scope here to discuss these results in detail; the interested reader is referred to Roe's study. What can be said is that these results support the conclusion arrived at in the discussion concerning social class and TV use, namely, that a refinement of the social-class variable is an essential task for future research if we are going to be able to come to grips with the complexities involved.

4.7. INTERACTION BETWEEN SOCIAL CLASS AND MEDIA USE

We know that different positions in the class structure will result in differential mass media use. Are there any reasons to suspect that the effect processes following the use of mass media will be different in different social strata? In other words, does social class or status interact with media use in producing differential effects of that use? The answer is, "yes", and there are some good reasons available in support of that answer.

Within a given social class there may be more or less pervasive perceptions and evaluations of a certain medium, of certain types of media contents and of certain media communicators; and those perceptions and evaluations may differ from those of other classes.

Mass media use, and the motives for that use, may differ from class to class. The members of one class, for example, may use television news for its entertainment value, whereas in another class it is primarily used to obtain information (Hvitfelt, 1977).

The media mix differs between different social groups. In one stratum television may be the unique source of information, whereas in another people turn to several other sources, such as newspapers and radio. We assume that when one is dependent on *one* medium, its impact will be greater than when there are functional alternatives (cf. Ball–Rokeach & DeFleur, 1976; Rubin & Windahl, 1982).

Education is unevenly distributed between different social classes. In some instances education will increase the effects of some content because one understands it better, in other cases education will help lessen the impact of what the media present.

Thus there are many reasons why mass media use may have differential effects in different social groupings. The area of differential effects along stratification lines seems to have been very little studied—if at all.

In Table 4.16 we present some data about the relationships between two media variables and political interest, as they stand out in our five socioeconomic subgroups. The media variables are habitual TV consumption and an index of preferences for TV programs about society and the community, for TV debates and TV news (cf. sec. 2.5). Political interest was measured by an index built on six attitudinal items, having an internal consistency of alfa = .89. (Note that the table is based on 10 different tables, the main tendencies of which are expressed by the betas.)

In the column of betas for the relationships between amount of TV and political interest the strongest relationship can be found in the top social-class category, whereas there is no relationship in the lowest. The relationships are negative in the two highest categories, with less clear directions in the others. The relationship between the same media variable and political interest, then, is highly differential in different social strata. Why is that so?

For the highest group we suggest that a lot of TV use in this category has a detrimental effect on political interest. We also believe, however, that the politically interested have little time for TV, compared with those who are only weakly interested in politics. For this high-status

Table 4.16.   Political Interest, Habitual TV Viewing, and Program Preferences in Different Social Classes. (MCA Beta Coefficients, Controlled for Gender; Vaxjoe Study; Third Wave, Grade 9)

				Political Interest and
				Preference for programs about society
Social class			Amount of television	
		n	Beta	Beta
High	1	49	.53	.63
	2	102	.17	.43
	3	46	.10	.41
	4	101	.15	.46
Low	5	143	.01	.63

group TV is not the main source of information. The result may also indicate that interest in politics does not have the same meaning in the highest and lowest social-class categories. For the latter, the political significance of TV may be almost nonexistent. Television is watched for other purposes than for politics. The low selectivity of this category, one may assume, also leads to little specific interest as an effect of watching.

Thus we have two interpretations of the differential relationship in the different social-class categories: political interest as an outcome of TV watching, and political interest as influencing TV watching. In both cases, differential perception of TV may be an important contingent variable. The two interpretations, of course, are not mutually exclusive. On the contrary, over time, they may very well reinforce each other.

The right-hand column of Table 4.16 suggests that there is also a strong relationship between preferences for societally oriented programs and political interest. This result may be interpreted as a mutual validation of our measures. If we prefer to look at the result as nontautological, it is an open question whether the preference variable is the independent one or not. It seems reasonable to assume that influence goes in both directions.

From a class perspective it is interesting to note that the relationship is strongest in the highest and the lowest social-class categories. We can only guess what this means. It may be that in the lowest category political interest leads to preferences for politics on TV, because in this group there are fewer alternative sources. But then, what about the highest category? What kind of process is at work there? Perhaps this category uses the political content of all types of mass media.

Regardless of which interpretation we prefer, it is quite clear that we have clearly demonstrated two cases of interaction between social class and different aspects of media use. In order to understand such interactions fully, it will be necessary to turn to socialization theory. Social class as such is a rather abstract phenomenon. In actual social life it manifests itself in a number of concrete social agents. Especially important are the agents of socialization. The family (often representing social class) is one such agent; the mass media (often representing general and/or class-specific culture), another. Agents of socialization seldom operate one by one. The family and the mass media often interact in a complex way. In the following chapter we will have rich opportunities to study the complex pattern of interaction between various agents of socialization.

4.8. SOCIAL CLASS, MEDIA USE, AND MEDIA EFFECTS—A CONCLUDING DISCUSSION

In this chapter we have shown that social class is an important antecedent to mass media use among adolescents. This is hardly surprising. On the basis of our theoretical arguments, supported by empirical data, we conclude, however, that the nature of the relationship is much more complicated than what is commonly assumed. One complication is the relation between class and status, in our studies often operationalized as education.

We have often used the education variable for comparisons with social class. More than once, education has come out as the better background variable. After all, media use is a cultural activity, part of intellectual and cultural capital. But mass media use is also something other than an outflow of education or the exploitation of cultural capital. For instance, it may be an expression of class identity.

The notion of social class is often used rather unreflectively. In this chapter we have differentiated between three different types of dimensions of class of origin, class of context, and class of destination. The three types of social class must be supposed to be related, and yet often to have a quite different impact on the lives and media use of adolescents. Our results show that media use does indeed vary in meaningful ways along all three dimensions of social class. Hopefully, future research on the relationship between social class, media use, and media effects will be able to draw on this insight.

One area in which it seems especially important to heed the three dimensions is the old question of whether the influence of social class on media habits, and so forth, increases or decreases as children and adolescents grow into adults. We hypothesized that the influence of class of origin would decrease with time, while that of class of destination would increase, and that of class of context remain more or less constant. Since we measured class of context only among ninth graders of the third wave, we could not test our hypothesis in this case. With class of destination we found an interaction effect with class of origin: The expected increasing influence was only found for youngsters having a middle-class origin. The influence of class of origin, on the other hand, showed the expected decrease over time across the board (as did background status measured as parental education).

Another aspect worthy of much more detailed attention in future research is the notion of curvilinearity in the relationship between class and media use. Roe (1983a) has pointed out that it may be questioned whether we can talk about a homogeneous working class. Our results support his critique and call for a finer gradation of our measures of class. In addition, the interaction of gender and class should be given increased attention. Class and status influence seems to be stronger for girls than for boys.

Combining our theoretical distinctions between different dimensions of class with the methodological demand for heeding possible curvilinearity in effects on television habits, we found curvilinearity for all three types of social class. When combined, the different dimensions of class interacted in creating a "television heartland" among the middle strata of society.

This chapter has also dealt with the relationships between class and three concepts that are of special interest to the uses and gratifications approach. Motives, selectivity, and dependency are all building-blocks in uses and gratifications models. In such models we may chronologically order them like this: Media use is regarded as, at least partly, motivated; the motives stemming from the needs and resources of the individual, which, in their turn, are to a large extent determined by class. These motives may then guide the selectivity of media use, influencing content preferences. (Selectivity is a very important aspect of the notion of activity in gratifications research.) One result of media use, selective or nonselective, may be dependency regarded as a case of mild addiction. (Dependency, it will be remembered, may also be conceptualized as a structurally determined lack of functional alternatives.)

Our inquiry into the motives part showed a generally stronger motivation for watching television on the part of working-class and lower education categories. Taking a closer look at the habit motive we found a tendency among the lower education categories to have an increasingly stronger relationship between the habit motive and amount of television viewed. This points to a process in which the low-educated heavy user becomes more and more habituated. For the higher-educated adolescents it is the other way around, especially for girls.

In the case of what we call preselectivity (whether one decides in advance what television program to watch) we found a parallel to what was just described. Among middle-class adolescents selectivity increases with age, among working-class adolescents it decreases. From such data it is easy to form the impression that young people from a lower educational and lower social-class background tend gradually to become more habituated and less selective. As an hypothesis, it seems to be well worth further testing.

When it comes to dependency, the differences between the middle and working classes are small, although the dependency score is higher for working-class than for middle-class children. We were able to measure dependency only with a one-item measure and we feel that there is a need to come to grips with this important variable using a better indes. (This has been attempted recently within the media panel group; cf Höjerback, 1985.)

In general the background factors of class and status tend to have very different impacts in different situations. In addition, the development over time of their influence is highly differentiated. Thus, our main conclusion is that the relationship between class and adolescent mass media use is a much more complex phenomenon than is generally assumed. The scope for future research is indeed great.

One way to understand better the relationships between class and media use is to turn to the processes mediating the influence of the former on the latter. That is the task to be undertaking in the following chapter, in which we will apply a socialization perspective.

5

Media Use and Socialization

The dual theme of this chapter relates two important and prolific traditions of research, both of which are characterized more by their wealth of perspectives and approaches than by their conceptual clarity or unambiguity of results. The two traditions have much to gain by a confluence. Socialization research has a rich theoretical heritage to offer mass communications research, and an ever increasing part of socialization is being carried out by the mass media. The task of relating the two must be repeatedly attempted. This chapter tries to undertake that task.

In the first section of the chapter socialization theory is discussed and related to mass communications research in general and the Media Panel Program in particular. In sec. 5.2. we deal with the general phenomenon of interaction, so basic to all socialization. Sec. 5.3. presents three different processes of socialization: modeling, reinforcement, and interaction. The complex relations between the four most important agents of socialization in the lives of children and adolescents—family, peers, school, and the mass media—are discussed in sec. 5.4. Sec. 5.5 deals with the content of socialization, more specifically with what are usually called media effects. In the last section of the chapter, we make an attempt to summarize and relate to each other the various lines of argumentation pursued in the chapter.

5.1. SOCIALIZATION: NOTES TOWARD A FRAMEWORK[1]

5.1.1. An Embarrassment of Riches

The theme of socialization is as old as humanity itself, for it covers the twin stories of becoming human, and of molding "newborn barbarians" into civilized people. The term "socialization" gained currency in the 1930s and obtained its hallmark in the 1950s. It is widely used in anthropology and in general social psychology. It is also applied in

---

[1] This section draws heavily on Rosengren (1985b).

subspecialties, such as political sociology and economic psychology, and it is becoming increasingly important in mass communications research. A rapidly growing number of overviews, handbooks, and bibliographies bear witness to the topicality of the term and the theme in various contexts (Albrecht, Thomas, & Chadwick, 1980; Brim, 1968; Brown, 1965; Burton, 1968; Child, 1969; Goslin, 1968; Greenstein, 1968; Halloran, 1976; Whiting, 1968; Zigler & Seitz, 1978).

The burgeoning literature on socialization is replete with terms, definitions, and distinctions, creating a true embarrassment of riches to the scholar trying to obtain a conceptually coherent picture of the area. In an attempt to bring some order into the potentially fruitful chaos, one may structure the distinctions into three main areas of problems: the content of socialization, the process of socialization, and the agents of socialization. The three following sections each deals with one of these areas.

5.1.2. The Content of Socialization: 3 dimensions

What is the content of socialization? What does society transfer through its various socializing agents such as family, peer and work groups, schools, and the mass media? What does the child acquire as it grows into a well-socialized adult?

A distinction often made is that between, on the one hand learning and teaching specific social roles and statuses, and on the other learning and teaching culture at large—beliefs, values, and evaluations pertaining not only to social roles and social structure, but to all other domains of the world as well. This distinction is sometimes referred to by means of the terms socialization and enculturation, respectively (Whiting 1968, p. 545). In enculturation, knowledge and norms primarily *about* the self, society, and the surrounding world are learned and taught. In socialization knowledge, norms and skills primarily *in* activities pertinent to various positions, roles, and statuses are learned and taught.

The distinction between enculturation and socialization is related to, but not at all identical with, that between primary and secondary socialization. Primary socialization as a rule refers to basic and general knowledge, norms, and skills learned and taught early in life, pertinent to basic positions, roles, and statuses in society and thus part of the culture more or less common to all members of society. Secondary socialization refers to specific knowledge, norms, and skills related to specific positions in the social structure (Berger & Luckman, 1967, pp. 129ff.).

A dimension common to both distinctions referred to above (encul-

turation/socialization; primary/secondary socialization) is generality/
specificity. Disregarding other differences, both enculturation and primary socialization are general, while both secondary socialization and
socialization (as opposed to enculturation) are specific.

The two partly overlapping distinctions are visualized in Figure 5.1.
It will be seen that there is one empty cell, and that the three empirically
meaningful cells could be "unfolded" onto a second-order dimension
of generality/specificity, with enculturation to the left, primary socialization in the middle, and secondary socialization to the right.

Quite another type of distinction concerns socialization within different areas or sectors of society: political socialization, economic socialization, and so forth. In the final analysis, such distinctions derive
from a small number of ultimate values furthered in different sectors
of society. These ultimate values may be ordered by means of two basic
dimensions: expressive vs. instrumental value orientation, normative vs.
cognitive value orientation. In combination, these two dimensions define
the four ultimate values of truth, utility, beauty, and righteousness/
holiness, on which are built the large institutions of society: economy,
polity, religion, and so forth. The institutions may be ordered in a
circumplex (Gutman, 1954; Shepard, 1978) defined by the two dimensions. This circumplex constitutes the "Great Wheel of Culture in

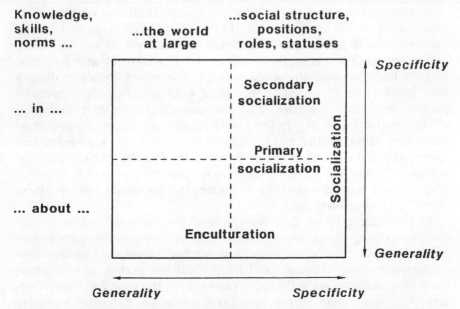

Figure 5.1. Two Overlapping Distinctions Referring to Content of Socialization

Society" presented in Figure 5.2. (For further discussion of the figure, see Rosengren, 1984.)

In principle, all types of content of socialization may be defined by means of the three dimensions visualized in the wheel of culture. In a given society, content of socialization may to advantage be characterized as more or less central/peripheral, more or less expressive/instrumental, more or less cognitive/normative. Enculturation and primary socialization take place primarily in the central regions of the wheel, secondary socialization primarily in the more peripheral regions. Subject specific socialization (political, economic socialization, etc.) takes place in the various sectors of the wheel, each of which is "loaded" to a varying degree on the two dimensions (expressive/instrumental, cognitive/normative) defining the circumplex and the four ultimate values. (Note here that distance from the center of the wheel is measured on a plane different from the two dimensions just mentioned.)

The comparative study of the content of socialization taking place in different societies (cf., e.g., Ellis et al., 1978; Whiting & Whiting, 1975) may be carried out in terms of comparisons between more or less different "wheels of culture". In the Media Panel Program we study only one society, that of Sweden (actually as represented in one large and one middle-sized city in southern Sweden). We can say nothing, therefore, about variations between national cultures, and only a little about variations within the national culture.

In terms of the wheel of culture the socialization and enculturation under study in the program is rather central: knowledge and norms "about," much more than knowledge, norms and skills "in"; and knowledge and norms not only about social structures and positions therein, but also about the world at large. The wheel of culture defines four broad types of socialization: moral (and/or religious), expressive (and/or aesthetic), cognitive, and instrumental (directly or indirectly related to practical work). In the Media Panel Program we are primarily concerned with cognitive and instrumental socialization: knowledge and norms about the world at large, particularly Swedish society and the adolescent's position therein. But we have also paid attention to moral and expressive socialization, for instance, the important role of music in the lives of adolescents.

In fact, our original data were spread over several sectors of the circumplex: art, the polity, economy, and so forth. Unfortunately, not all of them were as fit for analysis as we had hoped, and besides, our resources in time, personnel and money did not permit us to analyze but part of the data we collected. As is so often the case, our theoretical ambitions were more far-reaching than our actual empirical analyses. That is the fate of much theorizing. Nevertheless, our theoretical con-

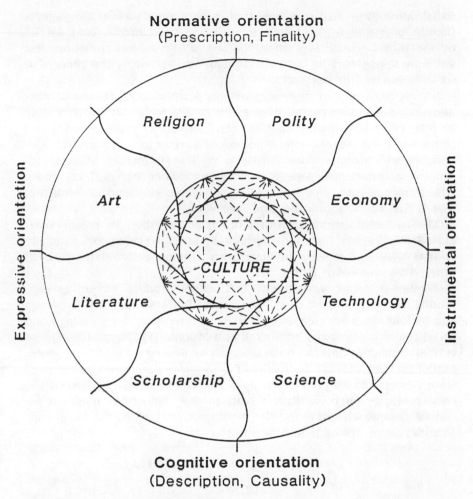

Figure 5.2. The Great Wheel of Culture in Society (From Rosengren, 1984)

ceptions may be used to illuminate our empirical efforts. In fact, that is what theorizing is for, and that goes also for the wheel of culture as a means of understanding the content of socialization.

5.1.3. The Socialization Process: A Typology

Two parties are involved in the socialization process: society and the individual. For each of the two parties an important distinction has often been made in socialization research.

The individual may be seen as a more or less passive object of socialization by society as represented by its various socialization agents (family, peer and work groups, schools, the mass media, etc.). Or he or she may be seen as a more or less active subject, more or less willingly taking part in, and affecting in various ways, the process of socialization and its outcomes.

Society may be seen from a consensus perspective or from a conflict perspective. The two perspectives are very different, and yet they may be blended so that society may be seen as basically conflict-ridden and at the same time as showing a facade of harmonious consensus. Both perspectives encompass descriptive as well as normative aspects. Descriptive and normative aspects tend to go together. By and large, those who think society is characterized by consensus also tend to think that that is the way it should be, and vice versa.

The two distinctions are often discussed together, in recent years most perceptibly and forcefully, perhaps, by McCron (1976). Yet, strangely enough they do not seem to have been systematically related to each other. This is done in Figure 5.3.

Combined in this way the two distinctions produce a typology containing four main approaches to socialization research. The typology and its four types are clear-cut parallels to a typology for sociology and social research developed by Burrell and Morgan (1979, pp. 12–29) and related to mass communications research by Rosengren (1985a). Indeed, two of the terms for the four cells of the typology are directly borrowed from Burrell and Morgan's typology. The close similarity between the two typologies offers validation both to the distinctions made in socialization research and to the two typologies. It also puts the discussions in socialization research into perspective.

INDIVIDUAL

	Subject	Object
Conflict	Radical humanism	Radical structuralism
Consensus	Interactionist social psychology	Mainstream sociology

SOCIETY

Figure 5.3.   Four Approaches to Socialization Research (cf. Burrell & Morgan, 1979)

Most socialization research to date has been carried out in the lower right-hand cell. That is, it has been explicitly or (more often, perhaps) implicitly based on a consensual view of society and a view of the socialized individual as a more or less passive object of societal (and, sometimes, biological) forces. The perspectives of the three other cells, however, have been with socialization research for a long time, not to say right from the start. During the last 20 years or so they have been gaining increased momentum. The relations between the four types of socialization research, therefore, must shortly be commented upon.

According to Burrell and Morgan (1979, p. 19), the demarcation lines between the four types of sociology defined by their typology represent qualitative differences, in principle insurmountable, between radically different research paradigms. Rosengren (1985a; cf. 1987) prefers to see the two dimensions as continua, and, consequently, the barriers between the four cells as not at all insurmountable (although, for psychological and political reasons not often transcended, perhaps). Presenting some support for his contention, he maintains that a cross-fertilization between the four traditions may prove extremely fruitful to mass communications research. It may well be that this holds true not only for mass communications research but also for socialization research. At least, that is the view predominant in the Media Panel Program.

The program is by definition eclectic, hopefully in the positive sense of the word. Its empirical data have been collected by means of measuring instruments borrowed from a wide array of theoretical perspectives. They have also been put to use within various theoretical perspectives—witness the six doctoral theses produced to date within the program (Flodin, 1986; Hedinsson, 1981; Johnsson–Smaragdi, 1983; Jönsson, 1985; Roe, 1983a; Sonesson, 1979).

Within the Media Panel Program, then, we maintain that there is an overall consensus between basically conflicting social classes in present-day Swedish society. We also maintain that in the socialization process the individual is both subject and object. While for analytical purposes it may be useful, even necessary, to cultivate one at a time of the four perspectives visualized in Figure 5.3, in reality there is both consensus and conflict in any society, and all individuals are both subjects and objects (Rosengren, 1985a; cf. Thunberg et al., 1982, p. 171).

This may sound like a collection of bland platitudes. However, the fruitfulness of our inclusiveness of perspectives will, to some extent, be demonstrated when we turn to a short discussion of the specific parts of mass communication research which are relevant to socialization research (sec. 5.1.5). In a conflict-based society mass media may be regarded as contributing to—among many other things—consensus (or at least, consent, which, of course, is something rather different; cf. Hall 1982, p. 85). In her relations to the mass media the individual stands out both as a passive object and as an active subject. In principle, this holds true for all relationships with the various socialization agents, although some of these may be more inviting than others with respect to mutual interaction.

5.1.4. Four Agents of Socialization

The process and content of socialization is decisively influenced by the agent of socialization at work. All human societies, including the most undifferentiated ones, have three main agents of socialization: family and/or kin groups, peer groups, and work groups. In more differentiated societies we find also socialization by means of priests (often organized in churches), agents of law (often organized in courts), and teachers (often organized in schools cooperating with churches and courts). In addition, industrial and postindustrial societies have a number of large organizations with more or less specialized activities (unions, institutionalized popular movements, etc.) which often act as socializing agents as well. Such societies have yet another important group of socializing agents: a highly developed mass media system.

In our society, then, we have at least eight large groups of socializing agents: family, peer groups, work groups, churches, law authorities, schools, popular organizations, and mass media. In the Media Panel Program, focusing on mass media use by children and adolescents, four of these are especially important: family, peer group, school, and the mass media.

The culture transferred and received in the socialization process of small groups such as the family or the peer group tends to be concrete, implicit and "lived", while in formal organizations such as the schools it tends to be more abstract, explicit and formalized (disregarding for the moment the "hidden curriculum"). The knowledge, norms, and skills mediated by the mass media cover the whole of this range. The mass media of modern society, therefore, are able to take over large parts of the socialization carried out both in informal groups and formal organizations. This is also what actually happens, probably to an increasing degree. It has often been observed that the mass media are taking over the functions formerly fulfilled by the family, the churches, and the schools (cf., for instance, Gerbner, 1984; Noble, 1975; Postman, 1979, 1982).

The role played by the various socializing agents varies not only between societies and over historical time, but also over the life-span of the individual (cf. chap. 3). The period of life studied in the Media Panel Program ranges from the age of 6 to 15; from nursery school to the end of the primary school. During this period the child grows into a sexually mature adolescent, gradually turning away from home and parents to peers for interaction and mutual socialization. In terms of the mass media, television use first reaches a peak and then an all-time low during this period, the medium of television being quickly replaced by the medium of music (cf. secs. 3.3.1 and 3.4.8).

This is a period of highly differentiated socialization. It may indeed be *the* period of differentiation. As a counterweight against the more or less authoritarian socialization of various adults and their formal organizations, the adolescent may mobilize the supposedly more democratic socialization of the peer group (Johnsson–Smaragdi, 1983, pp. 42ff.; Youniss, 1980). The peer groups may or may not develop subcultures of protest and conflict, growing into enclaves of more or less different life-styles (cf. sec. 4.4.3). The two dimensions of conflict and difference define a typology of adolescent peer groups, visualized in Figure 5.4. It is obvious that the character, origins and consequences of mass media use are very different in these three types of adolescent peer groups (cf. Roe 1983a).

The majority of adolescents is probably found among what has been labeled "Conventional Youth," characterized by basic consensus and conformity with dominant value orientations of the adult world, "mainstream society." Adolescent subcultures are found where on the basis of age differences groups of adolescents develop tastes, habits, value orientations, etc., markedly different from those of adult mainstream

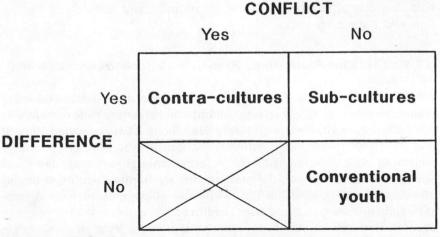

Figure 5.4.   Three Types of Adolescent Peer Groups (From Roe, 1983a)

society, without confronting in open conflict the adult world. Such subcultures may or may not develop into contracultures, in which the basic value orientations of the surrounding society are openly defied. Contracultures may be the last resorts of various types of dropouts, but they may also be built by highly successful individuals. In both cases they may be centers for, and sources of, innovation, sometimes heralding future societal change (cf. Merton's famous goals/means typology of deviance and innovation, and Harary's criticism of that typology; Harary, 1966; Merton, 1957). Typically, both subcultures and contracultures are numerically small. Few subcultures and contracultures are independent of the strong socializing agents. If nothing else, they depend on them as standards from which to deviate, as targets of protest and differentiation.

All through childhood and adolescence the individual is located in the center of an increasingly intricate and dynamic network of mutual relations with a host of socializing agents, in their turn interacting with one other and with society at large. Such networks have some general characteristics; typically, however, they vary considerably with age, gender, and social class. In adolescence, as in other periods of life, there are at least four great social worlds: the lives of male and female, the working class, and the middle class. In addition, there is also considerable variation within these social worlds.

The task of charting in detail all these variations would be truly herculean, and we shall not embark upon it. In this chapter our task is to concentrate on the mass media, particularly TV, as socializing agents interacting with other socializing agents, primarily the family, school, and peer group. That task is certainly difficult enough. Without half a century of international mass communications research, of course, it would have been impossible.

5.1.5. Mass Communications Research as Socialization Research

In general socialization research, the role of the mass media and mass communications is widely recognized but comparatively little researched. For instance, in Goslin's magnificent *Handbook of Socialization Theory and Research* (1969), mass communications research is given half a page (out of 1,200). In Albrecht et al.'s comprehensive textbook on *Social Psychology* (1980), the mass media are hardly mentioned in the 40-page chapter on socialization, while the 40-page chapter on aggression and violence contains 7 pages dealing with violence on TV, possibly because that subject has been conceived of more as a case of enculturation than socialization (cf. Figure 5.1).

Mass communications research has probably been more open to socialization research than the other way around—witness Halloran's extensive bibliography in *Mass Media and Socialization* (1976). After all, it is natural that an interdisciplinary field such as mass communications should draw on one of its mother disciplines. Yet it is only too obvious that much mass communications research has been carried out without heeding theories and empirical data collected and developed within socialization research. The need for a confluence, then, is strong. Very probably, both parties would profit from it.

The part of mass communications research most relevant to socialization research is that dealing with individual use of the mass media, its origins, and effects. The two main research traditions found in this research—effects research and uses and gratifications research—neatly correspond to the distinction between the individual as an object and as a subject (visualized in Figure 5.3). In terms of Burrell and Morgan's (1979) typology for sociology both traditions would be located predominantly in the lower right-hand cell corner. Nevertheless, it is obvious that uses and gratifications research grants more leeway than does effects research to the more or less consciously willed activities constituting individual mass media use (Palmgreen et al., 1985; Rosengren 1985a, 1985b). The confluence between the two traditions heralded by Windahl (1981) and many others will make possible the two-way traffic between the two perspectives long recognized as necessary in socialization research (Goslin, 1969, p. 15).

The other distinction of Figure 5.3—between a consensus perspective and a conflict perspective of society—has probably been more to the fore in mass communications research than in socialization research. To scholars of mass communications the time-honored question of how order can be maintained in a society of conflicting classes and (inherently) aggressive individuals has an obvious answer, complementary to the ones given by philosophers and social scientists over the centuries (Plato, Hobbes, Marx, Weber, and others). In societies such as ours, the maintenance of order, in spite of class conflicts and individual aggressiveness, to a large extent is made possible by mass communications. This insight is widely diffused among communications scholars of otherwise differing schools and loyalties (cf. Hall, 1982; McQuail, 1983). It has been perhaps most forcefully and convincingly argued by George Gerbner.

In a 15-year-long series of investigations, Gerbner and his associates have, by means of cultural indicators, set out to study the cognitions and evaluations of and about society and the rest of the world presented in the media, as well as the images of society and the rest of the world cultivated in the minds of the individuals consuming that media content

(Gerbner, 1969; Gerbner, 1984; Gerbner et al. 1980; cf. Hawkins & Pingree, 1984).

Gerbner's ideas have been widely discussed and sometimes acrimoniously criticized (cf. Gerbner et al., 1981; Hirsch, 1980). They have also been emulated and replicated in a number of studies carried out in several countries including Sweden (cf. Melischek et al., 1984). It is fairly obvious that they are highly relevant to socialization research.

More precisely, what Gerbner and his followers advocate is a turning away from the study of very specific, short-term, intended effects of specific mass media messages, to the study of more general, diffuse, long-term, often quite unintended, but nevertheless "functional" effects of the overall mass media content so interminably and monotonously disseminated among the population. In terms of Figure 5.3, Gerbner is one of the leading figures in the lower right-hand corner, the "dominating paradigm." But he has been strongly influenced by the ways of thinking of the three "dissident paradigms." In terms of Figure 5.1, Gerbner is more interested in enculturation than in specific secondary socialization. In terms of Figure 5.2, he is interested in the hub of the wheel of culture in society rather than the periphery. In this perspective, the very terms in which Gerbner has chosen to characterize his approach stand out as appropriate indeed: "cultural indicators" for measuring mass media content, and "cultivation research" for the study of the processes of mainstreaming, whereby potential conflicts between social classes may be dampened if not totally extinguished. In these terms, cultivation is a special case of enculturation: the enculturation exercised by the mass media, particularly by television (cf. Gross & Morgan, 1983).

In terms of mass communications research, cultivation research is primarily a special case of effects research. To the extent, however, that it is being realized that the media use by means of which cultivation comes about is subject to a host of initiating and modifying sociological and sociopsychological circumstances, it becomes a very fine example of uses and effects research (cf. sec. 1.3.2). This is increasingly becoming the case. A recent example is found in Rothschild (1984), who maintains that cultivation processes must be studied in relation to the groups forming the close surrounding of the individual whose pictures of society and the rest of the world are being mainstreamed by TV and other mass media. This development also recognizes the fact that the mass media represent only one of several main agents of socialization, other important ones being the family, the peer group, and the school.

In mass communications research the notions of "family communication patterns," originally developed by the group around Chaffee and McLeod in Madison, Wisc., have gained some currency during the last decade (Chaffee et al., 1971, 1973; Jarlbro, 1986; McLeod & Brown,

1976; cf. Tims & Masland, 1985). Communication in the family, it is maintained, may to advantage be characterized along two dimensions called socio-orientation and concept-orientation. If socio-oriented, one tends to stress the importance of smooth social relations with other people. If concept-oriented, one tends to stress the importance of ideas and concepts. Empirically the two dimensions are almost orthogonal and when dichotomized and cross-tabulated they define a typology offering four types of family communication patterns (cf. Figure 5.5).

The typology has a certain amount of face validity, and similar typologies have been presented more than once. (A striking similarity may be found, for instance, between the Chaffee typology and the "Circumplex Model of Marital and Family Systems" presented by David H. Olson and his associates (Barnes & Olson, 1985; Olson et al., 1979).) The four types of the Chaffee typology are related to social class. Indeed, it has been maintained that they can be regarded as a manifestation of social class in family life (Hedinsson, 1981, pp. 66, 194).

It has been shown that the use of mass media, as well as the effects of such use, are dependent on the family communication pattern prevailing in the family of the user (McLeod & Brown 1976; for Swedish examples, see Hedinsson, 1981; Jarlbro, 1986). In terms of socialization research: there is interaction between the mass media and other socializing agents. Such interactions have also been demonstrated with respect to more specific attitudes toward TV prevailing in the family

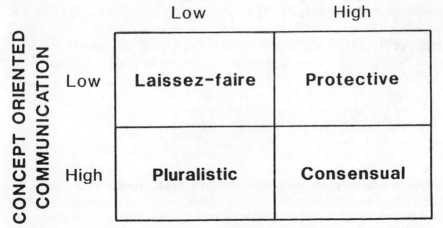

Figure 5.5. A Typology of Family Communication Patterns (From Chaffee et al., 1971, 1973)

(Brown & Linné, 1976; for a Swedish example, see Sonesson, 1979; cf. also sec. 5.3.3).

Both the general family patterns of communication and the more specific TV attitudes prevailing in the family may be supposed to relate to the even more specific motives for TV use embraced by the individual and influencing his or her choice of programs, and so forth (Greenberg, 1974; cf. sec. 3.3.5). Such motives may be regarded as products of a complex interplay between a number of socializing agents; family, peer group, school, and the mass media themselves.

Next to their family and besides the mass media, the most important socializing agents for children and adolescents are the peer group and the school. The interplay of mass media use with formal schooling has been creatively discussed by Murdock and Phelps (1973). Within the Media Panel Program, Roe (1983a), influenced by the French sociologists of culture and education Bourdieu and Passeron (1979), has studied the relations between the school and the mass media in the lives of adolescents, adding also the peer group as an important socializing agent, and differentiating with some success between the two agents of TV and popular music.

In the interplay between various socializing agencies the mass media, as a rule, have been regarded as a disturbing factor, imposing inappropriately on the more important and legitimate socialization processes taking place, say, in the family or at school. Excessive mass media use has been seen as eroding morals, debasing beauty, destroying knowledge and preventing much useful work (to express this Lutheran criticism in terms of the four ultimate values of the Great Wheel of Culture). But mass media use is not only an independent variable, as in the tradition of effects research. The social origins of mass media use have been continually stressed in uses and gratifications research (cf. Palmgreen et al., 1985), and one such origin may well be a shortcoming or even failure of another socializing agent—the school, for instance, or the family. Within the Media Panel Program, this latter standpoint has been forcefully argued by Roe (1983a). There is interaction not only between the individual and his socializing agents but also between the socializing agents (cf. also Jönsson, 1985). It is within the parameters of such double interactions that we are all continuously being socialized.

5.1.6. A Chapter on Socialization and Mass Media Use

The Media Panel Program has three main characteristics. It is built on a combination of a cross-sectional and a longitudinal design. Its two main panels cover the period from 6 to 16. Substantively, its variables represent a number of different subjects and problems. These three main characteristics make it possible to discuss and illuminate with empirical data the three main aspects of socialization mentioned in sec. 5.1.1: the process, the agents, and the content of socialization.

In the rest of this chapter each of these aspects will be treated at some length: socialization processes in sec. 5.3., socialization agents in sec. 5.4., and content of socialization in sec. 5.5.

Before dealing with the three aspects, however, some attention must be given to that basic medium of socialization: social interaction. All socialization presupposes social interaction of one type or another. In childhood and adolescence the pattern of social interaction is subject to drastic changes. This must have some effect on the process and content of socialization, as well as on the role of the agents of that process. The next section of this chapter, therefore, is dedicated to social interaction.

5.2. SOCIAL INTERACTION[2]

5.2.1. Introduction

In an oft-quoted chapter in Ray Brown's anthology, *Children and Television*, McLeod and Brown distinguish between three types of learning processes: modeling, reinforcement, and social interaction (McLeod & Brown, 1976, p. 209; cf. McLeod & O'Keefe, 1972). Effects of mass media use supposedly come about by means of all the three processes. The role of the three processes in shaping mass media use as such has been discussed much less.

Among the processes leading up to mass media use, reinforcement processes are either almost nonexistent (parents making few attempts directly to control their children's media habits) or very subtle and difficult to study directly in quantitative terms (cf., however, sec. 5.3.3). Modeling does occur in connection with mass media use (Johnsson–Smaragdi, 1983) and will be treated in sec. 5.3.2. What about the learning mechanism of social interaction as leading up to mass media use? That problem will be discussed in this section.

5.2.2. Adolescents' Orientation Toward Their Parties of Interaction

By definition, any act of social interaction is patterned by the mutual expectations about that interaction held by the parties of the interaction.

---

[2] This section draws heavily on ch. 8 of Johnsson–Smaragdi (1983).

Such more or less general expectations, in their turn, are colored by sets of attitudes, attitude clusters, and broad value orientations toward potential parties of interaction. In adolescence important types of such attitudes and orientations are those held toward the main agents of socialization of the period: family, peer group, school, and mass media. In sec. 3.1.2 we discussed in a general way how such attitudes and orientation change during the process of development. In this section, some empirical data on some such attitudes and orientations will be presented. (Just as in previous chapters, cross-sectional and panel data from the Malmoe and the Vaxjoe panels will be used alternately, as space and the organization of our data invite and admit.)

In the third wave of the Vaxjoe panel, the respondents were asked to name three activities they liked very much to do when out of school. Figure 5.6 presents the means of four such activities in grades 5, 7, and 9. "To be with one's friends" is the type of social interaction most preferred by our adolescents. "To be with one's family" is much less liked, and the liking for this type of interaction decreases monotonously as the adolescents grow older. Included in the figure is also the ado-

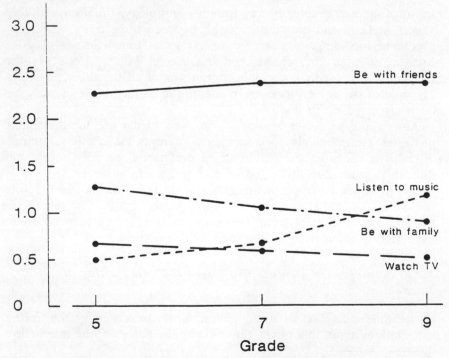

Figure 5.6. Preference for Different Types of Social Interaction and Other Activities. Vaxjoe Study, Third Wave (From Flodin et al., 1982)

lescents' liking for two types of media activities, music, and TV. The curves show how the liking for TV (a family-oriented medium) decreases, while that for music (a peer-oriented medium) increases. Quite naturally, then, and quite in line with other media panel results, we see that as the adolescents grow older they orient themselves away from their family of origin toward their peers, at the same time moving their preferences away from family-oriented media to peer-oriented media (cf. Flodin et al., 1982; Johnsson–Smaragdi, 1983; Roe 1983a; sec. 3.1).

The reorientation of attitudes toward parents and peers was studied in some detail by means of the well-known scale developed by Bowerman and Kinch (1959) and also used, for instance, by Stone et al. (1979). Ulla Johnsson–Smaragdi translated and adapted to Swedish conditions the scale which consists of items such as:

- Who do you think usually understands you best—your parents or your friends?
- Who do you think knows best about what is right or wrong—your parents or your friends?

Taking care of neutral and nonrelevant responses by means of the so called coefficient of imbalance technique, the scale was transformed to range from −1 (total parent orientation) to +1 (total peer orientation; cf. Roe, 1983a, pp. 214 ff.).

The reorientation of attitudes toward parents and peers observed in Figure 5.6 is clearly visible also in Figure 5.7. Regardless of gender and class, adolescents increasingly orient themselves toward the peer group. (Note, however, that, at least within the age interval under study, the peer group does not become as important as the parents were among the young children of grade 5.)

In Figure 5.8 we see that the changes in the preferences and orientation of Figures 5.6 and 5.7 manifest themselves in actual behavior. The adolescents' activities with their parents (measured by a multiplicative index of number and frequency of 14 activities) decrease with increasing age. A similar index of activities with peers, however, does not show any substantial increase with increasing age. As a matter of fact, the mean of the index diminishes with age. A possible explanation for this finding is that we were not able to find valid indicators, and/ or the right blend, of these activities (Johnsson–Smaragdi, 1983, pp. 176ff.). Another possible explanation may be long-term developments in adolescents' relations to peers and parents. The existence of such developments (over decades) has recently been demonstrated by Sebald (1986). It is also visible in Figure 5.8 (data for wave 3 higher than for

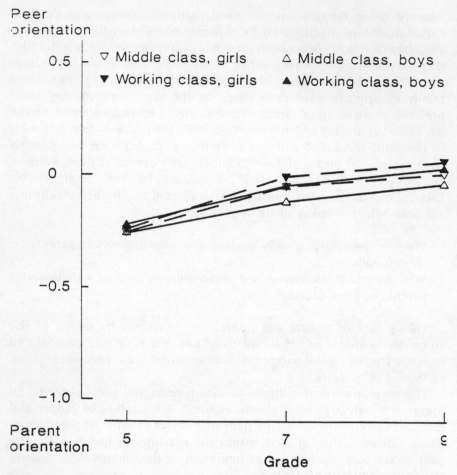

Figure 5.7.   Degree of Parent/Peer Orientation by Age, Gender, and Social Class. Vaxjoe Main Panel.

waves 1 and 2, which makes the panel's development slightly curvi-linear).

On the individual level, the two types of activities (with parents and peers) show strong correlations for the fifth graders (.60), and moderate correlations for the seventh and ninth graders (.38 and .29, respectively). In fact, the parent interaction of the fifth graders positively affects their peer interaction as they move into grades 7 and 9 (.29 and .25, respectively), while there is no indication of a reverse flow of influence (Johnsson–Smaragdi, 1983, p. 179).

Correlations such as these demonstrate that the two socialization agents of family and peer group interact to cultivate a social talent

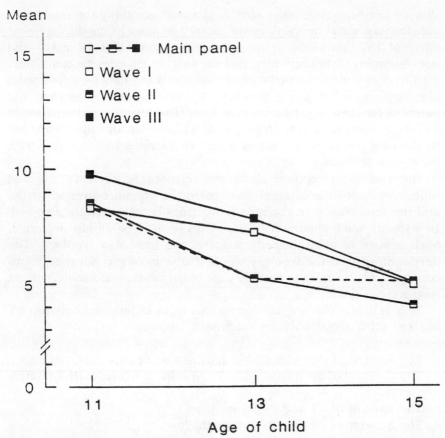

Figure 5.8.   Adolescents' Activities With Parents By Age. Vaxjoe Study, Three Cross-sections and Main Panel (From Johnsson-Smaragdi, 1983)

among adolescents. The correlations also show that some adolescents have and/or obtain less of this talent than do others. What are the implications of such interactions between socializing agents for the use of TV? How does TV use affect such interaction? These questions will be discussed in the next subsection.

5.2.3. TV Use and Social Interaction

Different social activities—such as TV use and face-to-face interaction—may be empirically independent, or (positively or negatively) correlated with each other. Functionally, they may be seen as independent, or as supplements, complements, or substitutes. It has often been maintained that TV competes with other activities, thus diminishing the time available for, say, social interaction with peers and parents: the displacement effect of TV. Conversely, it has also been argued that TV may—and does—reinforce other activities, that the various activities "accumulate". Finally, it has also been maintained that media use may be a functional alternative to other activities when, for one reason or another, the potential for these other activities is low. (The functional alternative of TV use is then sometimes regarded as valuable in the short run, but in the long run possibly "narcotizing," cf. Lazarsfeld & Merton, 1957; Rosengren & Windahl, 1972.)

The various conceptions about the relations between TV use and other social activities brought forward in the literature overlap partly, and the terminology in the area is far from being generally accepted. In addition, some important relationships seem to be all but neglected. Such a state of affairs usually suggests the lack of a typology. The development of such a typology would enable us to sort out the various concepts and also point to possible gaps in the conceptualizations current in the area.

Four variables characterize the various types of relations between TV use and other social activities referred to above:

- The valence of the relationship (positive or negative correlations);
- The direction of the relationship (TV or other activities main causative agent);
- The amount of TV use (high, low);
- The amount of other activities (high, low).

When combined, the four variables would yield 16 different types, but since the valence of the relationship is related to the various combinations of low and high TV use and other activities, the outcome is a typology with eight types, out of which at least two coincide. The four-dimensional typology is visualized in Figure 5.9. In the typology, the inner, dashed square represents four types of relations in which TV is the main causative agents. The outer triangles represent four types in which the other activities are seen as the main causative agents. (For the moment, we disregard the formidable problems of empirically ascertaining the direction of the relationships.) The valence of the relationship is given for the two triangles of each of the four squares.

As is so often the case, an explicit typology helps to clarify the argumentation. Before starting to use the typology, however, it should be underlined that we are dealing with a typology of ideal types: theoretical constructs which will seldom appear in pure form in empirical reality. Nevertheless, the ideal types will hopefully help us to think more clearly about empirical reality, always fuzzy and muddled.

Furthermore, it should also be underlined that we are dealing with a typology of relationships between different activities as such. Only the activities as such, and their relationships, are relevant, not their content and its possible effects on attitudes, beliefs, and so forth. In the terms suggested by Windahl (1981) it is a typology of *consequences* of media use as such (and of other activities as such). It is not a typology of the *effects* of the media content consumed (or about effects of other activities' content). Effects of media content consumed will be discussed in sec. 5.5.

The terms of the typology have been borrowed from the literature (as far as it takes us). As a consequence, the connotations of some terms reflect the widespread opinion that, as a rule at least, other activities are to be preferred to TV use. As a matter of fact, some terms specifically invented for the typology have been colored by the same assumption. That is only an assumption, however, and it should not be taken for granted. Media use may not always be the best among all conceivable activities, but in many cases it may be the best activity available. In some cases it may even be clearly preferable to some functional alternatives.

Finally, it should be noted that the typology visualizes the possibility that media use as such may have both negative and positive consequences. Regardless of how we evaluate media use as such, it may be either activating or pacifying—both of which consequences may be seen as either positive or negative.

After these preliminaries, let us turn to a more detailed discussion of the typology.

The four triangles of the typology running from the upper left corner to its lower right corner represent four different types of cumulativity (triangles 1, 5, 8, 4). In these types TV use and other activities are positively related, reinforcing each other. The four triangles running from the upper right corner of the typology to its lower left (triangles 2, 6, 7, 3) represent four different types of competition between TV use and other activities. In these types TV use and other activities are negatively related.

In terms of the two main traditions of mass communications research on the relations between the individual and the mass media—effects research and uses and gratifications research—the four inner triangles represent aspects of effects research (focused on consequences); the four outer ones, aspects of uses and gratifications research. Perhaps the fact that the typology covers both these traditions is a reason why the various types of the typology have not earlier been systematically related

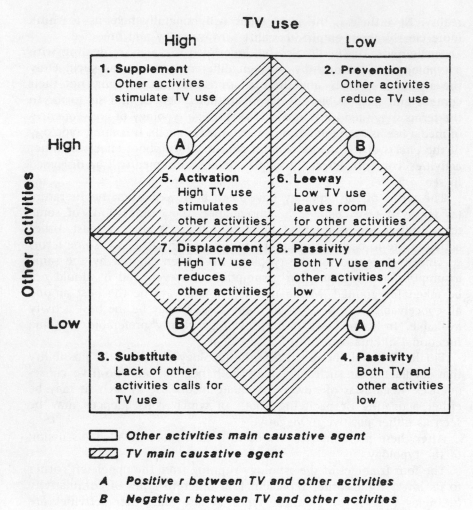

Figure 5.9.   A Typology of Relations Between TV Use and Other Activities

to one other. In any case, the Media Panel Program, merging the two traditions, needs the typology, for we must relate to one another some of the types defined by it.

Among the seven or eight types of our typology, type 7, Displacement, has, perhaps, been most often discussed. It represents the case when moderate or heavy TV use encroaches upon other activities. In a number of countries, studies of the introductory phase of television in particular have provided empirical evidence for it, for instance, England (Himmelweit et al., 1958), the United States (Schramm et al., 1961), Japan (Furu, 1971), Norway (Werner, 1971, 1972, 1982, 1986), Scotland

(Brown et al., 1974), Australia (Murray & Kippax, 1978), The Faroes (Forchammer, 1983), Canada (Williams, 1986). Studies of this type were reviewed by Cramond (1976) and Murray and Kippax (1981). A main finding seems to be that there are some displacement effects, in the introductory phase, but that they are by no means as strong and ubiquitous as is often imagined. [Note that the term "displacement effect" as a rule refers not to "effects" but to "consequences" (cf. above).]

The precise character of the displacement effects varies from country to country and from time to time as well as—one is tempted to add— from researcher to researcher. Nevertheless some general traits may be observed. In an introductory phase, displacement effects (i.e., consequences) of TV use on other activities seem to manifest themselves primarily in changes in the use of functionally related media (radio and cinema), and in a reduction of primarily unorganized leisure activities such as spontaneous play, conversations, hanging around, doing nothing, sleep, and so forth (cf., however, below).

Displacement effects after the introductory phase—that is, consequences of differential amount of TV viewing in a "TV society"—have been more difficult to demonstrate. Two main approaches have been used: studies of reactions to media strikes (Berelson, 1949; Cohen, 1981; de Bock, 1980; Kimball, 1959; Windahl et al., 1986), and various types of correlational studies (few of them longitudinal). The results have not been conclusive, but it seems safe to infer that not much support has been obtained for a theory of strong displacement effects. "Generally there was little support in our data for a theory that suggests that television viewing simply displaces other activities" (Medrich et al., 1982, p. 277).

For specific media activities, however, negative correlations have been found. For instance, Heyns (1976) reports a negative relationship between reading and watching television for schoolchildren. A representative sample of American grown-ups, on the other hand, showed positive correlations between various types of mass media use including TV viewing (Hornik & Schlinger, 1981; cf. Frank & Greenberg, 1980). In sec. 4.4.5 we saw that negative correlations between mass media activities were rare among our adolescents. We also saw that the degree of structuring among mass media habits varies considerably between various social subgroupings.

Cramond (1976, p. 267) equals "medium effects" with "displacement effects" and contrasts them to "content effects". A glance at the typology of Figure 5.9, however, tells us that there are at least three other "medium effects": Passivity, Leeway, and Activation. (Note that all these medium effects correspond to "consequences" in Windahl's [1981] terminology.)

"Activation" (type 5) is a consequence of TV use, a medium effect directly opposite to Displacement (type 7). It represents the case where moderate or high TV use leads up to other activities. While this type of relationship is rarely met in the general debate, some researchers do mention it as a possibility. "A fair amount of television viewing and participation in organized activities may not be incompatible" (Medrich et al., 1982, p. 220). It is a far cry, however, from the compatibility of TV use and other activities to establishing the covariation, not to mention the causal direction of the relationship (cf. Noble, 1975, p. 143). Therefore, cells 5 (Activation) and 1 (Supplement) must often be difficult to separate from each other in empirical research. Both of them manifest themselves in positive correlations between TV use and other activities, and in both cases TV use as well as other activities are high. It takes a panel design and advanced multivariate statistical analysis to differentiate between the two—a rather rare combination.

A very specific case of activation discussed at some length in the literature and given much attention in the general debate, is aggressiveness and aggression supposedly caused by excessive media use. Such aggressiveness should probably be seen more as an effect of media content consumed than as a consequence of media use as such. We shall return to that problem in sec. 5.5.

A milder form of activation sometimes taken up in the literature is discussions triggered by media use. Very often, however, the demonstration of this "coin of exchange function" or "basis for social interaction function" (McQuail et al., 1972) rests on cross-sectional correlations only, and could therefore equally well be interpreted as cases of the Supplement type (unless other circumstances forbid such an interpretation). In the Supplement type of relationship other activities lead up to TV use. Probably much family use of TV is of the Supplement type, although it tends to overlap with the Activation type. An additional problem in this connection is that consequences of medium use and effects of the content consumed are especially difficult to keep apart here. Furthermore, TV use itself is an activity, and it is pursued in parallel with a number of other activities (Levy & Windahl, 1985).

In principle we meet with much the same problem, should we want to distinguish empirically between cells 7 (Displacement) and 3 (Substitute). This time, however, both types manifest themselves in negative correlations (the causal directions of which are opposite). The substitute type of relationship may be expected to turn up in cases of so called media dependency (lack of other resources creates dependence on the mass media; cf. secs. 3.3.4 and 4.5.5). TV as substitute has been allegedly demonstrated over and over again (Bailyn, 1959; Himmelweit et al., 1958; Maccoby, 1954; Riley & Riley, 1951; Rosengren & Windahl, 1972, 1977) sometimes without any attempt to distinguish it from the Displacement type of relationships which theoretically is very different.

The same problem is met with also when trying to distinguish between the two types we call Prevention and Leeway (cells 2 and 6, respectively). Again we have two cases of negative correlations, but this time TV is low instead of high (in contrast to Displacement and Substitute). Neither of these two types has been very much discussed, probably because both represent a "good" combination (TV low, other activities high).

Low use of TV is characteristic also of the types covered by cells 4 and 8. Since in both cases other activities are also low, the theoretical distinction between TV or other activities as main causative agent breaks down and both types are referred to by the term Passivity. These types probably cover a rather small group of individuals. They contain the poor in spirit and acts, probably more or less identical with the "chronic know-nothings" of information campaigns as classically portrayed by Hyman and Sheatsley (1947).

Trying now to sum up the research being done on the seven or eight types of relations visualized in our typology, we find that the graces have been rather unevenly distributed. Displacement and substitute have received most attention, the former within the effects tradition, the latter primarily within uses and gratifications research. Both displacement and substitute are based on negative correlations between TV use and other activities. If, for the moment, we exclude aggressiveness (presumably caused more by media content consumed than by media use as such) the corresponding twin pair of activation and supplement (based on positive correlations) have been given much less attention. Probably these types have been less interesting to researchers because of the widespread ameliorative attitudes prevalent in the research community. The increasing interest in prosocial effects of TV have centered mainly on effects of content consumed rather than on consequences of TV use as such, and the same thing could be said, *mutatis mutandis,* about aggressiveness as an effect of TV.

Drawing on Ray Brown's theory of functional reorganization (which we used as one of the organizing devices of our developmental chapter) Brown et al. (1974) maintains that the hypothesis of displacement of functionally similar activities does not contain the whole truth. Looking beneath the surface of things, they maintain, one may find drastic functional reorganizations behind seemingly small changes with respect to time use. In their study of the introduction of television into three Canadian communities, Williams (1986, p. 186) tend to agree with

Brown et al. (1974), using also corroborating results from Murray and Kippax (1978).

The difference between the two hypotheses probably has to do with the distinctions between different aspects of media use discussed in sec. 2.2. In terms of amount of consumption, the hypothesis of functional similarity may well be applicable, while in terms of content preferences and functions of the content consumed, the hypothesis of functional reorganization may be equally applicable. The two hypotheses, then, refer to consequences vs. effects as distinguished between by Windahl (1981). In terms of consequences, the hypothesis about displacement along the lines of functional similarity may well be valid, while in terms of effects, the hypothesis of functional reorganization may be more applicable.

Prevention, leeway, and passivity have been given very little attention indeed by mass communication research, perhaps because they build on low TV use. Nevertheless they deserve some interest, not least within the context of adolescent media use. The reorganization of media use which takes place during adolescence could to advantage be interpreted in terms of prevention and leeway. Passivity, finally, is what is often feared as an outcome of TV use. The admittedly rather theoretical possibility that it could arise as a consequence of low TV use has not been given much thought.

After this taxonomic overview, let us turn back to some empirical data from the Media Panel Program. What have our own data to say about the relationships between TV use and other social activities?

In preschool the Malmoe children were asked whether or not they had a best friend (Sonesson, 1979, pp. 165ff.). A large majority had a best friend, but 12% replied "no." These children may be said to be interactionally low, especially when it comes to supposedly important close relationships. In terms of our typology, the media use of inter-actionally deprived children may be regarded in the light of either substitute, displacement or passivity, while those normal or high on interaction may be discussed in terms of supplement/activation or lee-way/prevention. What do our empirical data tell us in this respect?

Table 5.1 (adapted from Sonesson, 1979) clearly shows that we have to think in terms of passivity and supplement/activation rather than in terms of substitute/displacement or leeway/prevention. More than children having no best friend, those having such a friend tend to

- Prefer TV as favorite pastime,
- Have knowledge of adults' programs in general,
- Recognize Kojak,
- Have had a frightening TV experience,
- Have a positive TV situation.

That is, contrary to much earlier research, our findings indicate that socially somewhat passive children do not use TV more than do socially active ones. On the contrary, those socially active are also more involved with TV. They are more familiar with TV and have a socially better TV situation (do not watch alone to the same extent, etc.), but they have also been more often frightened by TV, probably when viewing programs for adults—Kojak, for instance. In short, for better and for worse, their experiences are richer, both socially and TV-wise, than are those of children without a best friend.

Since we are here working with cross-sectional data we cannot differentiate between the activation and supplementation types of relationship. That is, we do not know whether social activities stimulate TV use or whether high TV use stimulates social activities. What we do know is that among our preschool children we have found no support for the displacement or substitute theories so often aired in earlier research and in the general debate. What do our Vaxjoe panel data tell us?

In her study of TV use and social interaction, Johnsson–Smaragdi (1983) had the opportunity to study the relationships between TV viewing and social interaction of three different types:

1. Interaction with parents (measured by an index of 14 different items);
2. Interaction with peers (measured by an index of 11 different items), and,

Table 5.1. Having a "Best Friend," and Some Characteristics of TV Use (Percentage, Malmoe Study, Preschool)

	Having best friend $n = 220$ %	Having no best friend $n = 33$ %
Prefer TV as pastime	45	33
Knowledge of adults' programs low	22	55
Recognize Kojak	55	28
Have had a frightening TV experience	73	59
Positive TV situation	55	43

3. Socially organized leisure activities (a three-item index of sports, hobbies, and club membership).

The peer activities scale included activities such as sports, playing games, listening to music, doing homework, sitting down talking, being out dancing and being "out on the town." The family activities scales included activities such as watching TV, talking about what has happened at school, watching sports events, doing household work, going to the movies. In all cases we measured how often each activity was performed.

Johnsson–Smaragdi applied LISREL techniques to the main Vaxjoe panel and was thus in a position to infer something about the causal relations between TV use and other social activities. As is so often the case in such situations, her results show that the relations among TV, interaction and, social activities are probably more complex than is generally assumed.

The LISREL model of Figure 5.10 shows that in grade 5, when the children were about 11 years old, high TV use leads to high interaction with parents (in terms of our typology: activation). But in grade 9, when we are dealing with 15-year-old adolescents, high interaction with parents leads up to high TV use (supplement in terms of our typology). In both cases, however, we find positive relationships. TV integrates parents and children, and integrated families watch more TV. No negative relationships were found. In terms of our typology, we have not obtained any support for displacement/substitute or leeway/prevention. Is peer interaction different from parent interaction in this respect?

Figure 5.11 again shows positive relationships, but in this case only from TV to peer interaction, not the other way round. TV in grade 5 leads to higher peer interaction both in grade 5 and grade 7: in terms of our typology, a case of cross-sectional and longitudinal activation. Again we find no negative relationships, no support for displacement/substitute or prevention/leeway. (In grade 9 the importance of TV has waned, presumably to be succeeded by that of music and other media activities considered appropriate to that age bracket.)

These results are supported by similar results regarding TV relations and peer interaction, originally presented by Hedinsson (1981) and rendered in Table A.5 in the Appendix. They show that in grade 5, but not in grade 9, there is a significant positive relationship between peer interaction and involvement in the television content consumed. Not only amount of consumption, then, but also degree of involvement seem to be positively related to other activities.

When it comes to the relationship between TV viewing and organized leisure activities, however, we find a somewhat different picture: two (weak) negative relationships. But note the direction of the arrows.

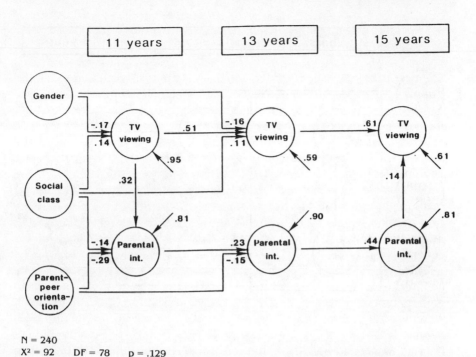

N = 240
X² = 92   DF = 78   p = .129

Figure 5.10. A LISREL Model of TV Use and Parent Interaction (From Johnsson-Smaragdi, 1983)

They point from activities to TV. Our data do not suggest that TV displaces other activities. On the contrary, they show that in grades 5 and 7, organized leisure activities may to some extent reduce the amount of TV viewed. In terms of our typology: a case of prevention (or, possibly, substitution), not one of displacement. (In grade 9, TV again seems to be less relevant to the social activities of adolescents.)

In this connection it may be instructive to recall Figure 3.8 from sec. 3.3.4, which shows a steady decrease in parental habitual viewing as the children grow up and pass through the school system. In the terms of our present discussion this trend may be interpreted as a case of a diminishing tendency among the parents to use TV as a substitute for activities outside the home, activities out of reach for those compelled to the privilege of staying at home with their preschoolers. (By the time we meet the parents of the preschoolers, of course, their media dependency must already be on the wane from the time when their children needed parental attention round the clock.) When the family situation gradually admits a freer choice of parental activities the role of TV in the lives of the parents declines. Their media dependency has diminished (cf. secs. 3.3.4 and 4.5.5).

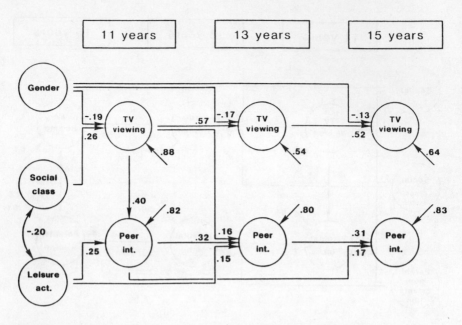

Figure 5.11. A LISREL Model of TV Use and Peer Interaction (From Johnsson-Smaragdi, 1983)

At the same time as part of parental TV viewing has a substitute character, however, its relationship to other parental activities must be characterized as prevention (type 2 of the typology of Figure 5.9). The very same children who bind their parents to the home, before the screen, demand so much attention that independent parental activities— TV use and other activities—are heavily reduced. The parents' amount of viewing is clearly below the average of the population in the corresponding age brackets—about 1½ hours versus some 2 hours a day. They are simply prevented by various forms of child care and related activities.

Thus parents are doubly bound. Their time is scarce, and a large proportion of what time there is has to be spent at home. In this situation TV may be a welcome substitute. But when the double bind slackens, more free time being available, the substitute is left for the real thing. The parents are no less prone to grab opportunities for social activities than are their children. To both, TV is a resource rather than a hindrance.

For parents and children alike, from preschool to grade 9, over various aspects of TV use and social interaction, we have found that

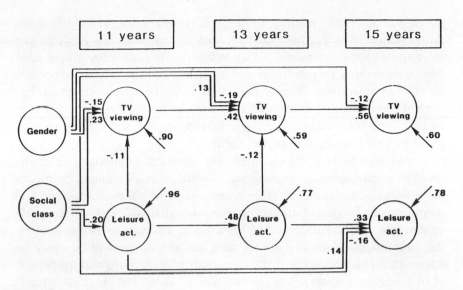

N = 314
χ^2 = 87   DF = 63   p = .026

Figure 5.12.   A LISREL Model of TV Use and Organized Leisure Activities (From Johnsson-Smaragdi, 1983)

TV does not reduce interaction. If anything, it does the opposite. Children high on TV are socially better integrated and more active. In preschool they are more apt to have a close friend. In grade 5, they interact more with parents and peers, and in grade 9 those who interact more with their parents also watch more TV. Only when it comes to organized leisure activities (sports, hobbies, etc.) did we find negative relationships. But here the influence ran from activities to TV viewing. A high amount of organized leisure activities reduced TV (prevention), a less amount of organized activities may have admitted—even called for—much TV (substitute). TV as substitute was found also for the parents. But TV did not reduce or admit the organized activities of the children (no displacement or leeway effects).

In contrast to much earlier research and to the tendencies of the general debate, we have found, then, that the influence of TV viewing on children and adolescents is socially activating rather than passifying. Actually, amount of TV viewing seems to be somewhat reduced by organized leisure activities.

While results such as these differ from early Anglo-American research (Bailyn, 1959; cf. also, for instance, Hendry & Patrick, 1977; Himmelweit et al., 1958; Riley & Riley, 1951), they are in line with more recent results produced outside the U.S. by, for instance, Noble (1975), Rosengren et al. (1976), Murray and Kippax (1978), Adoni (1979). It seems rather plausible to assume that TV's position in social life has changed since the 1950s (cf. also sec. 5.5.2). While in its early days it may have offered something extraordinary and attractive (not least to those socially isolated or disturbed), it now seems to have become a more or less normal phenomenon, integrated into regular social life. Consequently, its functions seem to be more those of supplement and activation than those of substitution and displacement.

It may well be that the so-called new media now about to enter the Swedish media scene on a grand scale—television distributed by means of various combinations of cable, videos, and satellite—at present find themselves in a period similar to the one that TV was in the early 1950s. The general situation of a medium, its way of being used by the individual and society during such an introductory phase, may be rather different from what is the case during later, more mature periods of the medium's history. The "moral panic" (Roe, 1985a; cf. sec. 1.2.1) which seems to accompany every introduction of a new mass medium, therefore, may be both justified and somewhat unnecessary in that the harm supposedly caused during the introductory phase may be quite real but, on the other hand, rather transient. The negative correlations between, say, videos and other activities at present reported in the literature probably are real enough (cf., for instance, Johnsson–Smaragdi, 1986; Johnsson–Smaragdi & Roe, 1986). But it is not at all sure that they will persist. In a future media landscape, today's "new media" may have grown as conventional and integrated as today's television seems to be.

In terms of our discussion about the active or passive individual in the socialization process (sec. 5.1.3) results such as those just presented point in the direction of an active, rather than a passive, individual. TV seems to encourage interaction with parents and peers. Interaction with parents leads to TV use, while organized leisure activities seem actively to prevent high levels of TV viewing.

The fact that TV goes with interaction and activities rather than with isolation and passivity does not mean, of course, that its role as a socializing agent must necessarily be diminished. On the contrary, the fact that it is coupled with social interaction may make it even more powerful. In the following section we shall turn to some of the specific processes of socialization in which TV may play a more or less important role—in its own capacity, and in interaction with other agents of socialization.

5.3. PROCESSES OF SOCIALIZATION

5.3.1. Introduction

Processes of socialization are (sometimes unintentional, even unconscious) processes of teaching and learning. The concepts and terms used to describe and analyze these processes offer a rich variety of often conflicting and contradictory ways of ordering the processes in meaningful ways. This section will draw on a simple tripartite scheme employed by McLeod and Brown (1976) in a discussion of the interplay of family, mass media, and other agents of socialization.

The socialization processes discussed by McLeod and Brown are three ideal type concepts: modeling, reinforcement, and social interaction. In terms of the two parties of socialization, the three types may be said to refer to the individual being socialized, the socializing agent, and to the interplay between them.

In modeling, the initiative, to a large extent, rests with the individual being socialized. (He or she uses agents and phenomena in the environment to "socialize oneself.") In reinforcement, the initiative rests more with the socializing agent, who draws on and reinforces, often by means of direct rewards and punishments, tendencies already discernible in the individual being socialized. Social interaction is basic to all socialization (cf. the preceding section). Yet some aspects, and some processes, of socialization may be best characterized and understood in terms of social interaction as transferring norms and values.

The three types of socialization processes are going on all the time in the life of a given individual. All the same it is tempting to conceptualize social interaction as being somehow in the beginning of the process, later on to be followed by modeling and reinforcement. In this section, however, we will first use our media panel data to illustrate and illuminate the concept of modeling, and then turn to reinforcement. The basic process of social interaction will be taken up only when the two more specific aspects have been dealt with.

5.3.2. Modeling

In the process of modeling the individual being socialized learns the behavior of another person, consciously or unconsciously. Among the specific psychological mechanisms behind modeling one may assume imitation of, and identification with, the individual(s) modeled.

The most basic example of modeling in connection with mass media socialization is probably modeling of mass media use itself. Children supposedly learn from their parents how, and to what extent, to use mass media. Similarities between the mass media use of parents and children have often been reported (Brolin, 1964; Himmelweit et al., 1958; Linné, 1964; cf. McLeod & Brown, 1976; Schramm et al., 1961). But similarities as measured, say, by cross-sectional correlations cannot be used to infer causal processes of the type we are after here. The relationships found may be contingent on background and intervening variables, and the direction of the relationship is always uncertain.

Within the Media Panel Program, Sonesson (1979, p. 57) demonstrated that the (weak to moderate) correlations between parents' and children's TV consumption found in the first wave of the Malmoe panel were contingent on social status. They were found only for the highest and lowest levels of education, not for the group in between. In his study of the first wave of the Vaxjoe panel Hedinsson (1981, p. 125) found moderate to strong relationships between parents' and children's TV viewing, even after control (by means of MCA) for social class of parents. These cross-sectional relationships were somewhat stronger in the ninth grade than in the fifth. In the main panel, on the other hand, we have found somewhat weaker relationships in grade 9 than in grade 5 (controlling for class). Results such as these clearly call for careful statistical controls, and for longitudinal data to ascertain the direction of the relationship.

Johnsson–Smaragdi (1983, pp. 155ff.) used LISREL techniques to analyze the relationships between parents' and childrens' amount of TV consumption within the main Vaxjoe panel. In this way, the control problem is taken care of as much as possible, and the direction of the relationships stands out clearly. The results are presented in Figure 5.13 and Table 5.2. (Note that, as mentioned in sec. 1.3.3, parental TV here is based mostly on data from and about the mothers of the children and adolescents. The differences between mothers' and fathers' TV viewing are small, however.)

It will be seen that the influence from parents' TV viewing on that of their children is strong and lasting. It makes itself felt both instantaneously and over time. For instance, the influence from parents' TV viewing when their children are 11 on children's TV viewing at age 13 is almost as strong as that from the children's own TV viewing at age 11. Although there is no arrow from parents' TV viewing to children's TV viewing at age 15, Table 5.2, presenting the direct, indirect and total effects of the parents' TV viewing on that of their children, clearly shows that there is a strong indirect effect also at this later age, when adolescents are otherwise on their way out from the family to peers and the surrounding society (cf. Roberts, 1981).

It deserves mention that these strong influences show up after con-

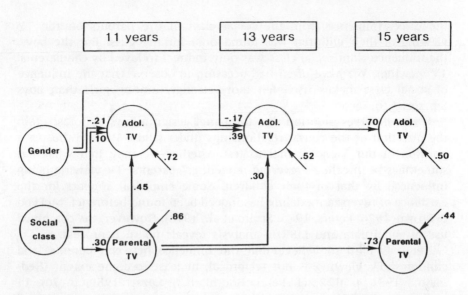

N = 375

X^2 = 116   DF = 96   p = .082

Figure 5.13.   A LISREL Model of the Modeling Hypothesis with Background Variables (From Johnsson-Smaragdi, 1983)

Table 5.2.   Direct, Indirect, and Total Effects of Parents' TV Viewing on Their Children's Viewing. (From Johnsson–Smaragdi, 1983)

Casual variable	Dependent variable	Direct effects	Indirect effects	Total effects[a]
Parents' viewing at time 1	Children's viewing at:			
	11 years	.45	.00	.45
	13 years	.30	.18	.48
	15 years	.00	.33	.33

[a] For instance, the total effects of parents' TV viewing on that of their children's is at 15 years (.45 x .39 x .70) + (.30 x .70) = .33. See Figure 5.13.

trolling in the model for the basic variables of gender and social class. In a later, two group analysis, Johnsson–Smaragdi (1983, p. 169) demonstrated that the basic causal structure visualized in Figure 5.13 turns up also when boys and girls are analyzed separately, both when it comes to the pattern of arrows and the size of the coefficients.

The fact that basically the same causal structure has been demonstrated for two different groups of individuals (boys and girls) is as strong a validation of the causal structure as may be wished for. However, the direct influence from the social class of the parents on the TV viewing of their children was found only for the girls. For the boys, the influence from social class was only indirect (relayed by the parents' TV viewing). We have often had occasion to observe that the influence of social class makes itself felt more strongly among girls than boys (cf. sec. 4.9).

It also deserves mention that the panel design allows us to ascertain the direction of the causal relationships under study. We are thus in a position in our Vaxjoe panel to test whether we may find what has sometimes been called "reversed modeling," parents' TV viewing being influenced by that of their children. Some empirical support for the existence of reversed modeling has indeed been found before (cf. McLeod & Brown, 1976; Peters, 1985; Surlin et al., 1978). However, the combined use of panel data and LISREL analysis reveals no such process.

Yet it is hard to believe that the influence between parents' and childrens' TV viewing is not reciprocal, at least to some extent (Hedinsson, 1981, p. 122; cf. Pearl, Bouthilet, & Lazar, 1980, p. 70). In exploratory LISREL analyses some signs of reversed modeling did indeed turn up, but they disappeared as the analyses were gradually refined (cf. Johnsson–Smaragdi, 1983, p. 161). In sec. 5.3.4, on the mechanism of social interaction, we shall return to this question.

All in all, then, a strong causal influence from the TV viewing of parents on that of their children has been demonstrated—stronger than that emanating from such otherwise powerful variables as gender and class. The influence also withstands controls for class and gender. No doubt this is socialization, but what process of socialization is it?

Few Swedish parents want their children to watch too much TV. So the process of socialization called reinforcement (cf. sec. 5.3.3) can hardly have been at work, at least not on a conscious level.

Much TV viewing by children and adolescents takes place in the company of parents and siblings. It must be assumed, therefore, that the influence from parents' viewing on that of their children to some extent is relayed by way of the socialization process of interaction. However, between 20% and 30% of children's and adolescents' actual viewing takes place in the absence of any company at all (sec. 2.6). It may be assumed, then, that some 50% of all adolescent viewing takes place in the absence of the company of parents. Furthermore, we have just seen that the influence of parents' TV viewing on that of their children stretches its long arm over at least 4 years, probably longer. So if there is an element of the socialization process of interaction in this influence, it cannot be the only one, probably not even the dominant one.

It is more plausible that what we have been able to demonstrate is a case of modeling. As the parents do, so do the children. Obviously this process of modeling has occurred gradually, over long periods of time, imperceptible, perhaps, to both parents and children. Yet is has occurred. The best advice to be given to parents complaining about the TV addiction of their youngsters, therefore, is this: "View less TV yourself. For your own TV viewing pattern is modeled by your children."

As we have just seen, TV viewing and a lot of social interaction go together. It is therefore only fair once again to point out that the modeling process occurs in conjunction with social interaction of the most diverse types. The problem of social interaction as a process of socialization will be taken up again in a later section. Before we treat that problem, however, let us turn to the socialization process of reinforcement.

5.3.3. Reinforcement and Conformity

In her study of the first wave of the Malmoe panel, Sonesson (1979, p. 82) asked both preschool children and parents who decided when the child should watch. The most frequent response combination (34%) was that children said parents decided, parents said children did. The next most frequent combination was that both children and parents said children decided (24%). Hedinsson (1981, p. 92) found very low frequencies of direct, successful restrictions in the first wave of the Vaxjoe panel (grades 5–7–9), both as reported by parents and by children.

The low frequencies of direct control found in such cases, and the sometimes contradictory results, have been taken as an indication that reinforcement as a means of socialization—more or less explicit rewards and punishments—may be less frequent in connection with mass media use than in other areas (Hedinsson, 1981, p. 32, 133; McLeod & Brown, 1976, p. 12; cf. Zahn & Baran, 1984). However, this is a matter of definition.

In a way, all socialization is reinforcement in the sense that some behavior is met with positive reactions, other behavior with negative reactions. The degree of explicitness may be (and often is) taken as a criterion for distinguishing between socialization by means of reinforcement and socialization by means of social interaction. A better criterion may be the one discussed by Younnis (1980) and, following Younnis, by Johnsson–Smaragdi (1983).

Younnis makes a distinction between socialization as conformity and socialization as cooperation. The former type is characterized by a relatively strong agent of socialization; the latter, by more equal parties of interaction. The former type is said to be prevalent in the parent–child relationship; the latter, primarily among peers and friends. One may have some doubts, though, about the egalitarian character of adolescent peer interaction. It is reasonable to assume that both conformity and cooperation are fairly frequent in both child–parent and peer–peer relationships.

The advantage of Younnis's distinction is that it does not demand a high degree of explicitness in rewards and punishments. The main requirement is that there is a strong norm-sender. The mechanisms of reinforcement may be very subtle—indeed, they may be partly unconscious to both the agent of socialization and the individual socialized. This is a situation which must be common in almost all socialization of children by parents. Children's behavior may conform with parents attitudes without any of the two parties being conscious of any reinforcement process having taken place.

By means of various attitude scales originally constructed by Brown (cf. Brown & Linné, 1976) and later developed and adapted to Swedish conditions by Sonesson (1979) we measured, in both the Malmoe and the Vaxjoe panel, the parents' attitudes toward TV in general and children's TV use in particular (cf. Hedinsson, 1981).

These are the seven scales developed by Sonesson (1979):

1. *Positive attitude:* Taps a basically positive, confident attitude to TV as a source of entertainment and relaxation both for parents and children. One of the items: TV is the best form of family entertainment.
2. *Addictive attitude:* Taps the degree of concern about the TV medium as being addictive and taking too much time from other activities. An item: Watching TV can easily become a habit with children and teen-agers.
3. *TV as stimulation:* Taps a belief that TV is a means to teach children to think independently about the realities of life. An item: TV really helps kids to think about things.
4. *TV as a base for discussions:* Taps a belief that TV provides material for discussions within the family. After having watched a TV program, I like to tell the children my opinion of it.
5. *Laissez faire:* Taps a liberal attitude to TV viewing, allowing the child to decide his or her own viewing pattern. One example of an item: Children may watch all kinds of TV programs, provided that their parents are with them.
6. *Control:* Taps a very restrictive orientation toward children watching TV. An example: Children should not be allowed to watch the TV news.
7. *Protective:* Taps a belief that TV is often unsuitable for children

and that children should be protected from some of the contents. An item: I do not like my child to watch TV programs that may frighten him or her.

These scales, of course, were only intended for the parents. It is to be expected, however, that such parental attitudes will to some extent influence children's TV behavior. This is also what we found.

In her thesis, based on the Malmoe panel, Jönsson (1985) adapted Sonesson's scales to her specific purposes (cf. sec. 5.5.3) and included them in a number of cross-sectional and longitudinal PLS analyses (cf. Appendix). She found significant cross-sectional influences from two parental attitudes called by her "TV confidence" and "TV control" on children's amount of TV consumption and type of TV content consumed. (The two attitudes correspond to scales 1 and 6 above.)

In preschool, grade 3, and grade 5, "TV confidence" was positively related to amount of TV consumption. In preschool, "TV control" was positively related to consumption of children's programs (mostly Swedish programs of a public service type), negatively related to consumption of TV fiction (often American detective stories). In grade 3, the same attitude was negatively related to consumption of TV fiction. (Since the results stem from PLS analyses they refer to the unique influence of the attitudes, after control for gender, social background, etc.)

The importance of maternal attitudes was convincingly demonstrated when, in a final longitudinal PLS analysis, Jönsson (1985, p. 136) found that even 6 years later, in grade 5, the maternal attitude of "TV confidence" as measured in preschool exerted an influence on children's consumption of TV fiction. (Again, this was a unique influence, after control for gender and social background, TV use in preschool and grade 3 etc.; cf. the model in sec. 5.5.3.) This longitudinal influence stands out as even more remarkable as TV confidence in grade 5 did not influence the fifth graders' consumption of TV fiction. The remaining effects of early socialization were stronger than the contemporaneous ones. Children may strive gradually to free themselves from parental influence. But that influence does have a long arm.

In grade 9, at the age of 15, adolescents are turning away from their family toward their peers, and TV is less in focus than before. Yet ninth graders of the Vaxjoe main panel having parents with a general positive TV attitude watched TV for some 10 hours a week, those having parents with a less positive TV attitude, for only about 8 (MCA analysis, beta = .13). The result cannot be due to any influence from parents' TV habits, for we controlled for parents' own TV viewing (as well as for social class and some other variables).

It is to be expected that the influence of parents' attitudes on their children's TV behavior will depend upon a lot of contingent circumstances. It is obvious, for instance, that parents have much better opportunities for bringing their child's TV behavior in accordance with their TV attitudes in one-child families, or with their eldest child, than with the middle or youngest child in families with more than one child. For the Malmoe panel, Sonesson (1979, pp. 202ff.) demonstrated that such is indeed the case. Among preschool children parental attitudes often had their strongest influence on the child's TV behavior in one-child families, or on the eldest child, whereas the same influence tended to be weaker for the middle or youngest child in families with more than one child.

Sometimes the tendencies in the different situations were quite contradictory, so that the overall connection between parental TV attitude and child's TV behavior was very low. In such cases sibling status had acted as a so-called suppressor variable (Rosenberg, 1968, p. 84). For instance, no overall connection was found between the child's TV habits (measured by a picture test) and the parental attitude of regarding TV as a positive stimulus for the child (gamma = −.04). However, the lack of relationship was due to the fact that the relationship was rather strong and positive for the eldest child (.41) and in one-child families (.39), whereas for the youngest and middle child it was rather strong and negative (−.26, −.39) (Sonesson, 1979, p. 207). In the latter cases it may well be that the causal sequence was reversed, so that heavy TV viewing by the child made some parents—who for lack of time had become less able to control the TV viewing of their children—somewhat skeptical about the stimulating capacity of TV for their child.

Naturally, parental TV attitudes do not grow out of nothing. They are related to the class position of the parents, which in turn influences the general family communication climate, which in turn forms a background for the more specific attitudes. We measured the general family communication climate by means of the scales developed by Chaffee and his colleagues (Chaffee et al., 1971; Tims & Masland, 1985; cf. sec. 5.1.5). The Wisconsin scales were translated and adapted to Swedish conditions. In the Swedish version of the family communication pattern scales, seven items form the socio-orientation scale; five, the concept orientation scale. For the sake of illustration we present two items from each scale (retranslation from the Swedish version):
Socio-orientation:

> We tell our adolescents that one's point of view, as a parent, is the correct one, and that it should not be challenged by a child.

Concept orientation:

We find it self-evident that our adolescents should be encouraged
to challenge our ideas and beliefs.

We say to our adolescents that expressing their point of view is
important, even if others do not like it.

It should be evident from the wording of these items that the social
and concept scales were presented to the parents. (In the third wave,
however, a reworded version of the scales was given to the adolescents
in the seventh and ninth grades.)

Both in grades 5 and 9 we found moderate relationships between
the Chaffee typology and positive and negative parental TV attitudes
(betas ranging between .11 and .25, controlling for class and parental
TV viewing). The overall influence of the family communication climate
on children's TV viewing was weak to moderate, but just as with that
of the more specific TV attitudes, it varied considerably between subgroups.

In grade 5, the influence of socio-orientation (controlling for concept
orientation) made itself felt especially for middle-class boys. Among
middle-class boys from families with low concept orientation, those
from high socio-orientation families watched about 6 hours more TV
a week than did those from low socio-orientation families (19.2. vs.
13.3. hours).

In grade 9, the influence of concept orientation (controlling for socio-
orientation) made itself felt especially for working-class girls. Among
working-class girls with high socio-orientation, those from families with
high concept orientation watched more than 4 hours less TV than did
those from families with low concept orientation (7.2. vs. 11.8 hours).

Concept orientation tends to go with middle-class status; socio-orientation, with working-class status. In both cases related above, then,
a family communication climate "at odds" with the class position of
the family seems to have influenced TV consumption considerably. Why
this is so, and why the phenomenon should turn up especially strongly
for middle-class boys in grade 5 and working-class girls in grade 9, we
do not know.

We do know, however, that parents' general orientations and specific
attitudes may have strong effects on their children's TV behavior, not
the least among specific subgroups, that is, after controlling for age,
gender, and social class. It is only natural to regard such phenomena
as instances of socialization by means of reinforcement, or better,
perhaps conformity.

5.3.4. The Socialization Process of Social Interaction

In sec. 5.2 we discussed the relationship between social interaction and TV viewing, finding on the whole positive relationships between children's TV viewing and their social interaction. In the light of much previous research, this finding was somewhat unexpected, but it did increase the importance of studying the socialization mechanism of social interaction. At the same time the task has become much more difficult. For if TV viewing—and perhaps other mass media use as well—goes with a lot of social interaction, how do we differentiate between the socialization processes connected with TV viewing and those connected with social interaction?

The answer to that question very often seems to be that we cannot thus differentiate. Perhaps we shall never be able to do so. In this situation what way out do we have? The answer is simple. We have to take a closer look at the ways in which mass media use is related to other types of social activities, trying to understand the socialization process of social interaction by way of understanding the supposedly meaningful patterns of that interaction.

For the main Vaxjoe panel we have data about the children's social activities with their friends (11 items) and their parents (14 items). We also have data about more organized activities such as sport, hobbies, and membership of clubs (cf. sec. 5.2.3). What patterns do these social activities form, and how do the patterns relate to the mass media use of children?

There are many ways of finding answers to these questions. We were interested primarily in the two main media activities of our panel: TV viewing and listening to pop music. It could be expected that the patterns of social interaction and media use were rather different, not only in the three waves of the main panel (grades 5, 7, and 9), but also between boys and girls from working-class and middle-class backgrounds (cf. chaps. 3 and 4). So for each of these four social categories we decided to take a look at the way in which the social activities on our lists were correlated with TV viewing and pop listening, including also book reading—a media activity interesting to parents and teachers, but otherwise not much studied in our research program.

Our data on social activities were largely structured along two dimensions: activities with parents versus activities with friends, and organized versus spontaneous activities. We therefore ordered the variables, a priori, in a quasi-circumplex built on these two dimensions (Figure 5.14).

In the center of each circumplex we could now represent the use of the various media, expressing the correlations between each medium

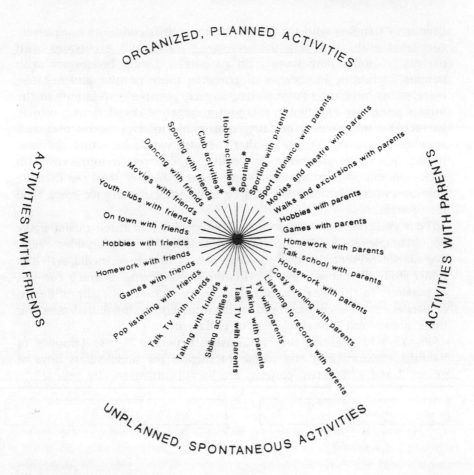

*) Not necessarily with parents or friends

Figure 5.14. A Quasi Circumplex of Adolescent Activities

and activities of the circumplex by means of a circle sector with a
radius corresponding to the strength of the correlation. For each circumplex we visualize six correlations, the three strongest positive and
negative correlations. In this way we get an intuitive comprehension
of the location of the medium in the social worlds of children and
adolescents. That location provides important information about the
processes of socialization going on in these social worlds. (Positive
correlations are symbolized by filled segments, negative correlations,
with empty segments. The radius of each circumplex corresponds to a
correlation coefficient of $r = .75$).

Suppose that a given medium in one social grouping is positively
correlated with such types of interaction as, say, "Being in town with

friends'', ''Dancing with friends'', ''Games with friends'', and negatively correlated with such activities as, say, ''Walks and excursions with parents'', ''Doing homework with parents'', ''Doing housework with parents'', while in another social grouping these positive and negative correlations have the opposite sign, so that positive correlations in the former group are negative in this group, negative correlations, positive. In such a case it would be fairly reasonable to hypothesize that as a socialization agent the role of that medium would be rather different in the two social groupings. In reality, of course, circumplexes with such clear-cut patterns are hardly ever found. But we shall see that the differences actually occurring will be quite sufficient to give some food for thought.

Four categories of adolescents, three grades and three media make 36 circumplexes (built on correlation matrices of 37 variables each). We cannot present them all. So for each of the three media activities under study we chose a pair of circumplexes offering as much contrast as possible. In this way we may graphically picture six rather different constellations of media use and social interaction, distributed over our three grades and four categories of children.

Figure 5.15 presents the relationship between TV use (amount of habitual consumption) and social interaction for middle-class boys of grades 7 and 9. The two patterns are literally diametrically opposed to

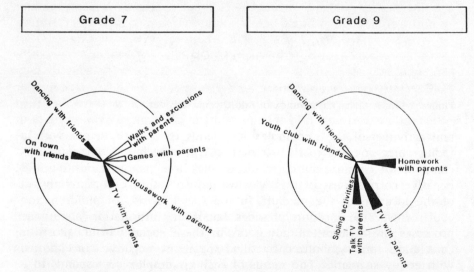

Figure 5.15.   Social Activities Positively and Negatively Related to TV Viewing; Middle-class Boys, Grades 7 and 9. (Length of Sector Proportionate to Strength of Correlation. Negative Correlation White; Positive Black)

each other. In grade 7, the TV use of the middle-class boys is positively correlated with social interaction with friends, negatively with social activities with parents. In grade 9, it is the other way around. TV is now positively related to homebound interactions with parents, negatively related to interactions with friends outside home. "Dancing with friends" even changes from a positive to a negative correlation, while, quite naturally, "TV with parents" shows positive correlations in both grade 7 and 9.

For our middle-class boys, then, TV in grade 9 is embedded in a pattern of social interaction rather different from that of TV in grade 7. In grade 7 it seems to offer a route from home and parents to peers and dances. For those who use it a lot in grade 9 it seems to be a link to home, parents, and school. As a socializing agent, therefore, TV seems to have changed character between the two grades. (Note that this change takes place for the very same individuals, controlling for gender and social class.)

In Figure 5.16 the social activities related to the book reading (number of nonschool books during last 3 weeks) of working-class girls and middle-class girls in grade 9 are presented. It will be seen that, for working-class girls, book reading is positively related to unplanned, spontaneous activities both within and outside the family ("In town with friends," "Talk TV with parents"), negatively related to more planned, long-range activities both inside and outside the family ("Sports," "Doing homework with parents"). For middle-class girls book reading is positively related to home-bound, rather unplanned activities ("Housework with parents," "Sibling activities"), negatively related to activities outside home ("In town with friends," "Doing homework with friends"). For working-class girls in grade 9, then, book reading seems to help differentiate between organized and spontaneous social interaction. For middle-class girls in grade 9, on the other hand, it seems to help differentiate between homebound and out-of-home activities. In both cases, however, book reading is not positively related to planned, intellectually or otherwise ambitious activities. Rather, it seems to be a medium of entertainment, on a par with the family medium of TV (positive correlations with "TV with parents" and "Talk TV with parents").

In combination with the social interaction of the types at hand, however, even the seemingly harmless entertainment of book reading may have somewhat unexpected consequences. In both cases there is a negative correlation between book reading and "Doing homework"— for working-class girls in the company of parents, for middle-class girls in the company of friends. The social interactions surrounding media use seem to be able considerably to change the socialization processes

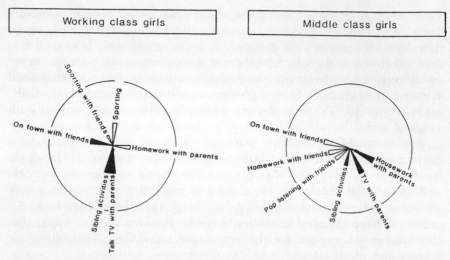

Figure 5.16. Social Activities Positively and Negatively Related to Book Reading; Grade 9, Working-class and Middle-class Girls

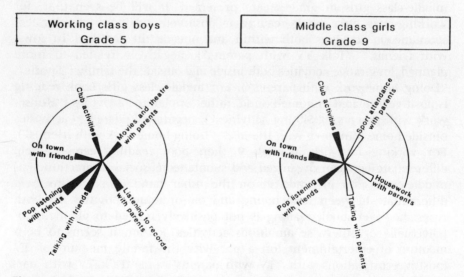

Figure 5.17. Social Activities Positively and Negatively Related to Pop Music Listening; Working-class Boys from Grade 5, Middle-class Girls from Grade 9

conventionally associated with the use of various media. (Much depends, of course, on the type of content chosen from the menu of the medium. In this particular case it is a fair guess that a large portion of the books read by our ninth-grade girls—both working-class and middle-class— would be greeted with only limited enthusiasm by their teachers.)

Figure 5.17 visualizes the relationship between pop music listening (from "never" to "every day") and other social activities for working-class boys in grade 5 and middle-class girls in grade 9. While in the two former cases our pairwise comparisons have been made between social categories rather similar to each other (middle-class boys in grades 7 and 9; working-class and middle-class girls in grade 9), we are now dealing with social categories as different as is possible within our material. There is a difference of 4 years, gender, and social class between the two groups. Small wonder, then, that the social activities surrounding listening to pop music are drastically different in the two groups.

Since, for all of us, time is a scarce commodity, indulging in one type of activity of necessity means that other types of activity must be neglected. Theoretically, this should lead up to bundles of positively and negatively correlated variables, something which has often been suggested in sociology and mass communications research. For the pop listening of working-class boys from grade 5, however, this line of argument does not seem to hold true. In this category pop listening shows only positive correlations, or a few correlations round zero. (Therefore, we have marked six positive correlations for this category.) Pop listening seems to be completely harmoniously integrated with the rest of social life, from record listening and moviegoing with parents to club activities and being in town with friends. This must be a rather happy constellation of social activities for those indulging in them. In a more or less ideal type shape it shows up for all four categories in grade 5. But it certainly does not appear in connection with the middle-class girls of grade 9.

As far as the middle-class girls of grade 9 are concerned, pop listening seems to polarize social life between social interaction with parents and with peers. It is strongly positively correlated with three activities out of home, strongly negatively correlated with three activities with parents. In more or less ideal type shapes, similar patterns show up for all four categories in grade 9. At this age, pop listening seems to be used as a means to express a belongingness to the social world of the peer group, a distance to the social world of home and parents (cf. sec. 5.4).

Listening to pop music, then, seems to be associated with rather different types of social interaction. At age 11, it tends to be compatible with overall integrative social interaction. At 15, it seems to be used as a means of social differentiation.

In terms of Figure 5.4, classifying peer groups into "conventional youth," "subcultures," and "contracultures," this development from integration to differentiation is suggestive of a development away from the type of conventional youth toward the two other types. In grade

5, an overwhelming majority belongs to what has here been called conventional youth. Presumably, most adolescents never really leave that safe fold. But no doubt there is a centrifugal force among the ninth graders, and pop music strengthens that force, just as in grade 5 it seems to operate as an integrating force. Thus the very same medium, being embedded in radically different types of social interaction, may have radically different socializing functions. This is a good example of the process which in our chapter on development was called the "functional reorganization of media use during adolescence" (cf. sec. 3.2). Thus the very same medium, being embedded in radically different types of social interaction, may have radically different socializing functions.

Our three pairs of circumplexes, picturing sometimes radically different relationships between media use and other social interactions, have shown—indirectly but clearly—that the process of social interaction as a means of socialization very probably decisively influences the ways in which the different mass media function as socialization agents. During the course of such processes, one and the same medium may fulfill radically different functions. Book reading may be used as a means of entertainment, encroaching upon the homework imposed by the very same school which once laboriously taught the child to read. Listening to pop music on radio, records, and cassettes may start as having a socially integrative function and end as a means of social differentiation.

Looking at the socialization process of social interaction, we have caught some glimpses of important changes in the role of different agents of socialization. In the next section of this chapter we shall try to enter more deeply into the problem of the agents of socialization.

5.4. Agents of Socialization[3]

In a modern society there are at least eight main types of socialization agents (cf. sec. 5.1.4). All of them are always active for all of us, but for children and adolescents, the four agents of family, peers, school, and mass media are the most relevant ones. Basically, the process of socialization—an interplay between the individual being socialized and the agents of socialization—is shaped by two structural factors: gender and social class (cf. sec. 4.3), and by one processual factor: development (biological, cognitive, and social development; cf. sec. 3.1). All this makes for an overall phenomenon of such subtle complexity that it is

---

[3] This section draws heavily on Roe (1983a).

indeed no easy task to try and describe it, not to mention attempts to explain (or even distinguish between) the roles played by this or that specific agent of socialization. That task is undertaken in this section.

Panel data and advanced multivariate statistical analyses are necessary to disentangle the complex web of mutual influences between the various agents of socialization and the individual socialized. To date, these preconditions have been met, within the Media Panel Program, primarily in the four doctoral theses by Roe (1983a), Johnsson–Smaragdi (1983), Jönsson (1985), and Flodin (1986). Among these, Roe is especially preoccupied with the problem of the relationship among different agents of socialization during adolescence.

Roe's focus is the interplay between two major agents of socialization, the school and the mass media, as it is being reshaped when, for developmental reasons, boys and girls gradually orient themselves away from the family in the direction of peers and the surrounding society. He questions the traditional view of this relationship, which regards mass media use as a potential threat to successful schooling. Instead, he literally turns the tables around, examining the possibility that mass media use may be the dependent variable, partly at least an outcome of success or failure at school.

Of the mass media Roe is primarily interested in the relationship between TV and listening to music by means of radio, records, and cassettes. He hypothesizes that as adolescents gradually reorient themselves from family to peers, their interest at the same time moves from the family medium of TV to more easily controlled media offering various types of popular music. As adolescents move through the school system, therefore, popular music should become an increasingly important agent of socialization—so important an agent, indeed, that it may well be able to influence one of the two or three most important decisions lying before adolescents, the decision about their future job.

Roe tests his arguments by means of two large LISREL models, one for boys and one for girls. The models are developed from an earlier LISREL model for both boys and girls, building in its turn on previous PLS models, and, before that, on a number of MCA analysis. The models deal simultaneously with 18 latent variables and 31 manifest ones (plus gender). The complexity of the models makes it difficult to visualize them graphically. For illustrative purposes, Figures 5.18 and 5.19 present simplified versions of the two models, leaving out the measurement models and a number of parameters and arrows not considered indispensable to the main points of the theoretical argumentation (for instance, stability coefficients for repeated measurements of the same variable).

It should be especially stressed that the large number of variables included in the model produces a large internal nonresponse. In combination with the type of analysis used (listwise deletion) this makes the number of cases in the models small, causing a problem of representativeness. The technique of pair-wise deletion would have given a higher number of cases, but then the different arrows of the model would have been built on partly different sets of individuals (cf. sec. 5.5.5 and Appendix). The problem inevitably turns up in all large multivariate analyses, and the only way out of the dilemma is that in future data collection procedures, increased attention be given to reducing internal nonresponse. For further technical details of the full models, the interested reader is referred to Roe (1983a).

Before entering a discussion of the substantive results offered by the two models, some information must be given about the variables used in them.

The background variable is parents' education, not class. Thus the model is a status model rather than a class model. Given the sociocultural emphasis of the theoretical arguments behind the models this is quite natural.

School achievement is measured by means of marks in Swedish and science given at the end of term in grades 6, 7, and 9 (no marks given in grade 5).

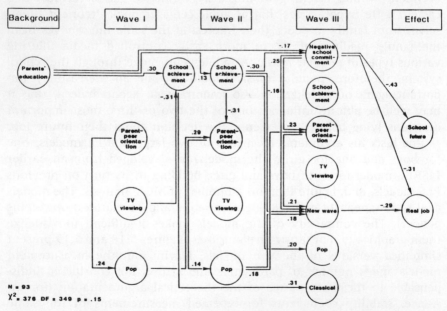

Figure 5.18. Agents of Socialization: An Illustrative LISREL Model (Parameters of Major Theoretical Interest; Boys; Vaxjoe Main Panel; From Roe, 1983a)

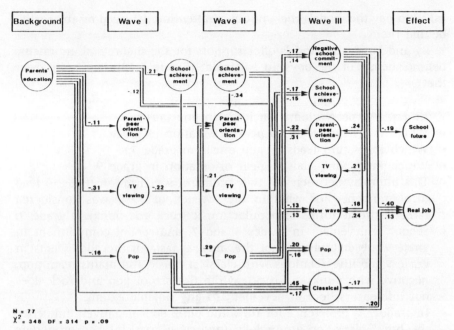

N = 77
χ² = 348 DF = 314 p = .09

Figure 5.19. Agents of Socialization: An Illustrative LISREL Model (Parameters of Major Theoretical Interest; Girls; Vaxjoe Main Panel; From Roe, 1983a)

Negative school commitment is a scale originally developed by Murdock and Phelps (1973) and applied to Swedish conditions in the Media Panel Program. School future concerns the choice of future education after compulsory school (various alternatives of high school, etc.).

The variables called Pop 1 and 2 represent use of popular music in general. The three music variables of wave three are preference scales obtained by means of factor analyses of a number of items tapping preference for 10 different types of music.

Real job concerns the plans for future jobs entertained by the adolescents (cf. sec. 5.5.5).

For further details about the latent and manifest variables of the model, the reader is referred to Roe (1983a).

Turning now to the substantive content of the two models, the first thing to be said of them as models is that in spite of the fact that they represent a considerable simplification of the full, original models, they are extremely complex. Some readers may indeed find them bewildering rather than clarifying. All the same, the sociocultural reality they represent must be infinitely much more complex and complicated. The readers possibly feeling some hesitation in the face of them are therefore asked to pay the models the amount of attention deserved by the reality behind them.

By and large, the models offer support for the theoretical arguments behind them. For the boys, in particular (Figure 5.18), it is quite clear that

- In grade 5, peer orientation leads to pop music;
- Which in its turn leads to peer orientation in grade 7;
- Which in its turn leads to pop music in grade 7;
- Which in its turn leads to peer orientation in grade 9.
- This interplay between the two agents of socialization tends to lead to a preference for what in the Sweden of 1980 was considered rather extreme forms of popular music (rock and punk) in grade 9.
- School achievement in grades 6 and 7, and school commitment in grade 9 are determinants of the musical taste of the adolescents in grade 9 (positive relations with classical music and mainstream pop, negative with punk and rock), while the use of pop and rock does not influence school achievement to any notable extent.
- In grade 9, a preference for rock and punk does negatively influence the boys' plans for future jobs (note that parental background is controlled for).
- TV seems to be rather irrelevant in the interplay of the agents of socialization as here conceived, especially in grades 7 and 9 (while TV in grade 5 does negatively influence school achievement in grade 6).

The girls' model (Figure 5.19) differs from that of the boys in several aspects, especially in that

- The influence from the parental status (education) is much more widespread and penetrant for the girls.
- An early interest in pop (grade 5) has long-lasting consequences, actually influencing school commitment and job plans 4 years later (grade 9).
- TV appears to be an agent of socialization much more central to girls than to boys.

The overall impression obtained from a comparison between the two figures is that the agents of socialization form a much more complex and structured network for the girls than they do for the boys, ranging from the influence of parents to that of the punk and rock so often despised by parents. This is in line with the observation made in sec.

4.4.5. about the differential influence of social class on the mass media use of boys and girls.

For both boys and girls, however, the net of interacting agents of socialization is quite formidable, and one may rightly wonder where in this complex web we can find the socialized individuals themselves? According to theory, socialization is an interplay not only between the agents of socialization, but also between these agents and the individual being socialized. By means of its agents of socialization, society puts its imprint on the individuals being socialized and, at the same time, these individuals themselves are active in the process of socialization, using for their own purposes the agents of socialization and what they have to offer (cf. sec. 5.1.3).

In socialization, then, individuals are both objects and subjects. In terms of mass communications research: In our study of socialization we are dealing with both the effects of mass media consumption and the use made of mass media by individuals. By and large, effects research is deterministic in its anthropology, and its methodology is causally oriented, while uses and gratifications research is voluntaristic in its anthropology, and its methodology is finalistically oriented (Rosengren, 1985a; Rosengren et al., 1983). By applying LISREL techniques to panel data we are in a position to combine the two approaches, a combination which over the decades has been often recommended but seldom achieved (Klapper, 1960; Rosengren & Windahl, 1972; Windahl, 1981).

In the context of mass media use it would seem reasonable to hypothesize that a finalistic, voluntaristic perspective is valid primarily in the short run, while a causal, deterministic perspective should be valid primarily in the long run. In the type of phenomena we are studying, intentions should as a rule manifest themselves in a perspective of, say, days or weeks, while effects will tend to need longer time to become visible: months or even years. In terms of our panel data and statistical models, this means that the intentions of acting subjects (say, intentional mass media use) should be studied by means of cross-sectional parameters; the effects on the objects of socialization agents such as family and peer groups, school and mass media, by means of longitudinal parameters (cf. Rosengren et al., 1983).

Figure 5.18 offers an opportunity for such combined analysis. In Figure 5.20 part of this figure has been cut out and simplified, so that the main tendencies will stand out more clearly for the reader unfamiliar with reading the more complex LISREL models. (Note that in order to increase clarity the stability coefficients were excluded from Figure 5.18. Together with the corresponding arrows they have been included in Figure 5.20, because of their theoretical importance in that figure.)

Concentrating on the interplay between parent–peer orientation and

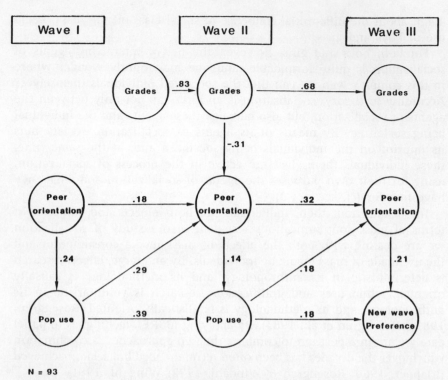

Figure 5.20. Boys' School Achievement, Peer Orientation, and Use of Pop Music at the Age of 11, 12, 13, and 15. Illustrative LISREL Model, Vaxjoe Main Panel.

the musical tastes of the adolescent boys, we see how peer orientation is cross-sectionally related to pop listening in grades 5 and 7, to punk and rock preferences in grade 9, while these activities and preferences in their turn longitudinally affect peer orientation (and finally the job preferences of the ninth graders; cf. Figure 5.18). That is, peer orientation is more or less intentionally expressed by means of the use of music, and that use causes peer orientation to increase over time. In terms of finality and causality, voluntarism, and determinism: a cyclical interplay between the individual socialized and the socializing agents (cf. above).

In its turn, this interplay has its origins and consequences. Behind peer orientation we find the school. In grade 7, low-achieving boys turn to their peers, in order, perhaps to retrieve at least a modest amount of the self-confidence and identity presumably lost in school. They thus enter a "spiral of interaction" (Thunberg et al., 1982) which finally will make them lower their aspirations for future jobs. Ironically, the sorting procedures of school are reproduced and reinforced by the very individuals sorted. They set in motion a type of self-fulfilling prophecy, more or less intentionally using the music of mass media to make the best of a difficult situation.

In this section we have been concentrating on the interplay between the individual socialized and differential agents of socialization. The data behind the arguments stem from the Vaxjoe panel as analyzed by Roe (1983a). In the following section we turn from the agents to the content of socialization. This will give us an opportunity to return to the interplay between family, school, and the mass media, drawing also on data from the Malmoe panel and covering an earlier period of childhood and adolescence.

5.5. THE CONTENT OF SOCIALIZATION: "EFFECTS OF MEDIA USE"

5.5.1. Some Introductory Remarks

As agents of socialization the mass media cover next to all aspects of society and culture. In terms of the "Great Wheel of Culture in Society" (Figure 5.2, sec. 5.1.2), they are not only normatively and cognitively, but also expressively and instrumentally, oriented. The potential effects of mass media use, therefore, may cover a plethora of phenomena. Thus, some distinctions must be made.

The very first distinction to be made in this connection is the distinction between what Cramond (1976) calls "medium effects" and "Content effects," and Windahl (1981) calls "consequences" and "effects," respectively. The distinction is analytically clear-cut but empirically more difficult to uphold. Yet it is convenient to respect it. Medium effects—consequences of media use as such—were treated primarily in sec. 5.2.3. In this section we are dealing primarily with content effects— effects of content consumed rather than consequences of media consumption as such.

Effects of content consumed have also been dealt with in the chapter on social class, for instance, in which we discussed the class-specific effects of TV use on political interest (moral and instrumental value orientations; cf. sec. 4.7).

In the rest of this section we shall try to follow, from preschool to grade 9, the content effects of TV use as they interact with the content brought over to children and adolescents by other important agents of socialization, mainly the school and the family. We start with what happens in preschool, trying as before to spread our examples over the various value orientations of the wheel of culture. Before we turn to a more detailed discussion of our empirical results in this area, however, we must insert some short methodological remarks.

A basic weakness of this section on content effects is that we lack good measures of TV content consumed. Our strongest consumption measure is the measure of amount of habitual consumption often used in previous sections and chapters. Among the content-oriented measures at our disposal, we should mention the preferences (cf. sec. 2.4), and the diary measures of the TV programs actually consumed (cf. sec. 2.3). The former show very little variation, the latter are only available for the third wave of our two panels. In this situation we have only to resort to our measure of habitual consumption.

The assumption underlying most analyses in this section, then, must be that more TV viewing means more TV content of the type relevant to the argument at hand. The validity of that assumption is by no means self-evident. On the other hand it is not obviously wrong. The basic homogeneity of mass media material has often been stressed in mass communications research, sometimes naïvely so in our opinion, but nevertheless with some justification. Be that as it may, for our argumentation is not completely dependent on the assertion of homogenity.

What we do assert is that the content effects found in the following sections are conservative estimates of the "true" effects supposedly lying behind the data. For we maintain that, if we can demonstrate content effects from overall consumption data, the effects demonstrated would have been stronger, had we been able to use content-specific consumption data. When our findings are negative, however, we cannot know whether we should have been able to find some effect, had we been able to use content-specific data. The same type of argument, it should be noted, is applicable with respect to the linearity assumed by some of our multivariate analyses, especially the LISREL analyses. (The MCA analyses, it will be remembered, are better at handling curvilinearity.) In some cases, we have showed that the relationships we study are not linear, but curvilinear (for instance, the relationship between social class and amount of TV viewing; cf. sec. 4.5.1). Had we been able to heed this curvilinearity in all our analyses, some of the relationships observed would have turned out to be stronger than what we have been able to demonstrate. Again our estimates are probably somewhat conservative.

Such is our predicament, shared by many working in the field. We have been able to live with it. Hopefully, our readers will be able to do so, too. At least, we have put up a sign of warning. (It should also be mentioned that in sec. 5.5.3, building on Jönsson [1985], we were indeed able to include some content-oriented measures of TV use.)

After these methodological preambles, let us turn to our results.

5.5.2. Aggressiveness, Anxiety, and Restlessness[4]

An overriding concern in the public debate on children's TV viewing has been its assumed effects on the character of viewers' behavior and personality. Directly or indirectly, this concern has lain behind much or most of the research on children's and adolescents' TV use, from the 1950s to the 1980s. In the forefront has been the theme of aggressiveness, while other important themes, such as anxiety and restlessness, have been less conspicuous. In terms of the Great Wheel of Culture, problems such as these are located within the expressive and normative quandrants.

In the studies based on the Malmoe panel a standing focus of interest has been what Sonesson (1979, 1982) calls emotional and social adjustment. Developing an instrument originally presented by William–Olsson (1973), Sonesson had parents and teachers rate children's behavior with respect to aggressiveness and anxiety at age 6 (preschool wave). Just as in most similar studies, the aggressiveness rated was rather mild: "pushiness" in class, quarrels with friends and family, boisterousness, incivility, and so forth, rather than the severe physical violence or criminal behavior perhaps suggested by the term itself (cf. Cook et al., 1985, p. 176). Similarly, the anxiety rated was by no means pathological—rather, a mild form of anxiety. The two scales as applied by parents and teachers were added to a composite index, dividing the preschool children into three groups: heavily symptom-laden, symptom-free, and an intermediary group (8%, 16%, and 76% of the children, respectively).

Sonesson (1979, pp. 158ff.) found that the symptom-laden children were heavy consumers of TV and more often viewed exciting programs, and programs for grown-ups. Not surprisingly they had also been more often frightened by something they had seen on the screen. Results such as these are more or less in accordance with most other research in the area. When it comes to the more subtle relations established with TV content consumed, however, Sonesson's results contradict some earlier findings.

With the small children under study here, it was out of the question to use the scales developed for older children within the program and measure capture, long-term and short-term identification, and so forth (cf. secs. 2.5 and 2.7). Therefore, single questions tapping "Identification

---

[4] This section draws heavily on Sonesson (1979, 1982, 1986).

of similarity" and "Perceived reality of TV persons" were used. As it turned out, the simple measurements necessitated by the age of the children resulted in clear-cut differences. Contrary to expectations, symptom-free children were almost twice as prone to identify with persons seen on the screen as were heavily symptom-laden children (60% vs. 34%). Also, they were more prone to perceive similarities between TV grown-ups and grown-ups of their acquaintance (54% vs. 31%).

These results are in line with the ones presented in sec. 5.2.3 and showing that, in the same preschool panel, children having a best friend tended to be TV fans, for better and for worse. They also agree with Noble (1975, pp. 75ff.) who supports with empirical data his belief that stable children are able to identify and interact with everybody—both with persons appearing on the screen and in reality. And they agree with Rosengren et al. (1976) who found that adolescents' parasocial interaction with personae on the screen was not a function of lack of real social interaction.

These results do not agree, however, with a long line of previous research, especially not with those from the early days of TV (Bailyn, 1959; Himmelweit et al., 1958; Maccoby, 1954; Riley & Riley, 1951; Schramm et al., 1961). These earlier results, however, refer to other time periods, other types of TV, and other societies than ours. This, then, may be a case where differences in media structure and societal culture produce different results (cf. sec. 1.1). In many ways, Sweden and Swedish TV in the 1970s and 1980s are different from the U.S. and American TV in the 1950s (as well as from Britain and British TV in the 1950s). Therefore, TV is used differently, and that use produces different effects.

Note, however, the often repeated fact that cross-sectional data such as these do not tell us anything about the direction of the relations found. The fact that heavily symptom-laden children watch a lot of TV may be interpreted in at least three ways. The same goes for the fact that heavily symptom-laden children seem to be less ready to establish close relations with the TV content they consume. Is TV cause or effect in these cases? Or is some hidden, third variable causing the relationship? On the basis of these data alone we cannot tell. Fortunately we have more data at our disposal.

When the preschool children had reached the age of 11 (grade 5) they were ready for more precise measurements of their TV consumption. Furthermore, since it was felt that we had won the confidence of their teachers and parents we were able to use longer and better rating scales measuring the social and emotional adjustment of the children. To the scales used in earlier waves of her panel, therefore, Sonesson (1982) added Kaufman et al.'s (1979) scale of restlessness, developed and adapted to Swedish conditions. After factor analyses, and so forth, we thus had three scales, with good internal consistency, tapping aggressiveness, restlessness, and anxiety. Here are the results of these measurements in grade 5 (based on teacher's ratings; cf. Sonesson, 1982).

Boys were rated as more aggressive and restless than girls, while gender did not influence the degree of anxiety at all. Children of parents with intermediate education were less aggressive, restless, and anxious than children of parents with low or high education. Moderate to weak relationships between TV consumption and aggressiveness, restlessness, and anxiety were found. Gender and status differences were also found in these relationships between TV consumption and the three dimensions of emotional and social adjustment.

The relationship between TV and aggressiveness does not hold true for girls (gamma = .07), only for boys, for whom it is strong (gamma = .57).

The relationship between TV and restlessness is strong for boys (G = .50), weak to moderate for girls (.23). For children of parents with high education it is strong (.60), for those with low education, weak to moderate (.23).

The weak relationship between TV and anxiety results from the fact that education here acts as a strong depressor variable (Rosenberg, 1968). For children of parents with low education it is clearly negative (G = .33), for those with intermediary or high education it is strongly or moderately positive (.46, .28).

For boys in particular, then, TV is positively related to aggressiveness and restlessness. For children of parents with intermediary and high education it is also positively related to anxiety. For children of parents with low education, it is negatively related to anxiety.

We cannot go into any detailed study of the social-psychological processes which must lie behind such interactions between TV, gender, and social status. Suffice it here to note that the results do concur with what could be expected, given, for instance, existing gender roles. The negative relationship between anxiety and TV consumption for children of parents with low education may have something to do with the socio-oriented climate of family communication (protective and consensual) predominant in low status families (Hedinsson, 1981, p. 67).

Another confounding variable, of course, may be the gender of the teacher carrying out the ratings. In a later follow-up of the same Malmoe panel in grade 8, we controlled for this. No significant relationships between teacher's gender and the ratings were found, but there are weak tendencies for female teachers to rate boys as more aggressive than did male teachers, while, on the other hand, male teachers showed a weak tendency to rate girls as more anxious than did female teachers.

Similarly, female teachers found boys more restless than did male teachers, while male teachers found girls more restless than did female teachers. All in all, then, there is a weak but statistically nonsignificant tendency for teachers to be somewhat more negative toward the negative sides of students of the opposite sex. The tendency is hardly strong enough to have disturbed our analyses. If anything, it may have made our estimates somewhat conservative.

The important thing to note here is that we have again found strong to moderate relationships between amount of TV consumption and emotional and social adjustment, just as in the first wave of the same preschool panel. Once again, however, we do not know the direction of the relationships. Are we talking about effects of TV use, or is TV use an effect of personal predispositions, and so forth? In order to find an answer to such questions we must make more intense use of the opportunities offered by our panel design.

The problem of aggressiveness as a long-term effect of TV consumption has been with TV research right from the beginning (see Andison, 1977, for an overview; cf. also Cook et al., 1985). Recently, two large American panel studies have come up with radically different results. On the basis of their large 3-year panels, NBC researchers Milawsky et al. (1982) maintain that there are no such effects (cf., however, Cook et al., 1985; Huesman, 1984; Kenny, 1984). Huesman et al. (1984), on the other hand, on the basis of comparative panels in several countries, maintain that there are such effects, possibly in the shape of circular patterns such as the ones we visualized for other variables in sec. 5.4.

The question is by no means settled. New data and new arguments are constantly presented (cf., for instance, Pearl, 1985; Singer et al,. 1984; Wurtzel & Lometti, 1984). What do the media panel data have to offer in this context?

Rosengren et al. (1983) presented a LISREL model of the interplay between boys' aggressiveness and amount of television viewing in preschool, grades 3, and 5 of the Malmoe panel. The model did not reach significance however, which may be due to many circumstances, for instance, curvilinearity, or stability problems associated with the difficulty of measuring those subtle phenomena over periods covering passages between early developmental stages (cf. sec. 3.1). The MCA analysis is better at handling curvilinearity than is LISREL.

In Table 5.3, TV consumption in preschool (as rated by parents) is related to aggressiveness in grade 5 (as rated by teachers), in an MCA analysis controlling for gender, parents' education, child's aggressiveness in preschool, and TV viewing in grades 3 and 5. It will be seen that for the large majority of the children there is only an irregularly curvilinear relationship between amount of TV viewing and aggressiveness. But the small group with very high TV consumption (more than 2 hours a day) does show clearly higher aggressiveness, even after simultaneous control for five strategical background and intervening variables. This result is interesting from both methodological and substantive points of view.

Methodologically, Table 5.3 reminds us that while LISREL's strength is its capacity to handle a large number of latent and manifest variables, the strength of MCA is its capacity to handle nonlinear relationships, so that groups in the middle or extremes of the variable range may be heeded. A small deviant group runs the risk of being washed away in the large LISREL analysis, while in the smaller MCA it may be clearly visible.

Substantively, Table 5.3 tells us that there is a moderate influence on fifth graders' aggressiveness already from TV in preschool. This influence is concentrated almost exclusively on a small group of heavy viewers. In grade 5, at the age of 11, those who watched more than 2 hours TV a day while in preschool, tend to have a level of aggressiveness rated almost twice as high as those having watched less TV while in preschool, even after control for aggressiveness in preschool, as well as for a number of other relevant variables.

From this finding, we may draw at least two conclusions, one methodological, and one substantive. The methodological conclusion runs like this: In order to understand the effects of television on children we need both the overview offered by the LISREL model and the more detailed view offered by the MCA analysis. And the substantive conclusion is: The influence of TV use on aggressive attitudes and behavior may well be concentrated to a small proportion of children and ado-

Table 5.3. Television Viewing in Preschool and Aggressiveness in Grade 5. (MCA, Controlled for Gender, Parents' Education; Aggressiveness in Preschool; and TV Viewing in Grades 3 and 5. Malmoe Panel)

TV viewing in preschool	n	Aggressiveness in grade 5	
		Unadjusted	Adjusted for independents and covariates
0–5 hrs/week	13	4.6	4.5
5.5–7	46	5.9	5.9
7.5–10.5	30	3.4	4.1
11.0–14.0	29	4.2	4.6
14.5 and up	17	10.4	8.6
Total	136	eta = .34	beta = .28

lescents, so small, indeed, that it runs the risk of disappearing in linear analyses of whole populations (cf. Cook et al., 1985, p. 175). This conclusion is well in line with results obtained by Fetler (1985), recommending that effects research concentrate on subgroups of viewers, namely, those who "report watching either a great deal of television or very little."

The call for concentrating on subgroups has yet wider implications, however. If the effects of television differ between subgroups of national or regional samples, a fortiori, they may very well differ between samples from different countries, characterized by different media structures and different national cultures. In this connection we should remember that our data refer to Swedish conditions. We have already noted a couple of times that Swedish TV, representing a public service system with an outspoken social responsibility ideology, tries to avoid showing the crudest forms of violence and aggressiveness (cf. secs. 1.2.1 and 2.5). In countries and times with other, perhaps more violent TV fare, other results may well turn up. On the other hand, "our" aggressiveness is a rather mild one: pushiness, and so forth, among friends and in the classroom (cf. above). This gives some credence to our results, and to those of the Huesman–Eron group referred to above. For if viewing of Swedish TV, with its comparatively mild TV violence fare, does indeed tend to exert some influence on later aggressiveness (albeit the rather mild form of pushiness or incivility measured in our studies), then it is only to be expected logically that a heavy diet of more violent TV fare should have effects of the type demonstrated by Huesman, Lagerspitz, and Eron (1984).

In terms of socialization and the Great Wheel of Culture, this is what the data from the Malmoe panel presented in this section tell us: One effect of TV content on young people seems to be a negative influence on the expressive and normative sides of our four basic value orientations: an interplay with aggressiveness, restlessness, and anxiety. The nature of the relationship and the small size of the group (some 10%) tend to attenuate this effect in population studies working with linear relationships. Nevertheless there is such an effect, and the group is large enough to have been visible again and again to teachers working closely with children (witness innumerable complaints from teachers in different countries and periods of time). To individual parents and children finding themselves in this situation, the problem certainly may be a very real one.

This is a point where more information to, and education of, parents, teachers and children may be very important and may have a chance of being successful. To be really successful, of course, such measures should be accompanied by changes in media structure and media content.

Unfortunately, the increasing internationalization of the electronic media following the large-scale introduction of satellites and cable systems makes such changes increasingly difficult and increasingly improbable.

In the next section we shall turn to other effects of the use of TV content, and to other dimensions of the Great Wheel of Culture as communicated by television in interplay with the family and school.

5.5.3. Television and School Achievement[5]

In the previous section we dealt with socialization in the expressive dimension. We found positive relationships between amount of TV viewing and aggressiveness and restlessness among boys, and between TV viewing and anxiety among children of intermediary and highly educated mothers. This may seem to be something quite different from the institutions of art and literature located at the expressive pole of the Great Wheel of Culture. But no doubt it is an example of what popular art and literature dramatized in the medium of television may foster among its audience.

Staying among the children of the preschool panel, we turn in this section to effects of TV in the cognitive dimension. We shall see that the effects of TV viewing are no smaller in this dimension than in the expressive one. In a large PLS model encompassing 17 latent and 47 manifest variables Jönsson (1985, 1986) examined the interrelationships between

• Children's TV situation in preschool;
• TV use in preschool as well as in grades 3 and 5;
• Motives for watching TV;
• School test results in grade 1, and
• School marks in grades 3 and 6.

Before entering a discussion of the many complicated relationships revealed by the model, a short presentation of the variables in the model will be given.

The sheer size of a model attempting satisfactorily to cover 6 years of interrelated processes between children's relations to TV, home, and school necessitated some parsimony when selecting the variables for the model. The exogenous variables of gender and social background (mother's education and occupation) were clearly essential. Among the endogenous variables several difficult choices had to be made.

---

[5] This section draws heavily on Jönsson (1985).

The TV situation in preschool encompasses three latent, attitudinal variables: "TV treatment," "TV control," and "TV confidence." These variables are based on the Brown–Sonesson scales for parental TV attitudes already referred to (scales 4: Discussion, 6: Control, 1: Positive attitude; cf. sec. 5.3.3). The same variables were also measured in grades 3 and 5, but owing to the relatively high stability of these parental attitudes, it was felt that the measurements taken in the first wave were sufficient (Jönsson, 1985, p. 133).

TV use was measured by the three variables: consumption of children's programs and fiction programs (preschool, grades 3 and 5), and documentary programs (grade 5). (The variables build on picture tests in preschool and grade 3; in grade 5, on TV diary data.) It was felt that in a situation of too many variables competing for inclusion, sheer amount of TV consumption had to yield to these more content-oriented consumption variables. Within the overarching perspective of the Media Panel Program this makes for some diversity, for with few exceptions (Sonesson, 1979) we have often had a somewhat unfortunate tendency to fall back on amount of consumption alone as the central variable of TV use.

In grade 5, two motives for watching TV, called "routine" and "knowledge" were also included (based on scales originally developed by Greenberg [1974, 1976] and adapted to Swedish conditions within the Media Panel Program; cf. secs. 3.3.5, 4.5.3, and 5.3.3).

For this cohort of Malmoe children, marks were not given in grades 1 and 5, only in grades 3 and 6. (The fact that grades were available for grade 6 was a happy coincidence, which made the time sequence behind the causal relationships somewhat easier to disentangle.) In grade 3, marks in Swedish, mathematics and general subjects were used; in grade 6, the children obtained marks also in English, and these were included. In grade 1, school tests tapping spatial capacity, speech understanding, letter knowledge, reading, and writing were available and used instead of marks.

All these choices—sometimes quite difficult to make—were based on a number of previous statistical analyses ranging from Pearson correlations matrices to MCA analyses to factor analyses and preliminary, cross-sectional, and longitudinal PLS analyses. For further technical details the reader is referred to Jönsson (1985).

The model itself is presented in Figure 5.21. Note that only the "inner" structural model is presented. It should also be mentioned that in order to make the model more surveyable, the strong and ubiquitous influences from the exogenous variables of gender and social background were not included in the graphical model (although they were included, of course, in the statistical analysis behind the model). The same goes for relationships between TV-use variables in the same panel wave. For the outer, measurement model, as well as for the omitted types of relationships, the interested reader is referred to Jönsson (1985), where one may also find the preparatory models on which the model here presented was built.

A model such as this, covering various aspects of TV use as well as its origins and its effects, is a true combination of uses and gratifications research and effects research (cf., for instance, secs. 1.1 and 5.4). The technique of analysis used at the same time produces a wealth of interesting details and a certain amount of overview. The model deserves some verbal comments. Indeed, to be understood fully, it needs them.

From a uses and gratifications perspective it is again interesting to see how children's TV use is influenced, as late as in grade 5, by the setting offered by parental TV attitudes in preschool (an arrow of .21 from parental TV confidence in preschool to consumption of fiction programs in grade 5, after control for gender and social background, previous TV habits, and so forth).

From the same perspective it is also interesting to have a confirmation of the assumption that the same medium in a different setting may become an agent of socialization with radically different effects (cf. sec. 5.3.4). In preschool, consumption of children's programs is partly an outcome of parental TV control (.28) and lack of confidence in the medium as such (−.16). Under these premises, the consumption of children's programs has a direct positive effect on school test results a

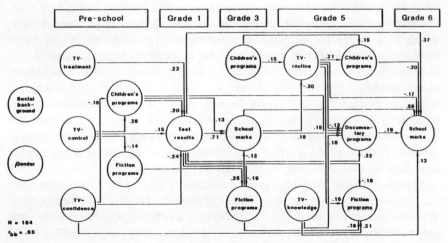

Figure 5.21.   A PLS Model of TV Use and School Achievement. Malmoe Panel. (From Jönsson, 1985)

year later, in grade 1 (and, indeed, indirect effects stretching up to marks in grade 6).

In grade 5, however, consumption of children's programs is partly an outcome of the TV-viewing motive of routine, in its turn negatively influenced by marks in grade 3. Children's program consumption of this type has a unique, negative influence on marks in grade 6 (controlling for such things as social background, earlier school achievements, earlier TV setting, and habits, and so forth). Some less successful children seem to turn to children's programs for the comfort of easy routine. As an unforeseen and unhappy result of this quite natural reaction, they later on become even less successful.

From an effects perspective, our interest is naturally focused on the effects of TV use on school achievement. Are they positive or negative? Since the introduction of TV three decades ago, both points of view have been represented in research and the general debate (Jönsson, 1985, pp. 33ff.; Roe, 1983, pp. 15ff.). The discussions have been intense but, in general, the point of view that TV is something negative has been predominant. Based as it is on advanced multivariate statistical analysis of three-wave panel data from a representative sample and stretching over 6 years, Figure 5.21 offers an opportunity to take a close look at this classical problem of mass media research. Basically, what the model of Figure 5.21 tells us is that the problem of TV and school has been twice posed in the wrong way.

In the first place, TV use is not only a set of independent variables; school, not only a set of dependent variables. On the contrary. School influences TV as much as TV influences school, and this holds true not only for TV but for other mass media as well. This is a point of view forcefully driven home by Roe (1983a) and discussed at some length in sec. 5.4. Here we get strong independent confirmation of its basic soundness (the details of which will be discussed in a moment).

Secondly, it is somewhat narrow-minded to assume that in its capacity as an independent variable, TV use should have exclusively positive or negative effects (although, in the heat of the debate, such an assumption may be quite natural, and also quite effective). The truth is that TV has both positive and negative effects, and this simple but often overlooked truth is made graphically visible in the model of Figure 5.21 (the details of which will be discussed in a moment).

Together, these two important features of the model neatly express the basic perspective of the Media Panel Program. This perspective involves an effort to merge the effects tradition with the uses and gratifications tradition in order to understand the mass media use of children and adolescents as a series of positive and vicious circles. The notions of "positive" and "vicious" are obviously dependent on the perspective employed: the perspective of time, and the perspective of the viewer (cf. Rosengren & Windahl, 1978; Rosengren et al., 1983). Glimpses of both positive and vicious circles have already been given in the previous discussion of the model. In this context it is striking to observe the importance of the early TV setting for future TV habits and school achievements.

Those parents who feel that children's use of TV should be controlled and that their TV experiences should be discussed make their children watch children's programs when they should be watched (in the preschool period) and make them watch fewer fiction programs. All this positively affects test results in grade 1, thereby starting a positive circle which ends up with a positive influence on marks in grade 6.

Parents who, at the time of their children's preschool days, have less belief in the need for control and more confidence in TV, influence the consumption of children's program in preschool negatively, the consumption of fiction programs positively. This starts a vicious circle: fewer preschool children's programs, more preschool and school fiction—worse marks—more routine motivated TV, fewer informative programs in grade 5, more fiction and children's programs—worse marks in grade 6.

Thus, depending on the circumstances, TV use may have both positive and negative effects. That is, it is both cause and effect—as is what happens at school. The overall effects of these positive and vicious circular processes may be substantial. Table 5.4 presents the direct, indirect, and total effects of consumption of children's programs as measured in the three different waves on the consumption of other types of programs, and on school achievement in grades 1, 3, and 6.

It will be seen that the effect on school marks of consumption of children's programs in the preschool days is very persistent. Actually, it grows ever stronger as the children proceed through school. The total direct and indirect effects on marks in grade 6 of consumption of children's programs in preschool alone is .28 (controlling for social background, other TV consumption, earlier school achievement, and so forth).

Figures such as these give us a notion of the importance of media use in early childhood for future achievement. Yet it must be remembered that, all in all, the influence of TV use on school achievement is rather modest, not to say marginal, at least as it can be measured today, and especially compared with the more powerful sociocultural factors of class and gender. A coefficient of .28 corresponds to some 8% of the variation. The strongest predictor of success at school is earlier success: the total effect of the school tests in grade 1 on the marks in grade 6 is .87 (Jönsson, 1985, p. 140).

Table 5.4. Direct, Indirect, and Total Effects of Children's Programs on Later TV Consumption and School Achievement, Controlled for Social Class, Gender, and TV Environment. (From Jönsson, 1985)

Independent variable	Dependent variable	Direct effect	Indirect effect	Total effect
Children's programs in preschool	Fiction in			
	grade 3	—	-.04	—
	grade 5	—	-.01	—
	Informational programs in			
	grade 5	.15	.14	.29
	School achievement in			
	grade 1	.20	—	.20
	grade 3	.13	.14	.27
	grade 6	—	.28	.28
Children's programs in grade 3	Children's programs in			
	grade 5	.15	.03	.18
	Fiction in			
	grade 5	—	-.01	—
	Informational programs in			
	grade 5	—	-.02	—
	School achievement in			
	grade 6	—	-.08	—
Children's programs in grade 5	School achievement in			
	grade 6	-.20	—	-.20

Nothing succeeds like success, but who originally succeeds is to a large extent socially determined. The total effect of social background on marks in grade 6 is .59. (The difference between .87 and .59 to a large extent must be an expression of the unique effect of intelligence which—mostly for reasons of the *Zeitgeist*—we were unfortunately not able to measure as satisfactorily as we would have wished.)

Figures such as these make us realize that although we have found a substantial influence from TV on school achievement, there is no reason either for despair or for optimism. TV is a force for better and for worse in the lives of children and adolescents. It is an important agent of socialization, and as such it interacts with other agents of socialization; and with the individuals being socialized. It is both a cause and an effect, and its effects are both positive and negative.

What is hopeful in the results just presented is that they show the importance of the early TV setting offered by parents. This setting may be influenced and changed by parents themselves—and by children. Therefore, efforts should be made to inform children, parents, and teachers about the positive and negative effects of TV use. Such efforts of information about media effects on children and adolescents have been made many times already, but on the basis of sustained research programs such as the Media Panel Program, they may receive increased impetus (cf. Rosengren, 1986). In the long run systematic and specific teaching at school and in teachers' seminars will probably be necessary (cf. Carlsson & Sonesson, 1983).

5.5.4. Television and Mental Maps[6]

In this section we rely mostly on Hägred (1983), who has employed data from the main Vaxjoe panel to discuss the relationship between television viewing and the emergence of internal images of the environment, so called "mental maps" (Abler, Adams, & Gould, 1971; cf. Gould, 1975).

Mental maps are the result of an interaction between a number of socializing agents. Nobody would ever maintain that they are entirely the result of what we get from the media. To a large extent our mental maps are fed with direct experiences. However, we also have images of what we have never primarily experienced ourselves, and here the media are extremely important. Images of distant places are brought to us daily on the television screen and on the pages of newspapers. Some of these places are so frequently represented that they become increasingly familiar to the audience. Thus, a reasonable assumption is that consumption of media presenting and describing places beyond everyday reach of the individual can be used as a predictor of the characteristics of some mental maps.

In his study, Hägred (1983) found TV viewing to exert a powerful influence on one aspect of mental mapping. In the Vaxjoe study we asked the respondents the following question:

Imagine that you have to move away from Sweden. Which country would you most of all like to move to?

There are great variations in the answers of different subgroups. Throughout the material, however, two main tendencies may be found:

---

[6] This section draws heavily on Hägred (1983).

The older the respondents, the greater the likelihood that they will choose the U.S. as their preferred destination.

The more television consumed, the greater the likelihood that the U.S. will be picked as the country to move to.

As can be seen in Table 5.5, there are only small deviations from these main tendencies. (The table also shows that boys in the fifth grade seem to be more U.S.-oriented than the girls, although this difference is less pronounced in the ninth grade.)

The fact that the U.S. becomes more popular with age, and Norway less so, does not depend on television viewing alone, of course. The older the youngsters become, the greater their ability to communicate in an English-speaking country. Although in Swedish schools English as a subject starts in grade 3, for many fifth graders Norway will be the natural country to choose because of the possibility of making oneself understood. (Norway, being Sweden's closest neighbor, has a closely related language, permitting easy communication between Swedes and Norwegians.) The impact of television viewing is obvious, however, and the direction of the influence is easily understood. The U.S. is a country portrayed frequently on Swedish TV. (In 1980–1981 some 30% of all imported programs were of U.S. origin, whereas Norway was the source of only 3%.)

Hägred's data suggest that the impact of television on the choice of country to move to is greater in the fifth than in the ninth grade. On the other hand, we have seen that, for all subgroups, the U.S. is mentioned more often among the elder. The U.S. image relayed by TV may be especially well received by older adolescents. For Swedish youngsters the U.S. of television may stand for much of what they want to acquire: another life-style, a well-developed youth culture, and a challenge that is different from that which a country such as Norway can offer. In short, the U.S. as pictured by Swedish television is more likely to provide better material for the independence and identity that are sought in adolescence. Cognitive and instrumental aspects of the socialization process interact in producing the mental maps of adolescents.

The combined impact of social class, age, and gender in interaction with the mental mapping of TV is visualized in Figures 5.23 and 5.24 contrasting the mental map of grade 5 girls with low TV consumption to that of grade 9 boys with high TV consumption. It will be seen that this impact is considerable. To boys in grade 9, who are high on TV viewing, the world is dominated by North America. The first map of the three (Figure 5.22) featuring the "news map" of Swedish TV in 1975 (DSu, 1976, p. 13), is much more balanced than those of our

Table 5.5. Country of Destination by TV Viewing, Gender, and Age. (Percentage, Vaxjoe Main Panel)

Country to move to: TV consumption:	Grade 5						Grade 9					
	Girls			Boys			Girls			Boys		
	Low	Middle	High	Low	Middle	High	Low	Middle	High	Low	Middle	High
United States	3	4	19	18	18	53	32	44	43	30	38	55
Norway	41	31	21	29	35	15	23	15	9	33	25	17
Great Britain	16	18	14	13	11	13	7	13	6	10	9	9
Canada	—	—	—	11	11	5	1	—	—	5	4	3
Denmark	5	10	9	7	—	2	3	—	3	—	—	1
Sum of percentages	65	63	63	78	75	88	66	72	61	78	76	85
n	58	51	43	45	57	62	69	48	35	40	55	69

adolescents. This difference suggests that the TV impact may stem more from "fictional" than from "factual" TV content. (For similar news maps from other countries and media, cf. Gerbner & Marvanyi, 1977.)

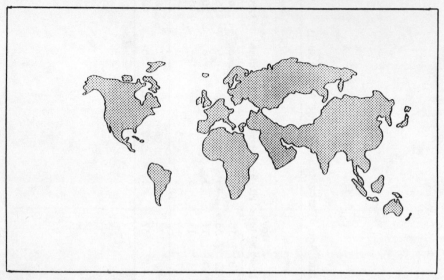

Figure 5.22.   Map of the World as Reported in Swedish TV News, 1975. (Source: DsU, 1976, p. 13)

Figure 5.23.   "Mental Map" of Girls Aged 11, Low TV Consumption

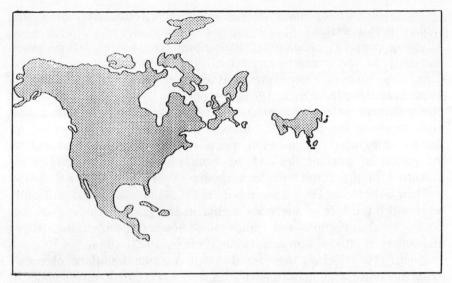

Figure 5.24. "Mental Map" of Boys Aged 15, High TV Consumption

5.5.5. Television and Occupational Plans[7]

In the previous sections we have been discussing socialization in the expressive, normative, and cognitive dimensions of the Great Wheel of Culture. In this section we turn to a discussion of socialization in the instrumental dimension. Our focus is one of the most important decisions in the life of the adolescent, the decision about future job.

This decision is never taken suddenly. It is true that it may sometimes be taken very quickly, but even in such cases adolescents take it against a more or less well-organized background of knowledge, beliefs, values, and evaluations of and about themselves, their society and the world at large. This background is constructed primarily from the four main socialization agents—family, peer group, school and mass media—as adolescents gradually start to shape for themselves a picture of their future position in a social world dominated by an instrumental value orientation, the world of work.

What use does the adolescent make of this knowledge, these beliefs, values, and evaluations in the process of making the important decision? In other, more effect-oriented terms: what influence do family, school, and mass media have on the occupational aspirations and on the choice

---

[7] This section draws heavily on Flodin (1986).

of occupation finally made by the adolescent? That question is the subject of this section.

Young people's occupational aspirations and choice of occupation represent an important research tradition in the sociology of work (Brown & Brooks, 1984; Sewell, Hauser, & Wolf, 1980; Sjöstrand, 1980; Watts, Super, & Kidd, 1981; Wernersson, 1983). In this tradition, however, very little attention has been bestowed upon the role of the mass media in the process. In mass communications research and in the sociology of communication much attention has been devoted to the picture of working life and the composition of the labor force as portrayed in print and broadcast media (Abrahamsson, 1983, 1985; DeFleur & DeFleur, 1967; Lowenthal, 1961; Signorielli, 1984). But only seldom has the role of the mass media in the gradual shaping of the occupational aspirations and choice of adolescents been studied (Himmelweit et al., 1958; Morgan, 1980; Werner, 1972, 1986).

Flodin (1986) brings together the two research traditions of occupational choice and mass media uses and effects in a novel way. A common feature of the two traditions is that of late both of them have been using structural equation models to analyze and present their data. It is thus quite natural that Flodin should confront formal models from the two research traditions with each other, in the process enlarging and elaborating both types of models. The end result of his labors is two LISREL models for the influence of social background, school achievement, and TV use on occupational plans of boys and girls in the main Vaxjoe panel of the Media Panel Program.

Before presenting the double model it is necessary briefly to discuss the variables included in the model.

In the Media Panel Program we have often had the opportunity to discuss the importance of gender in shaping the mass media use of children and adolescents, its causes, effects, and consequences. It is to be expected that this phenomenon should be especially important in connection with occupational plans, for at least three important reasons. In the first place, the labor market is highly differentiated according to gender. Women have fewer occupations to choose; occupations, furthermore, which are found to a great extent in the lower echelons of society, and often in the service sector (SOU, 1979, p. 56). Secondly, the picture of the occupational structure offered in the mass media, and not least on the TV screen, is even more biased than the social reality itself (Abrahamsson, 1983, 1985; Signorielli, 1984; Tuchman et al., 1983). Thirdly, we have seen in the preceding chapters that boys and girls use the mass media very differentially. For these and other reasons it is reasonable to keep boys and girls apart when studying the relationship between mass media use and occupational plans. That is done by presenting separate LISREL models for the two sexes.

We know from much earlier research that the occupational choice and aspirations of adolescents are strongly affected by social background (Brown & Brooks, 1984; Sjöstrand, 1980). Social background as an exogenous variable, therefore, is a requisite of any model of the process. Flodin (1986) used a composite index for both parents' occupational status as classified by the Swedish Central Bureau of Statistics (a classificatory scheme somewhat more elaborated than, but strongly correlated with, the one used by the rest of the Media Panel projects. [r = .81]). For technical reasons it was only possible to use this classification in the third wave of the main panel. Strictly speaking, therefore, it could not be used as a general background variable in a longitudinal design. However, the stability of social class is very high (.82 between first and third wave for the social class operationalization used in the rest of the Media Panel Program). Thus it was considered appropriate to use the new and better operationalization as a background variable. As used here, this variable has six values, ranging from the level of unskilled blue collar to the level of directors, managers, and professionals.

Flodin also utilized the composite index of the educational status of both parents, giving it five values. Parental occupational and educational status thus defined form the two manifest variables of the latent variable of "social background" in Flodin's models.

School achievement is the second obvious set of variables affecting adolescent occupational choice and aspirations (Härnqvist, 1980; Sewell, Hauser, & Wolf, 1980; Wilson & Portes, 1975). Flodin used the school marks of four subjects obtained in grades 6 and 7 (Swedish, mathematics, English, and what in Sweden are called orientational subjects). In grade 9, he used the marks of five subjects (Swedish, social studies, history, geography, and chemistry) as the manifest variables of the latent variable of school achievement. (The reason he chose different subjects in different grades was technical difficulties with calibrating subjects for which students are streamed on more than one level of qualification.)

In grade 9 (the last year of compulsory education) Swedish adolescents have to decide about their future educational plans. Some 85% go on to "past-compulsory" education (a welfare state variant of the so-called "gymnasium" of the continental European tradition, roughly corresponding to the American senior high school; cf. Abrahamsson and Göransson [1982]). There are a lot of qualitatively different alternatives available (lines of science, technology, economics, languages, social work, service jobs, industrial specialties, and so forth); but generally it could be said that the length of the course chosen is a good indicator of the future social status at which students are aiming. They may choose between gymnasium alternatives ranging from 1 to 4 years. The number of years chosen was used by Flodin as the operationalization of "planned secondary education."

In each of the three waves of the main Vaxjoe panel, occupational plans, aspirations and dreams were measured by two questions. The first question referred to the "dream job" of the adolescents. "If you could choose whatever job you liked—what job would you choose?" The second question referred to more realistic notions: "And in reality—what type of job do you think you will end up with?" The phenomena tapped by the first question have an interest of their own, but an added advantage of the first question is that it helps underline the expected realism of the replies to the second one. In his models, Flodin used the second question—expectations of their real future job—as a basis for his operationalization of the adolescents' occupational plans.

The responses to this question can be classified in a number of ways, the two main ways being vertical and horizontal. The vertical classification sorts the replies into categories of social class or status, while the horizontal sorts them into broad sectors of society, such as industrial production, service sector, and so forth. The classification scheme used by Flodin (cf. above) heeds both these aspects, separately and/or conjointly. In his thesis, he discusses at some length the horizontal differentiation of the responses of the adolescents, as well as its relation to the variables of interest to him (Flodin, 1986). In his structural models he concentrates on the vertical dimension. In these models his main dependent variable—Occupational plans—concerns the social class or status of the occupation with which the adolescents under study expect to end up.

A set of variables often used in studies in the tradition of occupational choice and aspirations is self-image, self-reliance, and so forth. Rosenberg's (1965) well-known self-image scales were included among our variables. Flodin (1986) related them to such potential variables of his structural models as TV use, school achievement, choice of education, and occupational plans, finding moderate first-order relationships with most of these variables. The explanatory value of self-image for occupational plans when controlling by means of MCA analyses for the basic variables of social background and school achievement was rather modest, however. All the same, Flodin included the variable in his preparatory, cross-sectional LISREL models. As implied by the MCA analyses, he found that its unique influence on occupational plans was next to negligible. He therefore decided to exclude it from his final longitudinal model.

In our presentation of the variables included in Flodin's models, we have so far stuck to the variables which traditionally lie in the focus of interest in the research tradition of adolescents' occupational aspirations and expectations. To these well-researched variables Flodin (1986) adds the variable of TV use.

The influence of the mass media in general, and television in particular, on individual occupational aspirations and choice have been much discussed but relatively little researched (cf., however, Himmelweit et al., 1958; Morgan, 1980; Werner, 1972, 1986). Theoretically, this influence may be expected to work in two ways. Because of the predominance of upper-class occupations in the world of TV it could be expected that heavy TV viewing would lead to higher occupational expectations. To the contrary, it could be argued that TV may have a passifying influence on the heavy viewer, which could lead to lower expectations (cf. Morgan, 1980). Flodin (1986) shows that there are indeed negative first-order relationships to be found between amount of TV consumption and occupational aspirations. But they are not too strong, and it is doubtful whether they can be expected to stand up to the stricter controls inherent in the structural models approach.

By means of MCA and LISREL techniques Flodin (1986) analyzed more closely the three types of TV consumption on which the main media panel TV consumption variable is built (TV consumption on weekdays, Saturdays, and Sundays), finding that consumption on weekdays as a rule was more strongly related to the variables central to his problems. (In retrospect, at least, it seems reasonable enough that viewing during weekdays—when most work is being done, inside school, and outside—should show stronger relations to variables such as job plans and school achievement.) As a consequence of this finding, in his final longitudinal model Flodin built his TV variable on TV viewing during weekdays, thus increasing his chances of finding an influence from TV use on occupational plans.

So much for the theoretical and technical background. For further information about theoretical and methodological considerations, such as detailed expectations about the relationships between the variables of the models, reliability, internal and external nonresponse, as well as other technical details in connection with Flodin's longitudinal models, the interested reader is referred to Flodin (1986).

Flodin's two models of the influence of social background, school achievement, and TV viewing on adolescent girls' and boys' occupational plans are presented in Figures 5.25 and 5.26. They are built on 9 latent variables and 21 manifest variables. As before, only the structural models are offered. (For the measurement models, see Flodin, 1986).

The very interested reader may wish to compare the parameters of the two models with corresponding parameters in models constructed by Johnsson–Smaragdi (1983) and Roe (1983a) and presented earlier in this book (secs. 5.3 and 5.4) and may find some discrepancies. Since the models are based on basically the same individuals these discrepancies must be due to substantive and/or technical differences in the data and/or the techniques of analysis lying behind the models.

Among the most important substantive differences should be mentioned first of all the simple fact that the different models are built on sometimes quite different concepts and variables. As the technique controls for influence from all relevant variables in the model, it is only to be expected that some differences in the resulting parameters should turn up. Other important but minor substantive differences include Flodin's social background variable, his use of weekday TV viewing, and his use of more school marks than Roe used.

Among the most important technical differences should be mentioned the fact that Flodin had the opportunity to use a later version of LISREL than the one available to Johnsson–Smaragdi and Roe (version VI vs. IV). Also, Flodin used so called pair-wise deletion; Johnsson–Smaragdi and Roe so-called list-wise deletion. In cases of internal nonresponse, pair-wise deletion retains more information but introduces other technical problems. Finally, Flodin used polychoric correlations as input data, while Johnsson–Smaragdi and Roe used Pearson r's (cf. Appendix 2, and Flodin, 1986). As a consequence of this, the X^2 test is not applicable.

In the light of these many differences between the conceptualization and data behind the various models, the basic similarities between the parameters of the various models offer support for the inherent soundness of the empirical data and the techniques of analysis used. As a rule the existing differences are small (in most cases the second decimal), and they do not substantially affect any arguments built on the models presented.

Nevertheless the differences should not be neglected. In cases where for some reason it is very important to choose between a parameter presented by Flodin (1986) and one presented by Johnsson–Smaragdi (1983) and/or Roe (1983a), it should be remembered that since the Media Panel Program is cumulative, the quality of the data used in the program is continually improved. So are the techniques of analysis used, as well as the technical skills of analysis possessed by all its members.

After these preliminaries, let us turn to the models themselves.

The first thing to note in connection with the two models is their basic similarity. The fact that much the same structural models and much the same parameters have been obtained for two entirely different subsamples of the same population offers strong validation for the underlying data, techniques of analysis and conceptualization. We shall return to the differences between the boys' and the girls' models in a

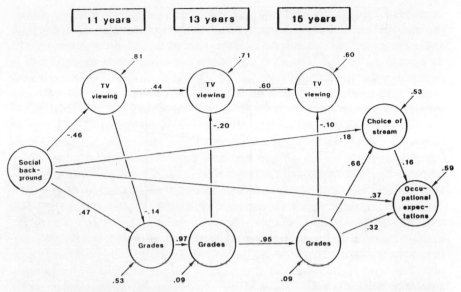

Adjusted goodness of fit index: .994

Figure 5.25. A LISREL Model of Girls' Occupational Expectations. Vaxjoe Main Panel. (From Flodin, 1986)

moment. For the time being, we are interested in characteristics common to the two models.

Common to the two models is above all the basic fact that TV exerts only a very marginal, indirect influence on the occupational plans of the adolescents. For both boys and girls the marks in grade 6 are negatively influenced by TV consumption in grade 5. This influence is then relayed on to school future and occupational plans by the marks in grades 7 and 9. By the time this influence has reached occupational plans it is minimal (−.04).

TV is related to marks in all three waves, but in the two cases when there is a choice as to the direction of the relationship (from the point of view of the time sequence) the arrows (probably basically reciprocal) point from marks to TV consumption. Again we have found support for the idea that school is not always—and certainly not only—to be seen as the dependent variable in its relation to other agents of socialization. In both of Flodin's models and in those developed by Roe (1983a; see sec., this volume), the influence from TV on school achievement is weak to negligible.

This is a result rather different from the one presented in the previous section. In the Malmoe panel we found an intricate interplay between TV use and marks. Two circumstances explain the differences. In the

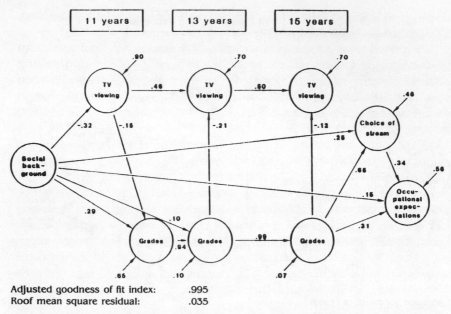

Adjusted goodness of fit index: .995
Roof mean square residual: .035

Figure 5.26.   A LISREL Model of Boys' Occupational Expectations. Vaxjoe Main Panel. (From Flodin, 1986)

first place, Jönsson's result presented in the previous section builds on content-oriented TV consumption variables, while Flodin's models build on quantity of consumption alone. It may well be that Flodin would have found some influence from TV on school achievement, perhaps even on occupational expectations, had he been able to introduce content-oriented variables into his models. But we doubt very much that such an influence would have been very substantial.

The reason for our doubts is simple enough. As the adolescents move through the school system, TV occupies a diminishing place in their lives. The consumption of TV may still be quite high for some students, but it has no longer a central location in the style of life preferred by most adolescents. Other media, primarily music from radio and cassettes, take its place. It is logical, therefore, that we should find no longitudinal influence from TV on school achievement in grades 7 and 9 (cf. Roe 1983a, p. 167).

This negative result also convincingly demonstrates the advantages of the structural modeling approach. Using zero-order relationships or controlling only for a small number of variables, Flodin (1986) found weak to moderate relationships between TV consumption and occupational expectations. Locating the TV variable in the context of a large longitudinal model, we see that these relationships are mostly artifacts, due to the close and long-lasting relationships among social background, TV use, and school marks.

The very strong influence of social background and school marks on the occupational expectations of adolescents is the other outstanding common feature of the two models. For boys and girls alike, between 40% and 50% of the variation in occupational expectations is due to social background and marks. This is also where the two models differ, however.

In the girls' model, the strongest total effect on occupational plans comes from social background (.61), while the influence from marks in grade 9 is weaker (.43). With the boys it is the other way around. Here the total effect from marks in grade 9 is strongest (.54), while the influence from social background is somewhat weaker (.45). Both the fact that social background and marks exert a strong influence on the occupational plans of adolescents, and the fact that girls are more influenced by class and status than boys, are familiar from common-sense and much earlier research, including our own (cf., e.g., Figures 4.1 and 4.2). It shows that the main results of the two models are reliable and valid.

We may be fairly convinced, then, that TV consumption does not, to any considerable extent, influence the vertical dimension of our adolescents' occupational plans. This is not to say, of course, that it does not influence the horizontal dimension of adolescents' occupational plans, or that other media, or specific TV content do not exert any such influence, on whole populations of adolescents, or on specific subgroups. But it does offer an opportunity to clarify some speculative theorizing on the role of mass media in our society.

From Marxist and functionally oriented sociologists of communications alike, it has often been maintained that in a modern society the mass media contribute to the maintenance and reproduction of the societal structure, not the least its class character and occupational structure (cf., for instance, Hall, 1982; Parsons, 1942; Wirth, 1948). No doubt this is a plausible hypothesis, even if empirical support may be less easibly available than is sometimes assumed. What our data have shown is that this reproductive function of the mass media is probably not fulfilled by way of an influence on individuals' location in the given societal structure of classes and occupations. Mass media do not seem to exert an influence on individual mobility or stationarity in these societal structures. Rather they may help reproduce the structures as such, in society and in our perceptions of society.

In the socialization process leading up to the occupational expectations entertained by adolescents, the mass media in general, and television in particular, may offer important information shaping adolescent perceptions of occupations and occupational structure. But TV consumption has not been shown to exert any influence on the vertical dimension of occupational expectations as such. These expectations are primarily influenced by the socialization content provided by those other two important agents of socialization: family and school.

5.6. MEDIA USE AND SOCIALIZATION: A CONCLUDING DISCUSSION

In the theoretical introduction of this chapter we presented two typologies: one for socialization research, and one for the content of the socialization process (more or less general aspects of society's culture). The rest of the chapter may be characterized as attempts to combine in empirical research various aspects of the two typologies.

One dimension of the socialization typology concerned the status of the individual socialized: whether to regard him or her as a subject or an object. We noted that this distinction was closely related to those two important traditions in mass communications research, uses and gratifications research and effects research. The former tends to regard the individual as a subject; the latter, as an object. The twin ambitions of this book, and particularly, perhaps, of this chapter, have been, first, to regard the individual as both a willing and acting subject and as an object of strong forces inside and outside the individual, *and*, secondly (something which amounts to much the same thing), to combine the two research traditions in what we like to call "uses and effects research."

The other dimension of the socialization typology concerns the nature of society: whether to regard it in the light of a consensus or from a conflict perspective. Again we maintain that a combination of the two perspectives is necessary and possible. All societies are characterized by both consensus and conflicts. This is clearly seen in the lives of our children and adolescents, and in their relations to the various agents of socialization trying to form them and their lives (television, for instance, primarily representing a consensual perspective fostered by the family; popular music, a potential conflict perspective fostered by the peer group; both perspectives being adroitly exploited by an international mass media industry). Again the study of such relationships implies a uses-and-effects approach.

Regardless of whether the empirical study of such relationships concerns the subject–object distinction or the conflict–consensus distinction, it is always extremely demanding. More specifically, it demands advanced multivariate analyses applied to panel data covering the various types of content categorized by the Great Wheel of Culture. This chapter has offered a number of such analyses.

Strictly speaking, the first of these analyses were content-free in that they concerned activity and interaction as such. Eight different types of relations between TV viewing and other activities were organized in a typology. Little or no support was found for the type of relationship called displacement (the view that television makes children and adolescents passive). Rather, the analyses offered a picture of the individual socialized as being an active subject much more than a passive object.

The following analyses were spread over the four value orientations of the wheel of culture, ranging from the expressive and moral orientations implied by the studies of aggressiveness and anxiety, to the cognitive and instrumental orientations implied by the studies of school achievement, mental maps, and occupational plans. More than once it was found that, in order really to understand the complex models resulting from the multivariate LISREL and PLS analyses, we must interpret the individuals *both* as willing and acting subjects using television and other media for their own purposes, *and* as more or less passive objects of strong influences from that same, originally self-willed, media use.

The final outcome of such an interplay between the individual socialized and a number of socializing agents is not as easily predictable as popular debate would have it. More often than not it may cut both ways. School achievement, for instance, was shown to be negatively or positively influenced by television viewing, depending on the type of content viewed, the context surrounding the viewing, and the location of the viewing among the developmental stages of childhood and adolescence. For a small group of boys viewing a lot of television in preschool, aggressiveness may be a very real outcome of their viewing, but for the whole population of children and adolescents television viewing can explain less than 10% of the variation in aggressiveness. Contrary to the firm beliefs of many parents and teachers, a preference for punk and rock (at the time despised by parents and teachers alike) may well have been an effect, rather than a cause, of school failure. The amount of television viewing does not seem to have any effect at all on the status of the job expectations held by adolescents, a finding which runs in the face of much functionalistic and Marxist speculation. On the other hand it would seem that the musical tastes and habits of the adolescents actually do exercise such an influence.

Regarding socialization in the light of the theoretical typologies presented in the first sections of this chapter, and in that of the empirical analyses presented in the later sections, has made some supposedly familiar phenomena look rather different. The vistas opening up toward continued research look promising.

6

Summary And Conclusions

6.1. INTRODUCTION: 2 PERSPECTIVES

Toward the end of a thoughtful research overview, Denis McQuail (1985) reflects, "With the Benefit of Hindsight," on uses and gratifications research. (McQuail, of course, for a decade or two has been a leading proponent and critic of that research tradition.) According to him, uses and gratifications research has had four main purposes, namely, to get to know more about the relations between mass media use on one hand, and culture, people, behavior, and society on the other. It is unlikely, he maintains, that any one model can serve all four purposes. Better to single out one of the problems—culture, for instance. The final paragraph of McQuail's article does indeed provide food for some thought, not least toward the end of an undertaking such as the Media Panel Program:

> The main thrust of the uses and gratifications tradition has been towards the construction of a major highway which serves to link all four purposes in one investigative enterprise. Real highways do facilitate very long, fast, journeys by large vehicles (research teams), but they also change the landscape they traverse, have restricted views and stimulate travel for its own sake or that of the vehicle. By comparison, the byway mapped out for reaching one rather limited goal of knowledge might be slow and winding, but should enable one to see more on the way and keep one generally in closer contact with nature (McQuail, 1985, p. 139).

In the rustic terms of McQuail, we should like to describe the Media Panel Program as a highway serving a rich and changing landscape full of enticing byways winding their way through fields and woods, from hamlet to town, from town to hamlet, sooner or later joining the highway leading to the city, where all the action is. Sometimes these charming byways end up in a blind alley.

Over time, our team has moved from small-scale, intensive studies to large-scale extensive ones, and back again:

From shoestring survey research on parasocial interaction among grown-ups (Rosengren & Windahl, 1972, 1977);

To qualitative studies of schoolchildren's essays on the use made of television, leading up to the construction of scales for the precise measurement of capture and parasocial interaction (Rosengren et al., 1976);

To extensive cross-sectional and panel studies of the use made of mass media by children and adolescents, as well as the causes and consequences of that use (Flodin, 1986; Hedinsson, 1981; Johnsson–Smaragdi, 1983; Jönsson, 1985; Roe, 1983a; Sonesson, 1979).

To qualitative follow-up interviews among small, purposive samples from our extensive panel surveys, validating important aspects of the survey results as well as the results of the qualitative interviews themselves (Jarlbro, 1986; Roe, 1983b).

On the basis of experiences gained during this prolonged undertaking, we have come to believe that the contradiction between highway and byway is by no means absolute.

The simile, in the first place, mingles two different distinctions: the distinction between an overall model vs. more specific ones, and the one between project team research vs. lone wolf research. In both cases, however, we firmly believe that—contrary to conventional wisdom—it is sometimes possible to have it both ways.

Individual, very specific research may be pursued within the ambit of a large teamwork project. Specific models may be developed within the overarching framework of an overall model. This is true especially for a research group working together for some time. Each member of the group puts his or her own specific knowledge and talent at the disposal of the group, and as time passes, the group members, and the group itself, move about in the empirical and theoretical landscapes, covering some miles of both highways and byways, producing a number of reports on the changing scenery, as seen from the highway, and from the byway.

In so doing one gradually realizes that it is indeed the same scenery all the time, although the scenery as seen from the highway may appear quite different from the one seen from the byway. Realizing this, one cannot seriously maintain that the highway view is better or worse than the byway view. They are just different. Similarly, the LISREL model is no less true than the two-by-two table or the novelette based on qualitative interviews, but the three are certainly different. An overall model of the whole blooming, buzzing thing is no better than a model of one specific aspect of it, and it is certainly no worse—just different.

It is precisely the difference between the specific models and studies and the overall ones which is the point. Indeed, more and more researchers of different schools have come to realize that a family of specific models, assembled and unified by means of an overarching, general one, is the best way theoretically to organize a large field of research dealing with some aspect of reality (cf., for instance, Boyd & Richerson, 1985, p. 24, and the several examples provided by these authors).

To return to McQuail's heuristic simile: In order to render the landscape faithfully we need the perspective from the highway just as much as the one from the byway. It is only when one tends to forget one for the other that one is in danger. The continuing discussions in a research group is an excellent way of keeping different perspectives open and alive. Differentiation becomes the key word, differentiation between elements of an integrated whole.

6.2. A DIFFERENTIATED DESCRIPTION

Differentiation has been the keyword of our concise travelog, this book. It remains the keyword also of its final chapter.

We started the presentation of results by differentiating the central concept of our study, mass media use, into four different concepts:

1.   Amount of consumption of the medium,
2.   Type of content preferred and consumed,
3.   Relations established with the content consumed,
4.   Type of consumption situation.

Three of these phenomena were related to each other in a longitudinal PLS model and found to have very little to do with each other. This finding could be regarded as an argument *for* the view that they all deserve a study of their own, an argument *against* the common practice of using amount of consumption as the one and only measure of media use. Unfortunately, because of technical characteristics of the other measures at our disposal, we ourselves to a large extent, but by no means exclusively, have been confined to having amount of consumption as our central variable. At least we have been aware of its limitations, the first among these being that it covers at least two quite different phenomena.

Amount of consumption may be differentiated into amount measured as a habit, and amount measured as actual consumption during a given period of time. The former, of course, is a measure of a disposition, similar to other dispositional measures, for instance, measures of attitude. It is an old truth in social science that habits and attitudes must not be mistaken for actual behavior in a concrete situation. Unfortunately, measures of habitual and actual media consumption are often used indiscriminately. As long as one knows what has been measured, one of the two is as good as the other. Each of them has their weaknesses, however.

The weakness of measures of actual media consumption is that they are very sensitive to accidental circumstances and thus not too well suited to be used in causal analyses of individual behavior. Several times we have confronted measures of habitual and actual consumption of television with each other, but as a rule we have used habitual consumption in the more elaborate analyses, for the reason mentioned, and for the simple reason that our measure of actual consumption was used only in the third wave of data collection.

The weakness of measures of habitual media consumption is that they run the risk of being unspecific—"As a rule, how much TV would you say you're watching?" In order to avoid this vagueness, our measure of habitual consumption is based on six different questions forming the basis of an additive/multiplicative index of half-hours of TV consumption a week.

Looking back on our many measurements of habitual television consumption by children, adolescents, and their parents, what is the main result to be reported? The simple answer to that question no doubt must be this: Television consumption among children and parents alike is differentiated to a very high degree.

In current audience statistics, it is customary to present results broken down in age categories, say, 9–14, 15–25, 35–50, 50–65, 65 and up. As a rule, the differences between the categories are quite visible. Differences within categories are assumed to be smaller. This is all very well, as far as it takes us. Unfortunately, it does not take as very far.

What our data have shown is that there is an immense variation in mass media consumption, especially, perhaps, when it comes to television and popular music. To begin with, there is variation between countries and cultures, depending on media structure and culturally influenced habits. Internationally, Swedish television viewing figures are rather low, probably mostly because of the restricted output of the monopoly system. Within this internationally low value, however, there is considerable variation.

During the period of life we have studied (6–15 years old), television reaches an all-time high in late childhood, only to reach an all-time low some 3 or 4 years later. On top of this temporal differentiation, there is differentiation along the dimensions of gender and social class.

Between them, the three basic variables of age, gender, and social class during childhood and adolescence create what can only be called different media worlds.

"We knew that already," it might be remarked with some justification. But because of its combined cross-sectional and longitudinal design the Media Panel Program has been able to demonstrate the existing differentiation in greater detail and with more clarity as to the persistence of, and the variation in, the overall pattern. In all of our three data collection waves, using cross-sectional as well as panel data, we have found that Swedish 11-year-old boys from the working class watch more than 2½ hours a day of television, while 15-year-old girls from the middle class watch little more than an hour a day. Within an age category which is often presented as homogeneous, there are differences between categories which amount to more than 100%.

This differentiation is not limited to the children and adolescents only. It is found also among the parents, something which, to the best of our knowledge, has not been reported before. It is well known that there are class, age, and gender variation in adults' TV viewing. Our data show, however, that there is another important source of differentiation as well, namely, the location within the family cycle.

As their children grow from age 6 to 15, the parents in our study reduce their TV viewing from close to 2 hours a day to little more than 1 hour a day. On top of this there is the usual differentiation with respect to age, class, and gender. As a consequence, we found that working-class parents of 6-year-old children viewed more than 2 hours a day, while middle-class parents of 15-year-old adolescents viewed less than an hour a day. (There was next to no variation in parental viewing with respect to the gender of the child, and unfortunately we had to accept and adapt to the response habits of the parents, which means that in almost all the cases the parent responding was the mother.)

Thus we have shown that children and parents alike change their viewing habits heavily as the children pass through childhood and adolescence. From early to late childhood, children increase their TV viewing; during adolescence, they reduce it. During this whole period, their parents reduce their TV viewing. Lying behind these twin processes of change we may assume are the two phenomena of development and dependency.

6.3. A DEVELOPMENTAL PERSPECTIVE

Biological, cognitive, and social development in interaction are responsible for the changing media habits of children and adolescents. As children develop in various respects they become, first increasingly, then decreasingly dependent on television for information, entertainment and company. Qualitative changes in their needs and resources make for quantitative changes in the media habits of children and adolescents.

Very briefly, the changes in needs may be described as the introduction of strong, spasmodic, or cyclical needs for mood control, in addition to already existing needs for information, entertainment, and company. At the same time as these new needs necessitate an increased control over media content consumed, they are matched by increased capacities and resources for such control.

All these developmental changes in the lives of adolescents make them turn away from the family and the family medium par préférence (television), toward the peer group and its medium par préférence (popular music). Concomitantly with these changes we find parallel changes in other media habits (for instance, moviegoing, magazine reading) as well as in the motives and preferences lying behind these habits (for instance, decreasing strength of motives for television viewing, changing structure of newspaper content preferences). As an overall result of basic developmental changes, the media world of adolescents changes dramatically during the period between 12 and 14, the girls generally leading the changes by some 2 years, just as they do in biological development.

The explanation and understanding of the heavy reduction in parental television viewing is much less complex. Development is an explanatory factor only indirectly. The main explanatory concept is dependency, entering the process at least twice. The more, because of their development, the children grow independent of their parents, the less the parents must stay at home with the children, and the less the parents themselves become dependent of the family medium of television for information, entertainment and company. They are quick to use the new independence. For somewhat different reasons children and parents alike leave television for the real thing.

6.4. A SOCIAL-CLASS PERSPECTIVE

We have already noted that the outcome of the developmental processes may be quite different in different classes. Developmental processes do not take place in a social vacuum. They occur within the framework of a social structure. In most, if not all, societies, class is a basic dimension of the social structure.

Looking closer at the notion of social class, one soon finds out that it needs a lot of clarification and differentiation. First, the twin concepts of class and status must be differentiated between. In addition we maintain that there are at least three different types of class which must be heeded: class of origin, destination, and context. "Where do you come from, where are you going, and where are you right now?" Finally, the type of influence emanating from social class must be discussed, from more than one perspective.

A basic perspective from which to discuss the influence of class on mass media use is whether that influence is linear or curvilinear. Most models of analysis have presumed a linear influence, but in some cases indications have popped up, sometimes inadvertently, that the relationship under some conditions may be curvilinear. Our data provide some support for this idea. In our study the lower the class of origin of the children and adolescents, the higher the TV consumption—except in the very lowest stratum of the working class, where TV viewing again becomes relatively low. On the other hand, this curvilinearity does not turn up among the parents, and not always for the status dimension of education. It does turn up, however, not only for class of origin, but also for class of destination. The combined influence of the two curvilinearities makes the middle strata into the heartland of television viewing.

It may be assumed that the curvilinearity may make some linear estimates conservative with respect to the strength of the "true" relationship between class and media use. The "deviant" group is not so large, the curvilinearity not so strong, however, as to limit seriously the applicability of linear models of analysis. Nevertheless, the finding is one among many others telling us that differentiation in media habits is so pervasive that it must be a compelling task in future mass media research to pay increased attention to mass media use among various subgroups instead of continuing with overall analyses of whole populations. (This is a point where the "byway" has decisive comparative advantages over the "highway." Nevertheless, there will always be a need for basic data relating to whole populations.)

A second basic perspective from which we have discussed the influence of class is the question whether that influence increases or decreases during childhood and adolescence? In earlier research, answers pointing in both directions may be found. We hypothesized that, as our respondents moved through adolescence, the influence from class of origin would decrease, that from class of destination increase, while the influence from class of context would be much the same over time. We found some support for our hypotheses.

At the same time, we must conclude that this type of changing influence must be further specified, not only with respect to type of medium, but also with respect to type of class. We have seen how, for some media, the same type of class influence may increase, for others it may decrease. And we have seen that the influence from class of destination on amount of TV viewing increased for adolescents of middle-class origin, but not for those of working-class origin. Again we find differentiation, this time with respect not only to mass media use as such but with respect to the influence of social class on that use.

Further signs of complicated interaction between social background, mass media use, and other variables were found. For instance, among low-status children high TV consumption in preschool led to negative school attitudes in grade 5 (6 years later, and after controls for a number of intervening variables), while for high-status children there were no clear effects of this type. Conversely, in grade 9 there was a strong relationship between political interest and amount of television consumption among upper-class adolescents, but none whatever among the lowest strata of the working-class adolescents.

So far, we have not been able to find any psychological, sociological, or communications theories capable of explaining such empirical findings, nor have we been able ourselves to explain them in theoretical terms. It is obvious that empirical research in this area has run ahead of theory—a situation which is not too unusual and can be remedied. Socialization theory, for instance, if properly developed, should have something to offer.

6.5. A SOCIALIZATION PERSPECTIVE

It is self-evident that all mass media use may be regarded as potential socialization. Mass media are becoming increasingly important as agents of socialization, not least among children and adolescents, among whom they are very serious competitors to the more traditional agents of socialization: the family, the school, and the peer group. Indeed, for a long time they have been regarded as such serious competitors that they have been suspected of being capable of reducing not only the influence of other agents of socialization, but the very basis of that influence, the interaction itself between children and the most primary among agents of socialization, the family and the peer group. For every new mass medium appearing on the scene, a "moral panic" has occurred, one of the fears expressed having been that the new medium would deactivate youth, turning them into passive, more or less narcoticized victims of the new medium.

Similar fears were often expressed when about 30 years ago television was introduced on a large scale. They also received some, although not unqualified, support from the research of the time, and they are still very much alive in the general debate. Our research does not support this notion at all. On the contrary, like some other recent European and American projects, we have found that, if anything, television is related to increased, not decreased interaction with both parents and peers. We have also found some indications that, far from preventing them, television consumption may actually have to yield ground to more organized activities, such as sports and clubs.

Naturally, these results do not imply that earlier results pointing in the opposite direction are faulty or even downright wrong. Not at all. What our and similar results do show is that the television of the 1970s and 1980s is probably different from that of the 1950s and 1960s. Today, television is integrated in society. It is an activity among many others. There is nothing special about it. No longer does it have any power to lure defenseless children away from more healthy activities together with peers and family members.

Our results have also a wider implication, however. They show that today's moral panics about videos, cable, satellites, computer games and the like, may concern rather ephemeral phenomena. It may be true that for some time media novelties may have a capacity to spell-bind children, preventing them from other, perhaps better, activities. But it is probably also true that such an influence will be transient and will be greatly reduced or even vanish as the "new" media find their place in society. The power of a given mass medium to act as an agent of socialization will always be circumscribed by other agents of socialization. All socialization is interaction—between the individual socialized and the agents of socialization, of course, but also between various agents of socialization.

The period of adolescence is an excellent period in which to study this interplay between various agents of socialization. We have already seen that when for very basic, developmental reasons adolescents increasingly orient themselves away from their family, toward the surrounding society as represented by the peer group, they also reorient their media habits. That is, they rearrange the pattern of socializing agents surrounding them.

We have been able to show that in such a process of rearrangement, or reorganization, the meaning of one and the same medium to its users may change completely. Such changes become even more apparent if, to the effects stemming from developmental change, we add the structural effects of gender and social class. Listening to pop music, for working-class boys in grade 5, is positively related to a number of other activities, ranging from unorganized to spontaneous activities, from family-oriented to peer-oriented ones. It is not negatively related to any such activities. For middle-class girls in grade 9, on the other hand, listening to pop music shows strong negative relations with family-oriented activities (regardless of whether they are organized or spontaneous ones) and strong positive relations with peer-oriented activities (be they organized or spontaneous). In the former case, listening to pop music is a means of integration; in the second case, a means of profilation and differentiation. Although this age-related difference is most apparent in the two cases just referred to, it may be found in all gender and class groupings.

This rearrangement of the agents of socialization, and of the meanings they carry to the adolescents, is a process originally initiated by strong biological forces within the adolescent. It is also supported by a number of societal institutions. However, to a large extent it is nevertheless carried out by willing and acting individual adolescents, quite consciously taking their decisions and making their choices. The effects and consequences of these decisions and choices, again, may be quite serious and far beyond the control of the individual adolescent—or, for that matter, the control of anybody else. These effects and consequences, furthermore, are to a high degree contingent on the position of the adolescent within the social structure, and upon the character of that structure itself. The adolescent may thus be seen as a willing and acting subject who is at the same time a more or less helpless object of strong biological forces from within, and equally strong social forces from outside. Socialization is the interaction between finality and causality.

This interaction between finality and causality is a very basic pattern which we have been able to observe for a number of different contents being transmitted in the complex, composite, and complicated process called socialization. The process has been traced in socialization content covering all four basic value orientations constituting the Great Wheel of Culture, expressive and normative value orientations as well as cognitive and instrumental ones. An important characteristic of this process of double interaction is the fact that for some individuals it may have very negative consequences, while for other individuals the consequences may be neutral or even very positive, so that the overall impression may well be one of total absence of effects.

A case in point is that old question of controversy, whether television may have harmful effects on children and adolescents with respect to aggressiveness and violence. We have already seen that in general terms television seems to lead rather to adjustment and presumably healthy social interaction than to isolation and maladjustment. But looking somewhat more closely at a small group of high consumers of television in preschool, we found that 6 years later they did indeed show a much higher tendency to aggressiveness and social maladjustment, even after control for a number of background and intervening variables. The influence of television was not to be found in an overall model. It was visible only for a specific subgroup.

Another case in point is the interplay between the adolescent socialized and those four important agents of socialization—family, peer group, school, and mass media—when it comes to school achievement and expectations about future jobs. The main causative agents in this process are the individual and the family. Having a low-status background, a working-class origin, reduces considerably the adolescent's chances of success at school, as well as the tendency to nurse expectations about a high-status job in the future (especially if the adolescent happens to be a girl). But regardless of social background, the individual's school achievement itself is a powerful predictor of expectations about future job status (especially if the adolescent is a boy).

In our attempts to understand this interplay between family, individual, and school we must also heed the mass media, in their turn interacting in a complex way with the individual and his agents of socialization. In families with a somewhat reserved enthusiasm toward television, the child will be taught to watch TV with some caution, and his or her restricted television fare during preschool will be helpful, it appears, several years later in school, resulting in better grades. In families more naïvely positive toward TV, the child will learn to use it more or less indiscriminately, and such a catholic use of television will actually prove harmful some years later. Becoming adolescents, such children will tend to be somewhat less successful at school.

Adolescents who for various reasons do not do too well in school, show a tendency to orient themselves to the peer group. Presumably they do so in order to regain at least some modest amount of the self-respect which their failure at school will have taken away from them. Advanced, rapidly changing forms of popular music (at the time of our study: punk, hard rock, etc.) are the cultural emblems of peer groups of this type. School, peer group, and popular music (but in this case, it would seem, not television) thus form a "spiral of interaction," leading adolescents into a subculture, or even a contraculture, of dissent, protest, and conflict—a culture including also the expectations entertained about future jobs and their class of destination.

Having their given position within a structural framework of gender and class, finding themselves in the midst of the two difficult and sometimes turbulent processes of development and socialization, adolescents, when struggling to give some minimum of meaning to their sometimes poor lives, may themselves (as a rule unwittingly), help to reproduce the societal structure against which they so vainly try to rebel. In this process, covering a decade or more of childhood and adolescence, mass media play an important role. Media matter.

6.6. FUTURE RESEARCH

The need for longitudinal studies of and research about individual use made of television, its causes and consequences, has been repeatedly stressed (cf., for instance, Comstock et al., 1978; Pearl et al., 1980; Surgeon General . . ., 1972). While longitudinal studies were rare when they were first called for, a number of such studies have been initiated since—a validation as good as any for the soundness of the recommendation. During the last few years a number of such studies have also been published (cf., for instance, Gerbner et al., 1980; Himmelweit & Swift, 1976; Huesman et al., 1984; Milawsky, 1982; Morgan, 1980; Tims & Masland, 1985; Williams, 1986). The Media Panel Program, of course, is another example of the widely and strongly felt need for longitudinal research in the mass communications area. What next, one may well ask, now that a number of such studies have been published and are about to be published?

Forecasting is always a difficult art, but it seems to be a safe guess that the need for longitudinal research will continue to make itself felt for quite some time. Once a number of longitudinal studies have proved their mettle, it will become increasingly difficult to make any serious statements about mass media use, its character, development, causes, effects, and consequences without support from longitudinal data, preferably within the framework of a combined longitudinal/cross-sectional design.

It is in the nature of things that the more specific character of future longitudinal studies in the area cannot be foretold with much confidence. But some general trends seem already to be on their way. An increased interest has been expressed in the study of subgroups. This interest is well in line with our experiences in the media panel group. Given the fact that there are now a number of well-organized panel studies available, it would be surprising if some of them, drawing upon their earlier experiences and results, did not combine the need for continued longitudinal studies with an interest in subgroup studies.

Another trend on its way seems to be an interest in combined qualitative and quantitative studies. Again it may well be that this interest too will draw on available resources in the form of experience of longitudinal research, panel studies etc. Intense, qualitative, ethnographic studies of subgroups within panels, whose general media habits have already been charted in earlier extensive surveys may well prove to be a way toward an increased understanding of the fine mechanisms supposedly lying behind the quantitative relationships demonstrated by the longitudinal surveys.

A third trend is the growing interest in the use made of the so-called new media, as well as the potential effects and consequences of that use. The degree of novelty of the new media may be discussed, but it is an undisputable fact that research on the new media will have to draw on the experiences and resources made available by research on the old ones. Future studies of the new media, therefore, will very probably use longitudinal designs, preferably in combination with cross-sectional ones, and we believe they would do well in combining quantitative and qualitative approaches.

Last, but certainly not least, we must not forget the theoretical base of the empirical study. Mass communications research has often, and with some justification, been criticized for its lack of theoretical sophistication. However, the last 15 years or so have been characterized by an increasing interest in different theories and models of various aspects of mass media and mass communications. This tendency has been quite evident also within the tradition of uses and gratifications research.

In this development, two distinct tendencies may be observed. One is a demand for clarity and overview, a wish to regard the many single studies in the light of an overarching model or theory. Another is a wish for more specific and detailed studies, charting with more precision some delimited area of the whole wide field under study. Recent examples of these two tendencies may be found in a research overview by Palmgreen et al. (1985) and in the overview by McQuail (1985) quoted in the opening paragraphs of this chapter. Both presentations offer a graphic model to express their ideas as clearly as possible, Palmgreen et al. presenting an overall model and McQuail a more specific one.

The two models may be regarded as illustrations of the highway-vs.-byway perspective discussed above. We firmly believe that in future research on mass media use by children and adolescents—indeed, in all mass communications research—both the highway and the byway perspective will be applied. We think so for the simple reason that in order to reach a full understanding of such complex and subtle phenomena it is absolutely necessary that both of them be used. So both of them will be used.

For a long time, it was customary that the highway perspective was applied by some researchers, the byway perspective by others. There is an encouraging tendency in recent communications research, however, for both perspectives to be applied by the same researchers or groups of researchers. Although the Media Panel group has been mostly working within a highway perspective, we have indeed applied and used both. We hope to continue to do so in the future.

Appendix

A.1. RESPONSE RATES, NUMBER OF CASES, MISSING DATA, AND MISSING ITEMS

Over the years, the original *Malmoe sample* was reduced by geographical mobility from 303 to 256 individuals constituting the Malmoe preschool panel. (Those children moving from Malmoe but within Sweden were approached by mail questionnaires, and respondents have been included among the 256 individuals of the final panel.)

Among the final panel's 256 parents 66% took part in all three waves, 17% actively refusing participation for both themselves and their children, and some 13% refusing on their own part but allowing their children to partake, the rest of the parents choosing not to take part for a number of reasons.

Of the 256 children belonging to the definitive panel, 79% took part in all three waves. Of the children allowed to partake by their parents, only some 2%–3% refused to take part. The rest were absent one or more times on grounds of illness, special education, and so forth. Comparisons between respondents and nonrespondents among children and parents revealed only marginal differences (Jönsson, 1985; Sonesson, 1979).

Table A.1 gives the response rate for all grades in the three waves of the *Vaxjoe study*. (In waves 1 and 3, data were collected on two different occasions, separated by some 8 or 10 days.) The figures within brackets refer to the main panel. Some children, who originally belonged to the panel but moved away from Vaxjoe, have been excluded from the main panel and from the following cross-sectional samples. The final answer rates for the main panel are thus based on two figures: (1) On the original sample (509 children) and (2) On the final sample where all movers are excluded (464 children). Unless otherwise stated we shall be using (2). Naturally the question of which is the correct figure to use could be a matter for discussion. Our solution is partly based on practical grounds, partly on methodological grounds (very few among the movers answered our questionnaires, and the answers given by them were mostly of poor quality with a large proportion of non-answers). *N*'s for the main panel in the three waves will accordingly be 509 (fifth grade, 1976), 494 (seventh grade, 1978) and 464 (ninth grade, 1980). It will be noted that the response rate is very high. The 464 individuals reached in the final wave of the main panel represent 86% of those originally approached in the first wave. There were only marginal differences in the response rates of boys and girls.

Table A.2 offers the response rates for the parents. Note that in 1978 only the parents new to the study, the parents of the fifth graders and third graders, were interviewed. The other parents were not included because it was felt that the risk of response fatigue from the second wave could have negative effects on the response rate in the important and final third wave.

The response rates of the parents are also quite satisfactory. A detailed comparison between respondents and non-respondents among the parents, including register data, revealed only marginal differences (Johnsson–Smaragdi, 1978).

The problem of missing data due to nonresponse on single questions or items was similarly analyzed by Johnsson–Smaragdi (1978). A weak overall tendency was found, suggesting that important factors behind internal nonresponse may be lack of knowledge (by parents on account

Table A.1.   Response Rates (%) for the 3 Cross-sectional Waves and for the Main Panel: Children. (Vaxjoe Study. Figures within Brackets Refer to Main Panel. From Johnsson–Smaragdi, 1983)

Wave	I		II	III	
Year	1976		1978	1980	
Questionnaire	1	2	1	1	2
Grade 9	94	94	92	94	92
				(86)[a]	(84)[a]
				(94)[b]	(92)[b]
Grade 7	98	96	95	95	95
			(88)[a]		
			(97)[b]		
Grade 5	99	98	99	93	95
	(90)[a]	(90)[a]			
	(99)[b]	(99)[b]			
Grade 3			97		
Sample size	1003		1268	1018	
	(509)		(494)	(464)	

[a] Percentage of original sample.
[b] Percentage of final main panel.

Table A.2. Response Rates (%) for the 3 Cross-sectional Waves and for the Main Panel: Parents. (Vaxjoe Study. Figures within Brackets Refer to Main Panel. From Johnsson–Smaragdi, 1983)

Wave Year	I 1976	II 1978	III 1980
Grade 9	86	—	84 (75) (82)
Grade 7	86	—	77
Grade 5	84 (79) (86)	79	78
Grade 3		80	
Sample size	1003 (509)	509 (—)	1018 (464)

of children's habits etc.), and lack of relevance (among adolescents, for developmental reasons, etc.). As a rule, however, the amount of internal nonresponse was negligible (1%–2%). In most cases, the internal non-response to scale items was evenly distributed over scales and individuals, so that the validity of the scales was not threatened. In a few cases, single questions showed such large proportions of missing data that they could not be used. Two specific types of internal nonresponse did cause some problems, however: jokes and nonresponse to central, one-question variables.

The questionnaires were completed by individuals with a keen and quick sense of humor: children and adolescents. In some cases respondents could not resist the temptation to fool with the questionnaires, by means of providing funny answers, having their response pattern to Likert or Osgood scales form more or less beautiful or fanciful patterns, and so on. Whenever there was reason to suspect responses of this type, this was noted, and the frequencies of such behavior were subsequently calculated for different sections of the questionnaires. In the first wave, 7.3% of all respondents were classified as jokers with respect to one or more sections of the two questionnaires. Of these, 4.6% (= 63%) joked in one section only. All nonserious replies were regarded as internal nonresponse.

If single items were missing from scales composed of many items they were replaced by the average of the scale for that individual, for the whole sample or for the relevant subcategory of the sample, as the case might be. Missing answers to single-question variables could not be replaced in this way (but if possible, register data were substituted, for instance, in the case of parental occupations). For some combinations of central single-question variables all this means that internal nonresponse may become nonnegligible. This is especially the case for multivariate analyses, in particular, LISREL and PLS analyses, which often build on a large number of variables (cf. sec. A.2).

In order to give the reader a notion of the number of cases we are dealing with in our concrete analyses, we present in Tables A.3 and A.4 the *n*'s for some subgroups often used in our analyses. Many of the tables and figures are based on *n*'s of the size suggested in these tables. In such cases, therefore, no specific *n*'s are given in the tables and figures, in order to save space and the reader's patience. When, for some reason, the number of cases becomes markedly small, however, *n* will be provided so that the reader can judge for himself what trust to put in the results of the analyses. In the large multivariate analyses we will always provide the *n*'s.

For each of the subgroups of Tables A.3 and A.4, two values are given. The higher value represents the number of children in the subgroup as such; the lower one, the value obtained when also the commonly used variable of TV consumption has been included in the analyses.

Note that in the Malmoe study we frequently use mother's education as a main background variable, whereas in the Vaxjoe material we most often use parents' social class. This is mirrored in Tables A.3 and A.4. The numbers in Figure 1.3 a-c and Table A.1 on the one hand and Table A.4 on the other and corresponding values given for the Malmoe panel show that the variables of social class and education do cause a noticeable internal nonresponse, while the variable amount of TV hardly can be said to do so.

A.2. STATISTICAL TECHNIQUES

Besides the more common types of statistical analyses, three techniques used in this book may need to be presented somewhat more closely. These are Multiple Classification Analysis (MCA) and the two structural modeling techniques of LISREL and PLS.

The MCA Technique

Hedinsson (1981) lists the following advantages of using the SPSS MCA program (Kim & Kohout, 1975) for a data material of the type found in the Media Panel Program:

Table A.3. Number of Children in Different Subgroups of the Malmoe Study. (With and Without Inclusion of TV Variable)

Mother's Education	WAVE I		
	Boys	Girls	Total
Low	34	43	77
	(34)	(42)	(76)
Middle	22	32	54
	(22)	(31)	(53)
High	35	28	63
	(35)	(28)	(63)
Total	91	103	194
	(91)	(101)	(192)
	WAVE II		
Low	34	43	77
	(34)	(43)	(77)
Middle	22	32	54
	(22)	(32)	(54)
High	35	28	63
	(35)	(28)	(63)
Total	91	103	194
	(91)	(103)	(194)
	WAVE III		
Low	34	43	77
	(32)	(43)	(75)
Middle	22	32	54
	(22)	(31)	(53)
High	35	28	63
	(35)	(28)	(63)
Total	91	103	194
	(89)	(102)	(191)

1. MCA allows extensive controlling procedures, which means that one can better isolate the unique effects of the independent variables.
2. The MCA program presents results in a way that makes it easy to examine the linearity or curvilinearity existing between the independent and dependent variables.
3. The additive effects of several independent variables and groups of variables can be established by means of the technique.

Here we will discuss the Multiple Classification Analysis (MCA), taking

Table A.4. Number of Children in Different Subgroups of the Vaxjoe Study. (With and Without Inclusion of TV Variable)

WAVE I

	Grade 5			Grade 7			Grade 9		
	Boys	Girls	Total	Boys	Girls	Total	Boys	Girls	Total
Working	126	120	246	50	49	99	63	56	119
Class	(120)	(117)	(237)	(48)	(49)	(97)	(60)	(47)	(117)
Middle	110	97	207	49	50	99	41	37	78
Class	(108)	(97)	(205)	(49)	(47)	(96)	(38)	(32)	(70)
Total	236	217	453	99	99	198	104	93	197
	(220)	(214)	(434)	(97)	(96)	(193)	(98)	(79)	(187)

WAVE II

	Boys	Girls	Total	Boys	Girls	Total	Boys	Girls	Total
Working	83	52	135	116	112	228	50	49	99
Class	(81)	(50)	(131)	(109)	(105)	(214)	(47)	(41)	(88)
Middle	29	25	54	101	93	194	49	50	99
Class	(27)	(22)	(49)	(93)	(83)	(176)	(41)	(38)	(79)
Total	112	77	189	217	205	422	99	99	198
	(108)	(72)	(180)	(202)	(188)	(390)	(88)	(79)	(167)

WAVE III

	Boys	Girls	Total	Boys	Girls	Total	Boys	Girls	Total
Working	40	36	76	83	55	138	124	120	244
Class	(38)	(36)	(74)	(78)	(49)	(128)	(118)	(107)	(225)
Middle	42	35	77	45	31	76	104	93	197
Class	(40)	(34)	(74)	(42)	(25)	(67)	(91)	(77)	(168)
Total	82	71	153	128	86	214	228	213	441
	(78)	(70)	(148)	(120)	(74)	(196)	(209)	(184)	(393)

a simple table from Hedinsson (Table 1.6, 1981) as a point of departure. The description of how to read it follows the same author.

In the table we find two types of independent variables:

1. Nonmetric, categorical variables that are usually termed *factors* but are in the tables labeled *independents.*
2. Metric variables, called *covariates.*

The point of departure is the grand mean of the dependent variable (here 2.51). The first column of the table shows the means of the dependent variable for each value or category of the independent factor variable. These means are expressed as deviations from the grand mean. The values are called "unadjusted," that is, the influence from other independent variables has not been controlled for. We find that the

Table A.5. MCA of Adolescents' TV Relations by Peer Interaction, Leisure Activities, and Social Class Controlled for Family Communication Pattern and Parental TV Attitudes. Vaxjoe Study, Wave 1, Grades 5 and 9. (From Hedinsson 1981.)

Variables	Grade 5 Grand mean = 2.51					Grade 9 Grand mean = 1.41				
	N	Unadj.	Eta	Adj. for indep. Beta	Adj. for indep. Beta + covar.	N	Unadj.	Eta	Adj. for indep. Beta	Adj. for indep. Beta + covar.
Peer Interaction										
1 low	122	-.52		-.46	-.44	43	-.16		-.16	-.16
2 medium	121	-.26		-.26	-.29	59	.11		.08	.08
3 high	113	.85	.28	.78	.79	53	.01	.08	.04	.04
				.26	.26				.07	.07
Leisure activities										
1 low	114	-.27		-.20	-.23	57	-.21		-.22	-.22
2 medium	102	-.05		-.11	-.10	58	.28		.30	.30
3 high	140	.25	.11	.25	.26	40	-.11	.16	-.13	-.12
				.10	.10				.17	.16
Social class										
1 (high)	51	-.45		-.33	-.28	13	-.18		-.16	-.17
2	75	-.12		-.17	-.14	26	.06		-.03	-.03
3	40	-.26		-.18	-.08	21	-.08		-.04	-.04
4	78	.15		.18	.13	33	.19		.22	.23
5 (low)	112	.27	.13	.21	.16	62	-.06	.08	-.06	-.06
				.10	.08				.08	.09
Multiple R				.309	.346				.193	.195
Multiple R ^{2}				.096	.120				.037	.038

relationship between TV relations and peer interaction is linear: the more peer oriented, the closer the TV relations.

In the second column all other independent factor variables are controlled for (i.e., leisure activities and social class), and we obtain the so called "adjusted" category means. The values of the first and second columns may then be compared. In the case of the independent variable, peer interaction, we find that the linearity is not altered when the relationship is controlled for influence from the variables leisure activities and social class.

In the third column further control is introduced, namely, of the influence exerted by the covariates, which here happen to be social and concept orientation and parental attitude toward TV (which we assume to be approximately metric). The linearity found in the first two columns also holds in this column.

In order to ensure that the results of the MCA analyses were not distorted by interaction effects, the interaction option in the ANOVA program was used to test for such effects (cf. Kim & Kohout, 1975, p. 410).

There are two measurements of the strength of the independent–dependent variable relationships. Eta is the unadjusted nonlinear correlation measure. The adjusted correlation measure, beta, is equivalent to the standardized multiple regression coefficient. In our example, the eta for the relationship between peer relations and capture is .28, the beta is .26, and when both independents and covariates are controlled for, beta is again in this case .26.

As seen in our sample table, the MCA also gives us R^2, which indicates the amount of overall explained variance in the dependent variable, taking the additive effects of all independent variables into account. In our example, $R^2 = .096$ when the independents are used. When the explanatory power of the covariates is added, $R^2 = .12$.

We have used the MCA technique quite extensively in our analyses. The results of our analyses will be presented in tables of various types, but always so as to be understandable against the background information just given.

The LISREL and PLS Techniques

Two main traditions in multivariate analysis are the factor analysis of psychology and the path analysis of genetics, economics, and sociology. The factor analysis tradition is concerned with relationships between manifest and latent variables; the path analysis tradition, with relationships between manifest variables. For decades the two traditions grew more or less independently of each other; then, in about 1960, a confluence between the two speeded their joint development. This gave rise to a veritable breakthrough, and in a relatively short period of time a number of new combinations were created (Bentler, 1980; Fornell, 1982; Mullins, 1975; Pedhazur, 1982; Rogosa, 1979; Saris & Stronkhorst, 1984).

At the Department of Statistics at the University of Uppsala in Sweden, two main approaches for advanced multivariate statistical analysis of large sets of manifest and latent variables by means of computers were developed. They are LISREL (Linear Structural Relations), developed by Jöreskog and his associates, and PLS (Partial Least Squares), developed somewhat later by Wold and his associates (Jöreskog & Sörbom, 1981; Jöreskog & Wold, 1982; Lohmöller, 1981). In the Media Panel Program we have used both approaches, and a short presentation of the two will therefore be given.

Both LISREL and PLS build upon a measurement or 'outer' model (corresponding to the factor analysis tradition) relating manifest indicators to latent variables, and a structural or "inner" model (corresponding to the path analysis tradition) relating latent variables to each other, much as the original path analysis related manifest variables to each other.

Both PLS and LISREL build on large systems of equations representing the two types of models. In PLS, the equations are solved by iterations between the two models until the system converges into an optimal solution. LISREL solves the equation systems simultaneously. LISREL uses primarily the maximum likelihood approach; PLS, the least squares approach. LISREL is thus parameter-oriented; PLS, prediction-oriented. LISREL demands more assumptions about the original data, but it also squeezes out more information from them.

Since, at present, PLS can handle a larger number of manifest and latent variables at a lower cost in computing time, while LISREL seems to have a greater capacity for precision in the analysis, a good strategy may sometimes be to start with PLS for an overview analysis ("soft modeling"), and then to turn to LISREL for a more precise and detailed analysis (model testing and modification). This strategy has sometimes been used in the Media Panel Program.

LISREL has been extensively used in sociology and has also entered adjacent disciplines such as psychology (Horn and McArdle 1980), political science (Dalton 1980), and communication studies (Gerbner et al., 1980; Kuo, 1985; Milawsky et al., 1982; Tims & Masland, 1985; Weber, 1984). PLS has been less often used in communication studies. (For examples, see Lohmöller & Wold, 1984.)

In a few cases PLS and LISREL have been applied to the same original data set (cf. Knepel, 1981; Lohmöller & Wold, 1984). While the two approaches certainly do not offer any panacea for the social sciences (Huba & Bentler, 1982; Martin, 1982) they do present new and powerful techniques of multivariate analysis. They are eminently suited to the needs of the Media Panel Program.

The items of the many scales used in the program may be regarded as manifest variables tapping latent variables such as motives for TV use, family communication climate, and so forth (cf. Table 1.1). The relationship between the manifest indicators and the latent variables may be studied by means of the "outer" measurement model of the two approaches.

The latent variables tapped by the manifest indicators should then be causally related to each other, controlling for a number of antecedent and intervening latent variables. This may be done by the "inner", structural model of the two approaches.

LISREL also takes care of measurement error, and various tests of the fit of the inner, outer and total models are offered. Small wonder that LISREL in particular has been extensively used in the Media Panel Program, by Hedinsson (1981), Roe (1983a), Johnsson–Smaragdi (1983), Rosengren et al., (1983) and Flodin (1986). PLS has also been used by several members of the program, most extensively by Jönsson (1985). The use of the two approaches has been immensely facilitated by courses and seminars generously given to the group by professors Karl G. Jöreskog and Herman Wold.

A problem with the PLS and LISREL analyses—and, indeed, with all multivariate analyses—is that the many variables used in combination causes the total internal nonresponse to become nonnegligible. The number of respondents with complete responses to all the variables used in the models may be small. This problem becomes especially serious when the analyses build on "list-wise deletion" (individuals with one missing value on any of the variables included in the analysis being removed from the analysis). The total internal nonresponse may then be so large as to raise questions about representativeness. "Pair-wise deletion" (only variables with missing values, not individuals, removed from the analysis) causes less total internal nonresponse. On the other hand, different coefficients of the model will then build on partly different sets of individuals. Thus representativeness must be weighed against homogeneity of the sample analyzed.

In most of the LISREL analyses reported in this volume, list-wise deletion has been used. Homogeneity of the sample has been felt to be more important than representativeness, a decision which probably agrees with common praxis in the field, but nevertheless may, of course, be discussed.

Flodin (1986), however, using a later version of LISREL (VI instead of IV), had the opportunity to build his models on polychoric correlations (instead of Pearsonian ones), something which is recommended by the authors (Jöreskog & Sörbom, 1981) when the metric status of the variables used is uncertain (as is often the case in social science). LISREL analyses building on polychoric correlations do not admit list-wise deletion. Thus Flodin may have bought statistical appropriateness (polychoric correlations) at the price of an heterogeneous, although possibly more representative, sample (pair-wise deletion).

In an attempt to solve this dilemma, Flodin (1986, p. 95) ran a large number of correlations based on both pair-wise and list-wise deletion. The two sets of correlations were then regarded as individual measurements and correlated. The result was quite positive (r=.91), suggesting that at least for the variables used by Flodin, pair-wise deletion is about as good as list-wise.

The fact that this specific problem turns up with LISREL is a good example of a general advantage characterizing this type of analysis: It makes both the strength and weakness of ones data clearly visible. In future studies using advanced multivariate analysis, increased attention should be given to the problem of both internal and external nonresponse.

PLS and LISREL may be used for both simple and complex analyses, for both descriptive and causal purposes. The real strength of the two techniques shows itself in complex causal modeling, however. The formidable capacity of the two approaches simultaneously to analyze the interplay of a great number of variables is immensely valuable. No doubt it will considerably enrich communication research in the near future.

The capacity of the structural modeling techniques grows especially powerful when applied to longitudinal data such as those of the Media Panel Program. We have tried to draw on it as much as our resources in (computer) time, money, and personnel have admitted. In spite of the new and advanced techniques of analysis put at our disposal, however, the more traditional techniques of analysis continue to be indispensable (cf., e.g., sec. 5.5.2).

Somewhat more technical presentations of LISREL and PLS than the present one may be found in Roe (1983), Johnsson–Smaragdi (1983), Jönsson (1985) and Flodin (1986). For full technical presentations, the reader is referred to Jöreskog and Sörbom (1981) and Lohmöller (1981).

A.3. GENDER AND SOCIAL CLASS OVER TIME: INCREASE OR DECREASE IN HOMOGENEITY?

Table A.6.   Means, Medians, Standard Deviations, and Coefficients of Variance for the TV Viewing Index by Age. (Half-hours/Week, Vaxjoe Main Panel, From Johnsson–Smaragdi, 1983)

	Mean	Median	S.D.	Coeff. of Variance (S.D./Mean)
Overall				
11 years	31.6	30.9	14.3	.45
13 years	25.5	23.9	12.6	.49
15 years	19.2	17.0	11.1	.58
Boys				
11 years	34.6	33.9	13.6	.39
13 years	28.6	27.1	12.6	.44
15 years	21.2	20.1	11.1	.52
Girls				
11 years	28.3	26.1	14.2	.50
13 years	22.1	20.0	11.7	.53
15 years	16.9	14.1	10.5	.62
Middle Class				
11 years	27.2	24.9	13.2	.49
13 years	21.5	19.6	10.4	.48
15 years	16.7	13.9	9.9	.59
Working Class				
11 years	34.3	32.1	14.4	.42
13 years	28.0	27.0	13.0	.46
15 years	20.4	19.3	11.1	.54

References

Abelman, R. (1984). Television and the Gifted Child. *Roeper Review,* 7, 115–118.

Abler, R., Adams, J., & Gould, P. (1971). *Spatial organization: The geographer's view of the world.* Englewood Cliffs, NJ: Prentice–Hall.

Abrahamsson, B., & Göransson, U. (1982). *Från grundskola till gymnasieskola.* Stockholm: Board of Education.

Abrahamsson, U. (1983). *TV-världen och verkligheten. Delrapport 1: Människor och samhälle i TV-fiktion för barn och ungdom.* Stockholm: Sveriges Radio/PUB, No. 7.

Abrahamsson, U. (1985). *TV-världen och verkligheten. Delrapport 2: Kvinnor och män i teater och film.* Stockholm: Sveriges Radio/PUB, No. 16.

Adelson, J. (Ed.). (1980). *Handbook of adolescent psychology.* New York: Wiley.

Adoni, H. (1979). The functions of mass media in the political socialization of adolescents. *Communication Research, 6,* 84–106.

Adorno, T.W. (1941). On radio music. *Studies in Philosophy and Social Science, 9,* 17–48.

Albrecht, S.L., Thomas, D.L. & Chadwick, B.A. (1980). *Social psychology.* Englewood Cliffs, NJ: Prentice–Hall.

Andersson, B.E. (1969). *Studies in adolescent behaviour.* Uppsala, Sweden: Almqvist & Wiksell.

Anderson, D.R., Field, D.E., Collins, P.A., Lorch, E.P., & Nathan, J.G. (1985). Estimates of young children's time with television: A methodological comparison of parent reports with time-lapse video home observation. *Child Development, 56,* 1345–1357.

Andison, F.S. (1977). TV violence and viewer aggression: A cumulation of study results 1956–1976. *Public Opinion Quarterly, 41,* 314–331.

Arnman, G., & Jönsson, I. (1983). *Segregation och svensk skola.* Lund, Sweden: Studentlitteratur.

Avery, R.K. (1979). Adolescents' Use of the mass media. *American Behavioral Scientist, 13,* 414–418.

Bachen, C.M. (1981, May). *The application of social development theory to research on television and children.* Paper presented to the ICA convention, Minneapolis, MN.

Bailyn, L. (1959). Mass media and children: A study of exposure, habits and cognitive effects. *Psychological Monographs, 73.*

Baker, R., & Ball, S. (Eds.). (1969). *Violence and the media.* Washington, DC: U.S. Government Printing Office.

Ball–Rokeach, S.J. (1985). The origins of individual media systems dependency: A sociological framework. *Communication Research, 12,* 485–510.

Ball–Rokeach, S.J., & DeFleur, M.L. (1976). A dependency model of mass media effects. *Communication Research, 3,* 3–21.

Baltes, P.B., & Goulet, L.R. (1971). Explanation of developmental variables by manipulation and simulation of age differences in behavior. *Human Development, 14,* 149–170.

Baranowski, M.D. (1971). Television and the adolescent. *Adolescence, 6,* 369–396.

Barnes, H.L. & Olson, D.H. (1985). Parent–adolescent communication and the circumplex model. *Child Development, 56,* 438–447.

Barwise, T.P., Ehrenberg, A.S.C. & Goodhardt, G.J. (1982). Glued to the box? Patterns of TV repeat-viewing. *Journal of Communication, 32,* 22–29.

Bentler, P.M. (1980). Multivariate analysis with latent variables: Causal modeling. *Annual Review of Psychology, 31,* 419–456.

Berelson, B. (1949). What "missing the newspaper" means. In P.F. Lazarsfeld & F.N. Stanton (Eds.), *Communication Research 1948–49.* New York: Harper.

Berg, U. (1982). *TV, radio och andra medier. Konkurrens eller komplement?* Stockholm: Sveriges Radio/PUB No. 21.

Berger, P.L., & Luckman, T.L. (1967). *The social construction of reality.* New York: Anchor Books.

Bernstein, B. (1971–1975). *Class, codes and control* (vols. 1–3). London: Routledge & Kegan Paul.

Blumler, J.G. (1979). The role of theory in uses and gratifications studies. *Communication Research, 6,* 9–36.

Blumler, J.G. (1982). Mass communication research in Europe: Some origins and prospects. In M. Burgoon (Ed.), *Communication Yearbook, 5.* New Brunswick, NJ: Transaction Books.

Blumler, J.G., & Katz, (Eds.). (1974). *The uses of mass communications: Current perspectives on gratification research.* Beverly Hills, CA: Sage.

Boalt, A. (1981). *Bostadsområden i Stockholms Län.* Stockholm: Landstingets Regionplanekontor.

Borgatta, E.F., & Jackson, D.J. (Eds.). (1980). *Aggregate data: analysis and interpretation.* Beverly Hills, CA: Sage.

Bourdieu, P. (1977). *Outline of a theory of practice.* Cambridge, England: Cambridge University Press.

Bourdieu, P. (1980). The aristocracy of culture. *Media, culture and Society, 2*(3), 225–254.

Bourdieu, P. & Passeron, J.C. (1979). *The inheritors: French students and their relation to culture.* Chicago: Chicago University Press.

Bowerman, C.E. & Kinch, J.W. (1959). Changes in family and peer orientation of children between the fourth and tenth grades. *Social Forces, 37,* 206–211.

Boyd, R., & Richerson, P.J. (1985). *Culture and the evolutionary process.* Chicago: University of Chicago Press.

Brim, O.G. (1968). Adult socialization. In *International encyclopedia of the social sciences, 14,* 555–562. New York: Collier–Macmillan.

Brolin, H. (1964). *Barnpublikens storlek och reaktioner.* Stockholm: Sveriges Radio.

Brown, D., & Brooks, L. (1984). *Career choice and development.* San Francisco: Jossey–Bass.

Brown, J.R., & Linné, O. (1976). The family as a mediator of television's effects. In R. Brown (Ed.), *Children and television.* London: Collier–Macmillan.

Brown, J.R., Cramond, J.K. & Wilde, R.J. (1974). Displacement effects of television and the child's functional orientation to media. In J.G. Blumler & E. Katz (Eds.), *The uses of mass communications.* Beverly Hills, CA: Sage.

Brown, R. (1965). *Social psychology.* New York: Free Press.

Bruner, J.S. et al. (Eds.). (1966). *Studies in cognitive growth.* New York: Wiley.

Bryant, J., & Zillmann, D. (Eds.). (1986). *Perspectives on media effects.* Hillsdale, NJ: Erlbaum.

Burrell, G., & Morgan, G. (1979). *Sociological paradigms and organisational analysis.* London: Heineman.

Burton, R.V. (1968). Socialization: Psychological aspects. In *International encyclopedia of the social sciences, 14,* 534–545. New York: Collier–Macmillan.

Carey, J.T. (1969). Changing courtship patterns in the popular song. *American Journal of Sociology, 74,* 720–731.

Carlsson, G. (1958). *Social mobility and class structure.* Lund, Sweden: Gleerups.

Chaffee, S.H. et al. (1971). Parental influences on adolescent mass media use. *American Behavioral Scientist, 14,* 323–340.

Chaffee, S.H. et al. (1973). Family communication patterns and adolescent political participation. In J. Dennis (Ed.), *Socialization to politics.* New York: Wiley.

Chaney, D. (1972). *Processes of mass communication.* London: Macmillan.

Charters, W.W. (1933). *Motion pictures and youth: A summary.* New York: Macmillan.

Child, I.L. (1969). Socialization. In G. Lindzey (Ed.), *Handbook of social psychology,* (vol. 2, pp. 605–612). Cambridge, MA: Addison–Wesley. (rev. ed.).

Christenson, P.G., DeBenedittis, P., & Lindlof, T.R. (1985). Children's use of audio media. *Communication Research, 12,* 327–343.

Cohen, A. (1955). *Delinquent boys: The culture of the gang.* Chicago: Free Press.

Comstock, G. (1980). *Television in America.* Beverly Hills, CA: Sage.

Comstock, G., Chaffee, S., Katzman, N., McCombs, M., & Roberts, D. (1978). *Television and human behavior.* New York: Columbia University Press.

Comstock, G.A., & Rubinstein, E.A. (Eds.). (1971). *Television and social behavior.* Washington, DC: U.S. Government Printing Office.

Cook, T.D. et al. (1985). The implicit assumptions of television research. *Mass Communication Review Yearbook, 5,* 143–183.

Costanzo, P.R., & Shaw, M.E. (1966). Conformity as a function of age level. *Child Development, 37,* 967–975.

Cramond, J. (1976). The introduction of television and its effects upon children's daily lives. In R. Brown (Ed.), *Children and television.* London: Collier–Macmillan.

Dale, E. (1935). *Children's attendance at motion pictures.* New York: Macmillan.

Dalton, R.J. (1980). Reassessing parental socialization: Indicator unreliability versus generational transfer. *American Political Science Review, 74,* 421–431.

Danowski, J. (1975). *Informational aging: Implications for alternative futures of societal information systems.* Presented at the ICA convention in Portland, OR.

de Bock, H. (1980). Gratification frustration during a newspaper strike and a TV blackout. *Journalism Quarterly, 57,* 61–66, 78.

DeFleur, M., & DeFleur, L. (1967). The relative contribution of television as a learning source for children's occupational knowledge. *American Sociological Review, 32,* 777–789.

Denisov, R.S., & Bridges, J. (1982). Popular music: Who are the recording artists? *Journal of Communication, 32*(1), 132–142.

DiMaggio, P. (1982). Cultural capital and school success. *American Sociological Review, 47,* 189–201.

Dimmick, J.W. et al. (1979). Media use and the life span: Notes on theory and method. *American Behavioral Scientist, 23*, 7–31.

DsU. (1976). *TV's utlandsrapportering* (Vol. 13). Stockholm: Office of Education.

Elkind, D., & Weiner, I.B. (1978). *Development of the child.* New York: Wiley.

Elliott, P. (1974). Uses and gratifications research: A critique and a sociological alternative. In J.G. Blumler & E. Katz (Eds.), *The uses of mass communications. Current perspectives on gratifications research.* Beverly Hills, CA: Sage.

Ellis, G.J. et al. (1978). Supervision and conformity: A cross-cultural analysis of parental socialization values. *American Journal of Sociology, 84*, 386–403.

Erikson, E.H. (1968). *Identity: Youth and crisis.* New York: Norton.

Faber, R.J. et al. (1979). Coming of age in the global village: Television and adolescence. In E. Wartella (Ed.), *Children communicating: Media and development of thought, speech, understanding.* Beverly Hills, CA: Sage.

Feilitzen, C. von (1976). The functions served by the media: Report on a Swedish study. In R. Brown (Ed.), *Children and television.* London: Collier–Macmillan.

Feilitzen, C. von (1985). Om barns TV-tittande, bokläsning och fritid. In *PUB 84. Forskning om radio och TV.* Stockholm: Sveriges Radio/ PUB.

Feilitzen, C. von, Filipson, L., & Schyller, I. (1979). *Blunda inte för barnens tittande.* Stockholm: Sveriges Radio.

Feilitzen, C. von, & Linné, O. (1974). *Barn och identifikation i masskommunikationsprocessen.* Stockholm: Sveriges Radio/PUB, No. 146/73.

Ferrer, J. (1983). *Punkare och Skinheads.* Stockholm: Norstedts.

Fetler, M. (1985). Television viewing and school achievement. *Mass Communication Review Yearbook, 5*, 447–461.

Filipson, L. (1980). *Skolbarn och etermedier.* Stockholm: Sveriges Radio.

Filipson, L. (1981). *Barn, ungdom och radio.* Stockholm: SR/PUB No. 22.

Filipson, L., & Schyller, I. (1982). *TV- och videotittande bland barn och ungdom.* Stockholm: Sveriges Radios publik- och programforskning.

Findahl, O., & Gaspar, M. (1981). *TV-nyheternas publik. En djupstudie över tre dagar.* Stockholm: SR/PUB No. 2.

Findahl, O., & Höijer, B. (1974). *On knowledge, social privileges and the news.* Stockholm: SR/PUB No. 201.

Flavell, I. (1968). *The development of role-taking and communication skills in children.* New York: Wiley.

Flavell, I. (1977). *Cognitive development.* New York: Prentice–Hall.

Flodin, B. (1986). *TV och yrkesförväntan: En longitudinell studie av ungdomars yrkessocialisation.* Lund, Sweden: Studentlitteratur. (with a summary in English).

Flodin, B. et al. (1982). Primary school panel. A descriptive report. *Media Panel Report No. 17.* Lund, Sweden: Department of Sociology, University of Lund. (mimeo.)

Forchhammer, J. (1983). *Born for TV.* Copenhagen: Nord.

Fornell, C. (Ed.). (1982). *A second generation of multivariate analysis.* New York: Praeger.

Frank, R.E., & Greenberg, M.G. (1980). *The public's use of television.* Beverly Hills, CA: Sage.

Freud, S. (1905/1953). *Three essays on the theory of sexuality* (standard ed., Vol 7). London: Hogarth.

Frith, S. (1983). *Sound effects: Youth, leisure and the politics of rock'n roll.* London: Constable.

Frith, S., & McRobbie, A. (1978). Rock and sexuality. *Screen Education, 29*(Winter), 3–20.

Furhammar, L. (1965). *Filmpåverkan.* Stockholm: Norstedts.

Furu, T. (1971). *The function of television for children and adolescents.* Tokyo: Sophia UP.

Gahlin, A. & Wigren, G. (1981). *Hur många går på bio?* PUB informerar. Stockholm: SR/PUB.

Game, A., & Pringle, R. (1984). *Gender at work.* London: Pluto Press.

Gaziano, C. (1985). The knowledge gap. *Mass Communication Review Yearbook, 5,* 462–501.

Gerbner, G. (1969). Toward "cultural indicators": The analysis of mass mediated public message system. *AV Communication Review, 17,* 137–148.

Gerbner, G. (1984). Political functions of television viewing. In G. Melischek et al. (Ed.), *Cultural indicators. An international symposium.* Vienna: Akademie der Wissenschaften.

Gerbner, G., & Gross, L. (1976). Living with television: The violence profile. *Journal of Communication, 26*(2), 173–199.

Gerbner, G., & Marvanyi, G. (1977). The many worlds of the world's press. *Journal of Communication, 27*(2), 52–66.

Gerbner, G. et al. (1980). The mainstreaming of America. Violence profile No. 11. *Journal of Communication, 30*(3), 10–29.

Gerbner, G. et al. (1981). Final reply to Hirsch. *Communication Research, 8,* 259–280.

Golding, P., & Murdock, G. (1978). Theories of communication and theories of society. *Communication Research, 5,* 339–356.

Goodhardt, G.J., & Ehrenberg, A.S.C. (1969). Duplication of television viewing between and within channels. *Journal of Marketing Research, 6,* 169–178.

Goodhardt, G.J., Ehrenberg, A.S.C. & Collins, M.A. (1975). *The television audience: Patterns of viewing.* Lexington, MA: Lexington Books.

Goslin, D.A. (Ed.). (1969). *Handbook of socialization theory and research.* Chicago: Rand McNally.

Gould, P. (1975). *People in information space: The mental maps and information surfaces of Sweden.* Lund, Sweden: CWK Gleerup.

Goulet, L.R., & Baltes, P.B. (Eds.). (1970). *Life-span developmental psychology: Research and theory.* New York: Academic Press.

Greenberg, B.S. (1974). Gratifications of television viewing and their correlates for British children. In J.G. Blumler & E. Katz (Eds.), *The uses of mass communications.* Beverly Hills, CA: Sage.

Greenberg, B.S. (1976). Viewing and listening parameters among British youngsters. In R. Brown (Ed.), *Children and television.* London: Collier–Macmillan.

Greenberg, B.S., & Dervin, B. (1970). *Use of the mass media by the urban poor.* New York: Praeger.

Greenberg, B.S., & Dominick, J. (1969). Racial and social class differences in teenagers' use of television. *Journal of Broadcasting, 13,* 331–334.

Greenstein, F.J. (1968). Socialization: Political socialization. In *International encyclopedia of the social sciences, 14,* 551–555. New York: Collier–Macmillan.

Gross, L., & Morgan, M. (1983). Television and enculturation. In J.R. Dominick & Y. Fletcher (Eds.), *Broadcasting research methods.* Boston: Allyn & Bacon.

Gruber, H.E., & Voneche, J.J. (1977). *The essential Piaget.* New York: Basic Books.

Gustafsson, K.E. (1983). Mass media structure and policy in Sweden in the early 1980's. *Current Sweden* (Vol. 301). Stockholm: Swedish Institute.

Gustafsson, K.E., & Hadenius, S. (1976). *Swedish newspapers and newspaper policy.* Stockholm: Swedish Institute.

Gutman, L. (1954). A new approach to factor analysis: The radex. In P. Lazarsfeld (Ed.), *Mathematical thinking in the social sciences.* New York: Free Press.

Hadenius, S., & Weibull, L. (1980). *Massmedier.* Stockholm: Bonniers.

Hägred, P. (1983). Barns bild av omvärlden. *Media Panel Report,* No. 29. Lund, Sweden: Department of Sociology. (mimeo.)

Hall, S. (1982). The rediscovery of "ideology": Return of the repressed in media studies. In M. Gurevitch et al. (Eds.), *Culture, society and the media.* London: Methuen.

Halloran, J.D. (Ed.). (1976). *Mass media and socialization.* Leeds, England: Kavanagh.

Halsey, A.H. et al. (1980). *Origins and Destinations.* Oxford: Clarendon Press.

Harary, F. (1966). Merton revisited: A new classification for deviant behavior. *American Sociological Review, 31,* 693–697.

Härnqvist, K. (1980). Individers efterfrågan på utbildning. In S. Franke–Wikberg & U.P. Lundgren (Eds.), *Karriär och levnadsbana.* Stockholm: Wahlström & Widstrand.

Hawkins, R.P., & Pingree, S. (1984). The effects of television-mediated culture. In G. Melischek et al. (Eds.), *Cultural indicators: An international symposium.* Vienna: Akademie der Wissenschaften.

Hedinsson, E. (1981). *TV, family and society: The social origins and effects of adolescents' TV Use.* Stockholm: Almqvist & Wiksell.

Hedinsson, E., & Johnsson–Smaragdi, U. (1978). Primary school panel: Some descriptive data. *Media Panel Report,* No. 2. Lund, Sweden, Department of Sociology, University of Lund. (mimeo.)

Hedinsson, E., & Windahl, S. (1984). Cultivation analysis: A Swedish illustration. In G. Melischek et al. (Eds.), *Cultural indicators: An international symposium.* Vienna: Akademie der Wissenschaften.

Hendry, L., & Patrick, H. (1977). Adolescents and television. *Journal of Youth and Adolescence, 6,* 325–336.

Heyns, B. (1976). *Exposure and the effects of schooling.* Washington, DC: National Institute of Education.

Himmelweit, H., Oppenheim, A.N. & Vince, P. (1958). *Television and the child.* London: Oxford University Press.

Himmelweit, H., & Swift, B. (1969). A model for the understanding of school as a socializing agent. In P. Mussen et al. (Eds.), *Trends and issues in developmental psychology.* London: Holt Rinehart, & B. Winston.

Himmelweit, H., & Swift (1976). Continuities and discontinuities in media usage and taste: A longitudinal study. *Journal of Social Issues, 32*(4), 133–156.

Hirsch, P.M. (1980). The scary world of the nonviewer and other anomalies. *Communication Research, 7,* 403–456.

Höjerback, I. (1985). Högstadieungdomars massmedieanvändning. *Lund Research Papers in the Sociology of Communication* (Vol. 1). Lund, Sweden: Department of Sociology, University of Lund.

Höjerback, I. (1986) Video i Malmö. *Lund Research Papers in the Sociology of Communication* (Vol. 3). Lund, Sweden: Department of Sociology, University of Lund.

Horn, J.L. & McArdle, J.M. (1980). Perspectives on mathematical/statistical model building (MASMOB) in research on aging. In L.W.

Poon (Ed.), *Aging in the 1980's: Psychological issues.* Washington, DC: American Psychological Association.

Hornik, J., & Schlinger, M.J. (1981). Allocation of time to the mass media. *Journal of Consumer Research, 7,* 343–355.

Horton, D., & Wohl, R.R. (1956). Mass communication and para-social interaction. *Psychiatry, 19,* 215–229.

Huba, G.J., & Bentler, P.M. (1982). On the usefulness of latent variable causal modeling: A rejoinder to Martin. *Journal of Personality and Social Psychology, 43,* 604–611.

Huesman, L.R. (1984). Review of "Television: Ally or enemy?" *Contemporary Psychology*(4), 283–285.

Huesman, L.R., Lagerspetz, K., & Eron, L.D. (1984). Intervening variable in the TV violence-aggression relation: Evidence from two countries. *Developmental Psychology, 20*(5), 746–775.

Hultén, O. (1984a). *Mass media and state support in Sweden.* Stockholm: Swedish Institute. (2nd, rev. ed.).

Hultén, O. (1984b). *Video i Sverige. Vadan och varthän?* Stockholm: Sveriges Radio/PUB, 3.

Hultén, O. (1986). Video—bara för nöjes skull? *PUB 85/86. Forskning om radio och television.* Stockholm: Sveriges Radio.

Hvitfelt, H. (1977). *Verklighetsförträngning.* Lund, Sweden: Department of Sociology, University of Lund. (with a summary in English).

Hyman, H., & Sheatsley, P. (1947). Some reasons why information campaigns fail. *Public Opinion Quarterly, 11,* 412–423.

Janis, L., & Fadner, R. (1949). The coefficient of imbalance. In H.D. Lasswell et al. (Eds.), *Language of politics.* New York: G.W. Stewart. (pp. 153–169).

Jarlbro, G. (1986). Family communication patterns revisited: Reliability and validity. *Lund Research Papers in the Sociology of Communication* (Vol. 4). Lund, Sweden: Department of Sociology, University of Lund.

Johnsson–Smaragdi, U. (1978). Grundskolepanelen. Intern rapport. *Media Panel Report,* No. 3. Lund, Sweden: Department of Sociology, University of Lund. (mimeo.)

Johnsson–Smaragdi, U. (1981). Grundskolepanelen: Massmediekonsumtionen 1976 och 1978. *Media Panel Report,* No. 11. Lund, Sweden: Department of Sociology, University of Lund. (mimeo.)

Johnsson–Smaragdi, U. (1983). *TV use and social interaction in adolescence. A longitudinal study.* Stockholm: Almqvist & Wiksell.

Johnsson–Smaragdi, U. (1986). Tryckta kontra audiovisuella medier—konkurrens eller samexistens? *Wahlgrenska stiftelsens rapportserie* (vol. 3). Malmö: Wahlgrenska stiftelsen.

Jönsson, A. (1985). *TV—ett hot eller en resurs för barn?* Lund: CWK Gleerup. (with a summary in English).

Jönsson, A. (1986). TV: A threat or a complement to school? *Journal of Educational Television, 12*(1), 29–38.

Jöreskog, K.G., & Sörbom, D. (1981). *LISREL VI. Analysis of Linear Structural Relationships by Maximum Likelihood and Least Square Methods.* Uppsala, Sweden: Department of Statistics (mimeo.)

Jöreskog, K.G., & Wold, H. (Eds.). (1982). *Systems under indirect observation: Causality, structure, prediction.* Amsterdam: North Holland.

Kastenbaum, R. (1975). "Is death a life crisis?" On the confrontation with death in theory and practice. In N.. Datan & L.H. Ginsburg (Eds.), *Life span developmental psychology: Normative life crisis.* New York: Academic Press.

Katz, E., & Lazarsfeld, P.F. (1955). *Personal influence.* Glencoe, IL: Free Press.

Kerckhoff, A.C. (Ed.) (1980). *Longitudinal perspectives on educational attainment.* Greenwich, CN: JAI Press.

Kim, J.H., & Kohout, F. (1975). Analysis of variance and covariance: Subprograms ANOVA and ONEWAY. In N.H. Nie et al. (Eds.), *Statistical package for the social sciences.* New York: McGraw-Hill.

Kimball, P. (1959). People without papers. *Public Opinion Quarterly, 23,* 389–398.

Kimmel, D.C. (1974). *Adulthood and aging.* New York: Wiley.

Kinsey, A. (1948). *Sexual behavior in the human male.* Philadelphia: Saunders.

Kinsey, A. (1953). *Sexual behavior in the human female.* Philadelphia: Saunders.

Kjellmor, S. (1981). *Lyssnandet under tre år.* Stockholm: Sveriges Radios Publik- och programforskning.

Klapper, J. (1960). *The effects of mass communication.* New York: Free Press.

Kline, F.G. (1977). Time in communication research. In P.M. Hirsch et al. (Eds.), *Strategies for communication research.* Beverly Hills, CA: Sage.

Knepel, H. (1981). *Sozioökonomische Indikatormodelle zur Arbeitsmarktanalyse.* Frankfurt, West Germany: Campus.

Kohlberg, L. (1968). The child as a moral philosopher. *Psychology Today, 2,* 24–30.

Kroeber, A.L., & Kluckhohn, C. (1952). *Culture: A critical review of concepts and definitions.* Harvard University, Peabody Museum of American Archaeology and Ethnology Papers, 47(1).

Kuo, C. (1985). Media use, interpersonal communication and political socialization. *Communication Yearbook, 9,* 625–641.

Larson, R., & Kubey, R. (1985). Television and music. Contrasting media in adolescent life. *Mass Communication Review Yearbook, 5,* 395–413.

Lawrence, F.C., Tasker, G.E., Daly, C.T., Orhiel, A.L., & Wozniak P.H. (1986). Adolescents' time spent viewing television. *Adolescence, 21,* 431–436.

Lazarsfeld, P., & Merton, R.K. (1957). Mass communication, popular taste and organized social action. In B. Rosenberg & D.M. White (Eds.), *Mass culture.* New York: Free Press.

Lazarsfeld, P.F. et al. (1944). *The people's choice.* New York: Duell, Sloan, & Pierce.

Lefkovitz, M.M., Eron, L.D., Walder, L.O. & Huesman, L.R. (1972). Television violence and child aggression: A follow-up study. In G.A. Comstock & E.A. Rubinstein (Eds.), *Television and social behavior, III,* 35–135.

Levy, M.R. & Windahl, S. (1984). Audience activity and gratifications: A conceptual clarification and exploration. *Communication Research, 11,* 51–78.

Levy, M.R., & Windahl, S. (1985). The concept of audience activity. In K.E. Rosengren et al. (Eds.), *Media gratifications research. Current perspectives.* Beverly Hills, CA: Sage.

Lewin, K. (1951). *Field theory in social science.* New York: Harper.

Lindell, E. (1984). *Våldets läroplaner.* Pedagogiska skrifter, No. 266. Stockholm: Sveriges Lärarförbund.

Linné, O. (1964). *Barns reaktioner på våldsinslag i TV.* Stockholm: Sveriges Radio.

Lipset, S.M. (1968). Stratification, social: Social class. *International Encyclopedia of the Social Sciences.* New York: Macmillan.

Lohmöller, J.B. (1981). *LVPLS 1.6. Program manual: Latent variables path analysis with partial least squares estimation.* Munich: Hochschule der Bundesweher. (mimeo.)

Lohmöller, J.B., & Wold, H. (1984). Introduction to PLS estimation of path models with latent variables. In G. Melischek et al. (Eds.), *Cultural indicators. An international symposium.* Vienna: Akademie der Wissenschaften.

Lowenthal, L. (1961). *Literature, popular culture and society.* Englewood Cliffs, NJ: Prentice–Hall.

Lundgren, U.P. (1979). *School curricula: Content and structure and their effects on educational and occupational careers.* Stockholm: Liber.

Lull, J. (1983). *Communication alternatives for the modern youth culture.* Paper presented to the ICA convention, Dallas.

Lutte, G. (1971). *Le moi ideal de l'adolescent.* Brussels: Dessart.

Lyle, J., & Hoffman, H.R. (1972). Children's use of television and other media. In E.A. Rubinstein et al. (Eds.), *Television and social behavior (Vol. 4). Television in day-to-day life: Patterns of use.* Washington, DC: U.S. Government Printing Office.

Lyle, J., & Hoffman, H.R. (1976). Explorations in patterns of television viewing by pre-school-age children. In R. Brown (Ed.), *Children and television.* London: Collier–Macmillan.

McCain, T. (1986). Patterns of media use in Europe: Identifying country clusters. *European Journal of Communication, 1,* 231–250.

Maccoby, E. (1954). Why do children watch television? *Public Opinion Quarterly, 37,* 50–61.

McCombs, M. (1980). *Changing trends in newspaper readership in America.* Syracuse, NY: School of Public Communication, Syracuse University. (mimeo.)

McCron, R. (1976). Changing perspectives in the study of mass media and socialization. In J.D. Halloran (Ed.), *Mass media and socialization.* Leeds, England: Kavanagh.

McLeod, J., & Brown, J.D. (1976). The family environment and adolescent television use. In R. Brown (Ed.), *Children and television.* London: Collier–Macmillan.

McLeod, J., & O'Keefe, G.J. (1972). The socialization perspective and communication behavior. In F.G. Kline & P.J. Tichenor (Eds.), *Current perspectives in mass communication research.* Beverly Hills, CA: Sage.

McQuail, D. (1983). *Mass communication theory.* London: Sage.

McQuail, D. (1985). With the benefit of hindsight. Reflections of uses and gratifications research. *Mass Communication Review Yearbook, 5,* 125–141.

McQuail, D., & Gurevitch, M. (1974). Explaining audience behavior: Three approaches considered. In J.G. Blumler & E. Katz (Eds.), *The uses of mass communications. Current perspectives on gratifications research.* Beverly Hills, CA: Sage.

McQuail, D., & Windahl, S. (1981). *Communication models for the study of mass communications.* London: Longman.

McQuail, D. et al. (1972). The television audience: A revised perspective. In D. McQuail (Ed.), *Sociology of mass communications.* Harmondsworth, England: Penguin.

Martin, J.A. (1982). Application of structural modeling with latent variables to adolescent drug use. *Journal of Personality and Social Psychology, 43,* 598–603.

Mediapocket. Stockholm: Expressen.

Mediabarometern. Stockholm: Sveriges Radio.

Medrich, E.A. et al. (1982). *The serious business of growing up.* Berkeley: University of California Press.

Melischek, G., Rosengren, K.E. & Stappers, J. (1984). (Eds.). *Cultural indicators: An international symposium.* Vienna: Akademie der Wissenschaften.

Mendelsohn, H. (1964). Sociological perspectives on the study of mass communication. In L.A. Dexter & D.M. White (Eds.), *People, society and mass communications.* New York: Free Press.

Merton, R.K. (1963). *Social theory and social structure.* (rev. ed.). Glencoe, IL: Free Press.

Milawsky, J.R. et al. (1982). *Television and aggression: A panel study.* New York: Academic Press.

Miyazaki, T. (1981). Housewives and daytime serials in Japan. *Communication Research, 8,* 323–341.

Morgan, M. (1980). Television viewing and reading: Does more equal better? *Journal of Communication, 30*(1), 159–165.

Mullins, N.C. (1975). New causal theory: An elite specialty in social science. *History of Political Economy, 7,* 499–529.

Murdock, G., & McCron, R. (1976a). Consciousness of class and consciousness of generation. In S. Hall & T. Jefferson (Eds.), *Resistance through rituals.* London: Hutchinson.

Murdock, G., & McCron, R. (1976b). Youth and class. In G. Mungham & G. Pearson (Eds.), *Working class youth cultures.* London: Routledge & Kegan Paul.

Murdock, G., & Phelps, G. (1973). *Mass media and the secondary school.* London: Macmillan.

Murray, J.P. (1980). *Television and youth. 25 years of research and controversy.* Boys Town, NE: Center for the Study of Youth.

Murray, J.P., & Kippax, S. (1978). Children's social behavior in three towns with differing television experience. *Journal of Communication, 28*(1), 19–29.

Newcomb, H. (1978). Assessing the violence profile studies of Gerbner and Gross: A humanistic critique and suggestion. *Communication Research, 5,* 264–282.

Nilsson, C., & Nordström, B. (1980). *Lokalradions publik.* Stockholm: Sveriges Radio: PUB.

Noble, G. (1975). *Children in front of the small screen.* London: Constable.

Nordberg, J. (1984). *Kulturbarometern.* Stockholm: SR/PUB.

Nordlund, J.E. (1978). Media interaction. *Communication Research, 5,* 150–175.

Nowak, L. (1979). Information gaps. *Reflexions of Social Inequality*. Stockholm: SR/PUB No. 20.

Olson, D.H. et al. (1979). The circumplex model of marital and family systems: 1. Cohesion and adaptability dimensions, family types, and clinical applications. *Family Process, 18*, 3–27.

Ostman, R.E., & Jeffers, D.W. (1985). Life stage and motives for television use. *Journal of Aging and Human Development, 17*, 315–322.

Palmgreen, P., & Rayburn, J.D. (1985). An expectancy-value approach to media gratifications. In K.E. Rosengren et al. (Eds.), *Media gratifications research: Current perspectives*. Beverly Hills, CA: Sage.

Palmgreen, P., Wenner, L.A. & Rosengren, K.E. (1985). Uses and gratifications research: The last ten years. In K.E. Rosengren et al. (Eds.), *Media gratifications research: Current perspectives*. Beverly Hills, CA: Sage.

Parkin, F. (1979). *Marxism and class theory: A bourgeois critique*. London: Tavistock.

Parsons, T. (1942/1964). *Essays in sociological theory*. Glencoe, IL: Free Press.

Pearl, D., Bouthilet, L., & Lazar, J. (Eds.). (1982). *Television and behavior. Ten years of scientific progress and implications for the eighties*. Washington, DC: U.S. Government Printing Office.

Pearl, H.A. (1985). Theoretical trends in youth research in the USA. *International Social Science Journal, 37*, 455–473.

Pedhazur, E.J. (1982). *Multiple regression in behavioral research*. New York: Holt, Rinehart, & Winston.

Peters, J.F. (1985). Adolescents as socialization agents to parents. *Adolescence, 20*, 921–933.

Peterson, R.A., & Berger, D.G. (1975). Cycles in symbol production: The case of popular music. *American Sociological Review, 40*, 158–173.

Peterson, R.C., & Thurstone, L.L. (1933). *Motion pictures and the social attitudes of children*. New York: Macmillan.

Piaget, J. (1968). *Barnets själsliga utveckling*. Lund, Sweden: Gleerup.

Piepe, A. et al. (1975). *Television and the working class*. Farnborough, England: Saxon House.

Piepe, A. et al. (1978). *Mass media and cultural relationships*. Farnborough, England: Saxon House.

Pietilä, V. (1969). Immediate versus delayed reward in newspaper reading. *Acta Sociologica, 12*, 199–208.

Pietilä, V. (1974). *Gratifications and content choices in mass media use*. Tampere, Finland: University of Tampere.

Pinner, F.A. (1968). Cross-pressure. *International encyclopedia of the social sciences, 3*, 519–522.

Postman, N. (1979). *Teaching as a conservative activity.* New York: Delta.

Postman, N. (1982). *The disappearance of childhood.* New York: Delacorte Press.

Powell, G.B. (1976). Political cleavage structure, cross-pressure processes, and partisanship: An empirical test of the theory. *American Journal of Political Science, 20,*(1), 1–23.

Riegel, K.F. (1975). Adult life crises: A dialectic interpretation of development. In N. Datan & L.H. Ginsburg (Eds.), *Life-span developmental psychology: Normative life crises.* New York: Academic Press.

Riley, M.W., & Riley, J.W. (1951). A sociological approach to communication research. *Public Opinion Quarterly, 15,* 445–460.

Roberts, C. (1981). Children's and parents' television viewing and perceptions of violence. *Journalism Quarterly, 58,* 556–581.

Robinson, J.P. (1972). Toward defining the functions of television. In E.A. Rubinstein et al. (Eds.), *Television and social behavior (Vol. 4: Television in day-to-day life.* Washington DC: U.S. Government Printing Office.

Roe, K. (1981). Video and youth. *Media panel report,* No. 18. Lund, Sweden: Department of Sociology, University of Lund. (mimeo.)

Roe, K. (1983a). *Mass media and adolescent schooling: Conflict or coexistence?* Stockholm: Almqvist & Wiksell.

Roe, K. (1983b). The influence of video technology in adolescence. *Media Panel Report,* No. 27. Lund, Sweden: Department of Sociology, University of Lund. (mimeo.)

Roe, K. (1985a). The Swedish moral panic over video 1980–1984. *Nordicom Review of Nordic Mass Communication Research* (June), 20–25.

Roe, K. (1985b). *The programme output of seven cable TV channels.* Lund, Sweden: Department of Sociology, University of Lund. (mimeo.)

Rogosa, D. (1979). Causal models in longitudinal research. In J.E. Nesselroade & P.B. Baltes (Eds.), *Longitudinal research in the study of behavior and development.* New York: Academic Press.

Rosak, T. (1971). *The making of a counter culture.* London: Faber.

Rosenberg, M. (1965). *Society and the adolescent's self-image.* Princeton, NJ: Princeton University Press.

Rosenberg, M. (1968). *The logic of survey analysis.* New York: Basic Books.

Rosengren, K.E. (1974). Uses and gratifications: A paradigm outlined. In J.G. Blumler & E. Katz (Eds.), *The uses of mass communications.* Beverly Hills, CA: Sage.

Rosengren, K.E. (1984). Cultural indicators for the comparative study of culture. In G. Melischek et al. (Eds.), *Cultural indicators: An international symposium.* Vienna: Akademie der Wissenschaften.

Rosengren, K.E. (1985a). Communication research: One paradigm or four? In E.M. Rogers & F. Balle (Eds.), *The media revolution in America and Western Europe.* Norwood, NJ: Ablex.

Rosengren, K.E. (1985b). Media linkages of culture and other societal systems. *Communication Yearbook, 9,* 19–56.

Rosengren, K.E. (1985c). Growth of a research tradition: Some concluding remarks. In K.E. Rosengren et al. (Eds.), *Media gratifications research: Current perspectives.* Beverly Hills, CA: Sage.

Rosengren, K.E. (Ed.). (1986). *På gott och ont. TV och video, barn och ungdom.* Stockholm: Liber.

Rosengren, K.E. (1987). Paradigms lost and regained. In B. Dervin et al. (Eds.), *Paradigm dialogues in communication: General issues.* (Forthcoming)

Rosengren, K.E., & Windahl, S. (1972). Mass media consumption as a functional alternative. In D. McQuail (Ed.), *Sociology of mass communications.* Harmondsworth, England: Penguin.

Rosengren, K.E. & Windahl, S. (1977). Mass media use: Causes and effects. *Communications, 3,* 337–351.

Rosengren, K.E. & Windahl, S. (1978). The media panel program—A presentation. *Media Panel Report, No. 4. Lund, Sweden: Department of Sociology, University of Lund. (mimeo.)*

Rosengren, K.E. et al. (1976). Adolescents' TV relations: Three scales. Communication Research, 3, 347–365.

Rosengren, K.E., Roe, K., & Sonesson, E. (1983). Finality and causality in adolescents' mass media use. *Media Panel Report,* No. 24. Lund, Sweden: Department of Sociology, University of Lund. (mimeo.)

Rosengren, K.E., Wenner, L.A., & Palmgreen, P. (Eds.). (1985). *Media gratifications research: Current perspectives.* Beverly Hills, CA: Sage.

Rothschild, N. (1984). Small group affiliation as a mediating factor in the cultivation process. In G. Melischek et al. (Eds.), *Cultural indicators: An international symposium.* Vienna: Akademie der Wissenschaften.

Rotter, J.B. (1966). Generalized expectancies for internal versus external control of reinforcement. *Psychological Monographs, 80,* 1–27.

Rotter, J.B. (1975). Some problems and misconceptions related to the construct of internal versus external control of reinforcement. *Journal of Consulting and Clinical Psychology, 43,* 56–67.

Rubin, A.M. (1977). Television usage, attitudes and viewing behavior of children and adolescents. *Journal of Broadcasting, 21,* 355–369.

Rubin, A.M. (1979). Television use by children and adolescents. *Human Communication Research, 5,* 109–120.

Rubin, A.M. (1981). An examination of television viewing motivations. *Communication Research, 8,* 141–165.

Rubin, A.M., & Windahl, S. (1982). Mass media uses and dependency. *Media Panel Report,* No. 21. Lund, Sweden: Department of Sociology, University of Lund. (mimeo.)

Rubin, A.M., & Windahl, S. (1986). The uses and dependency model of mass communication. *Critical Studies in Mass Communication, 3,* 184–199.

Rydberg, S., & Höghielm, R. (1974). *Snabbt performancetest på intelligens (ia). Svenskspråkig version.* Stockholm: Skand. Testförlag.

Saris, W., & Stronkhorst, H. (1984). *Causal modelling in non-experimental research.* Amsterdam: Sociometric Research Foundation.

Sarnoff, C. (1976). *Latency.* New York: Aronson.

SCB. (1980). *Alfabetiskt yrkesregister. Folk- och bostadsräkningen 1980.* Stockholm: SCB.

SCB. (1982). *Socioekonomisk indelning (SEI).* Stockholm: SCB. Meddelanden i samordningsfrågor, 4.

Schramm, W. (1949). The nature of news. *Journalism Quarterly, 26,* 259–269.

Schramm, W., Lyle, J. & Parker, E.B. (1961). *Television in the lives of our children.* Stanford, CA: Stanford University Press.

Schyller, I., & Filipson, L. (1979). *1000 och en siffra.* Stockholm: Sveriges Radio/PUB, No. 16/79.

Sebald, H. (1986). Adolescents' shifting orientation toward parents and peers. A curvilinear trend over recent decades. *Journal of Marriage and the Family, 48,* 5–13.

Selman, R.L. (1971). Taking another's perspective: Role-taking development in early childhood. *Child Development, 42,* 1721–1734.

Seltzer, V.C. (1982). *Adolescent social development: Dynamic functional interaction.* Lexington, MA: Lexington Books.

Severinsson, R. (1985). *Publiken möter kabel-TV.* Göteborg: Avd för masskommunikation, No. 4.

Sewell, W.H., Hauser, R.M. & Wolf, W.C. (1980). Sex, schooling, and occupational status. *American Journal of Sociology, 86,* 551–583.

Shepard, R.N. (1978). The circumplex and related topological manifolds in the study of perception. In S. Shye (Ed.), *Theory construction and data analysis in the behavioral sciences.* San Francisco: Jossey-Bass.

Siebert, F. et al. (1956). *Four theories of the press.* Urbana, IL: University of Illinois Press.

Signorielli, N. (1984). The demography of the television world. In G.

Melischek et al. (Eds.), *Cultural indicators: An international symposium.* Vienna: Akademie der Wissenschaften.

Singer, M. (1968). The concept of culture. *International encyclopedia of the social sciences, 3,* 527–543.

Sjöstrand, P. (1980). Teorier om yrkesval. In S. Franke–Wikberg och U.P. Lundgren (Eds.), *Karriär och levnadsbana.* Stockholm: Wahlström & Widstrand.

Sonesson, I. (1979). *Förskolebarn och TV.* Malmö: Esselte Studium. (Preschool Children and TV; with a summary in English).

Sonesson, I. (1982). TV—från förskola till mellanstadium. En deskriptiv rapport. *Media Panel Report,* No. 22. Lund, Sweden: Department of Sociology, University of Lund. (mimeo.)

Sonesson, I. (1986). Några negativa följder av massmedieanvändning. In K.E. Rosengren (Ed.), *Barn, ungdom och massmedier. En symposierapport.* Stockholm: Liber.

Sonesson, I. (1987). *Vem fostrar våra baru—videon eller vi.* Stockholm: Esselte.

SOU. (1979). *56 (Statens Offentliga Utredningar) Steg på väg.* Nationell handlingsplan för jämställdhet utarbetad av jämställdhetskommitt én. Stockholm: Ministry for Social Affairs.

Stein, A.H. et al. (1972). Television content and young children's behavior. In G.A. Comstock & E.A. Rubinstein (Eds.), *Television and social behavior, II.* Washington, DC: U.S. Government Printing Office.

Stenholm, B. (1970). *Education in Sweden.* Stockholm: Svenska Institutet.

Stone, L.H. et al. (1979). Parent-peer influence as a predictor of marijuana use. *Adolescence, 14*(53), 115–122.

Strid, J. (1983). *Ungdomars tidningsläsning.* University of Gothenburg, Sweden: Department of Political Science. (mimeo.)

Strid, J., & Weibull, L. (1984). *Läsvanor och läsintressen 1979–1983.* Gothenburg, Sweden: Unit of Mass Communication Research, Report No. 2.

Sturm, H., & Brown, J.R. (Eds.). (1979. *Wie Kinder mit dem Fernsehen umgehen. Nutzen und Wirkung eines Mediums.* Stuttgart, West Germany: Klett–Cotta.

Sugarman, B. (1967). Involvement in youth culture, academic achievement and conformity in school. *British Journal of Sociology, 18,* 151–164.

Super, D.E. (1984). Career and life development. In D. Brown & L. Brooks (Eds.), *Career choice and development.* San Francisco: Jossey–Bass.

Surgeon General's Scientific Advisory Committee on Television and

Social Behavior. (1972). *Television and growing up*. Rockville, MD: U.S. Government Printing Office.

Surlin, S.H. et al. (1978). *Parental control of children's television viewing behavior: Support for the reverse modelling principle*. Paper presented to the ICA conference.

Svärd, S. (1985). *Med sladdar och satelliter. Fakta och debatt om nya medier*. Oslo, Norway: Norbok.

Svenning, C., & Svenning, M. (1980). *Daghemmen, jämlikheten och klassamhället*. Lund, Sweden: Liber.

Svenning, C., & Svenning, M. (1982). *Massmedia som fostrare*. Lund, Sweden: Liber.

Tanner, I.M. (1962). *Growth at adolescence*. Oxford, England: Blackwell Scientific Publications.

Therborn, G. (1978). *What does the ruling class do when it rules?* London: New Left Books.

Thunberg, A.M. et al. (1982). *Communication and equality: A Swedish perspective*. Stockholm: Almqvist & Wiksell.

Tichenor, P.J., Donohue, G.A. & Olien, C.N. (1970). Mass media flow and differential growth in knowledge. *Public Opinion Quarterly, 34,* 159–170.

Tims, A.R., & Masland, J.L. (1985). Measurement of family communication patterns. *Communication Research, 12,* 35–57.

Tingsten, H. (1937). *Political behaviour*. London: Bedminster Press.

TS–boken. Stockholm: Tidningsstatistik AB

Tuchman, G. et al. (1978). *Hearth and home: Images of women in the mass media*. New York: Oxford University Press.

Vermeersch, E. (1977). An analysis of the concept of culture. In B. Bernardi (Ed.), *The concept and dynamics of culture*. The Hague: Mouton.

Wall, J., & Stigbrand, K. (1983). *Televisionsbarn*. Stockholm: Skeab.

Wallis, R., & Malm, K. (1984). *Big sounds from small peoples*. London: Constable.

Wartella, E. (1980). Children and television: The development of the child's understanding of the medium. In G.C. Wilhoit & H. de Bock (Eds.), *Mass communication review yearbook,* I. Beverly Hills, CA: Sage.

Wartella, E. et al. (1979). The mass media environment of children. *American Behavioral Scientist, 23,* 33–52.

Watts, A.G., Super, D., & Kidd, J. (Eds.). (1981). *Career development in Britain*. Cambridge, England: Hobsons.

Weber, R.P. (1984). Content-analytic cultural indicators. In G. Melischek et al. (Eds.), *Cultural indicators: An international symposium*. Vienna: Akademie der Wissenschaften.

Webster, J.G., & Wakshlag, J.J. (1982). The impact of group viewing on patterns of television program choice. *Journal of Broadcasting, 26,* 445–455.

Weibull, L. (1983a). *Tidningsläsning i Sverige.* Stockholm: Publica. (with a summary in English).

Weibull, L. (1983b). Newspaper readership in Sweden. *Newspaper Research Journal, 4,* 53–64.

Weibull, L. (1985). Structural factors in gratifications research. In K.E. Rosengren et al. (Eds.), *Media gratifications research: Current perspectives.* Beverly Hills, CA: Sage.

Werner, A. (1971). Children and television in Norway. *Gazette, 17,* 133–151.

Werner, A. (1972). *Barn og Fjernsyn.* Oslo, Norway: Universitetsforlaget.

Werner, A. (1982). *Utviklingstendenser i bruk av massemedier blant barn og ungdom 1967–1978.* Oslo, Norway: Institutt for presseforskning. (mimeo.)

Werner, A. (1986). *Oppvekst i fjernsynsalderen.* Oslo, Norway: Institutt for presseforskning.

Wernersson, I. (1983). *Könsroller och tidigare föreställningar om yrkesval.* Göteborg, Sweden: Pedagogiska institutionen. (mimeo.)

Westin–Lindgren, G. (1979). *Physical and mental development in Swedish urban school children.* Stockholm: Liber.

Westin–Lindgren, G. (1982). Kroppslig utveckling och mognad. In I. Naeslund (Ed.), *Boken om skolbarns utveckling.* Stockholm: Liber.

Whiting, B.B., & Whiting, J.W.M. (1975). *Children of six cultures.* Cambridge, MA: Harvard University Press.

Whiting, J.W.M. (1968). Socialization: Anthropological aspects. In *International encyclopedia of the social sciences, 14,* 545–551. New York: Collier–Macmillan.

Wigren, G. (1980). *Så tittade vi—publikåret 1979/80.* Stockholm: Sveriges Radio/PUB, No. 24/80.

Wigren, G. (1982). *TV-tittandet—säsongen 1981/82.* Stockholm: Sveriges Radio/PUB, No. 25/82.

Wigren, G., & Gahlin, A. (1981). *Publikåret 1980–81. Specialtema: Sommaren 1981.* Stockholm: SR/PUB, No. 25, 4–9.

Wilensky, H.L. (1964). Mass society and mass culture: Interdependence or independence? *American Sociological Review, 29,* 173–197.

William–Olsson, I. (1973). *Kognitiva funktioner hos emotionellt störda förskolebarn.* Stockholm: Pedagogiska Institutionen, Lärarhögskolan.

Williams, T.M. (Ed.), (1980). *The impact of television. A natural experiment.* Orlando, FL: Academic Press.

Willis, P. (1978). *Profane culture.* London: Routledge & Kegan Paul.

Wilson, K.L., & Portes, A. (1975). The educational attainment process: Results from a national sample. *American Journal of Sociology,* *81,* 343–363.

Windahl, S. (1981). Uses and gratifications at the crossroads. In G.C. Wilhoit & H. de Bock (Eds.), *Mass communication review yearbook,* II. Beverly Hills, CA: Sage.

Windahl, S., Höjerback, I., & Hedinsson, E. (1986). Adolescents without television: A study in media deprivation. *Journal of Broadcasting & Electronic Media, 30*(1), 47–63.

Windahl, S., & Rosengren, K.E. (1976). The professionalization of Swedish journalists. *Gazette, 22,* 140–149.

Windahl, S., & Rosengren, K.E. (1978). Newsmen's professionalization. *Journalism Quarterly, 55,* 466–473.

Wirth, L. (1948). Consensus and mass communication. *American Sociological Review, 13,* 1–15.

Wohlwill, J.F. (1962). From perception to inference: A dimension of cognitive development. In W. Kessen & C. Kuhlman (Eds.), *Thoughts in the young child.* Monographs in Social Research on the Child, *27,* 87–112.

Wohlwill, J.F. (1970). Methodology and research strategy in the study of developmental change. In L.R. Goulet & P.B. Baltes (Eds.), *Life span developmental psychology: Research and theory.* New York: Academic Press.

Wright, E.O. (1985). *Classes.* London: Verso.

Wrong, D.H. (1961). The oversocialized conception of man in modern sociology. *American Sociological Review, 26,* 183–193.

Youniss, J. (1980). *Parents and peers in social development.* Chicago: University of Chicago Press.

Zahn, S.B., & Baran, S.J. (1984). It's all in the family: Siblings and program choice conflict. *Journalism Quarterly, 61,* 847–852.

Zigler, E., & Seitz, V. (1978). Changing trends in socialization theory and research. *American Behavioral Scientist, 21,* 731–756.

Author Index

Stigbrand, K., 6, *286*
Stone, L.H., 175, *285*
Stronkhorst, H., 264, *284*
Sturm, H., xv, *285*
Sugarman, B., 153, *285*
Super, D.E., 232, *285, 286*
Surlin, S.H., 194, *286*
Svärd, S., 3, 6, *286*
Svenning, C., 5, 118, *286*
Svenning, M., 5, 118, *286*
Swift, B., xvii, 122, 127, 253, *275*

T

Tanner, I.M., 56, 67, *286*
Tasker, G.E., 21, *278*
Therborn, G., 112, *286*
Thomas, D.L., 160, *268*
Thunberg, A.M., 165, 212, *286*
Thurstone, L.L., xv, *281*
Tichenor, P.J., *286*
Tims, A.R., xvii, 171, 198, 253, 264, *286*
Tingsten, H., 115, *286*
Tuchman, G., 232, *286*

V

Vermeersch, E., 117, *286*
Vince, P., xv, xvi, 52, 66, 74, 137, 180, 182, 189, 191, 216, 231, 234, *275*
Voneche, J.J., 57, *274*

W

Wakshlag, J.J., 42, *287*
Walder, L.O., *278*
Wall, J., 6, *286*
Wallis, R., 105, *286*
Wartella, E., 58, 60, 61, 62, 76, 77, *286*
Watts, A.G., 232, *286*
Weber, R.P., *286*
Webster, J.G., 42, *287*

Weibull, L., 2, 9, 19, 20, 93, 95, 116, *274, 285, 287*
Weiner, I.B., 55, 56, 57, 59, 60, *272*
Wenner, L.A., 8, 64, 86, 87, 88, 169, 172, *281, 283*
Werner, A., xv, 21, 115, 180, 211, 232, 235, 254, *287*
Wernersson, I., 232, *287*
Westin-Lindgren, G., 56, 61, *287*
Whiting, B.B., 162, *287*
Whiting, J.W.M., 160, 162, *287*
Wigren, G., 4, 21, 30, 34, *273, 287*
Wilde, R.J., 54, 62, 63, 67, 91, 180, *270*
Wilensky, H.L., 35, 113, *287*
William-Olsson, I., 215, *287*
Williams, T.M., xvi, xvii, 181, 183, 253, *287*
Willis, P., 152, *287*
Wilson, K.L., 233, *288*
Windahl, S., 1, 2, 8, 9, 18, 19, 39, 40, 46, 80, 81, 116, 120, 137, 140, 142, 153, 169, 178, 179, 181, 183, 211, 213, 225, 243, *275, 278, 279, 283, 284, 288*
Wirth, L., 239, *288*
Wohl, R.R., 19, 39, *276*
Wohlwill, J.F., 57, *288*
Wold, H., 264, 265, *277, 278*
Wolf, W.C., 232, 233, *284*
Wozniak, P.H., 21, *278*
Wright, E.O., 112, *288*
Wrong, D.H., 55, *288*
Wurtzel, 218

Y

Youniss, J., 55, 167, 195, *288*

Z

Zahn, S.B., 195, *288*
Zigler, E., 55, *288*
Zillman, D., 8, *270*

Subject Index

0